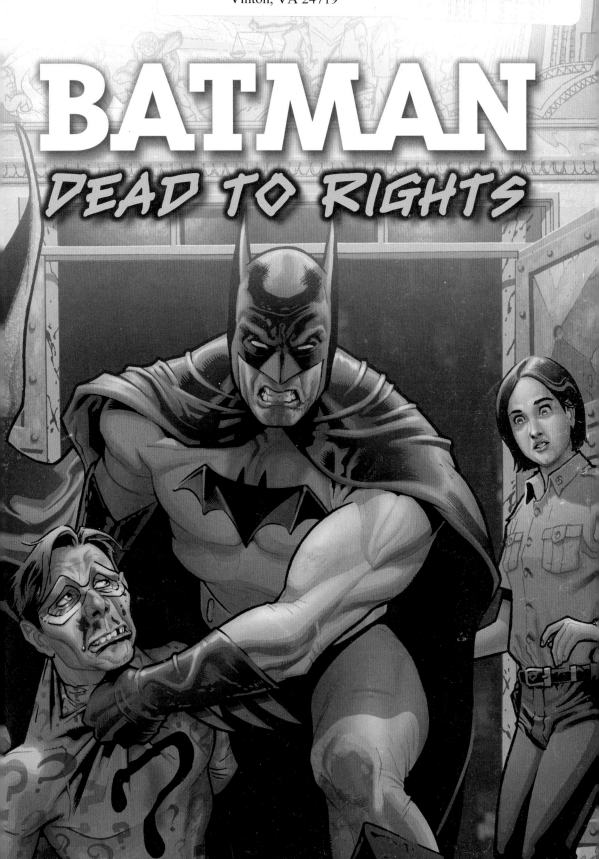

BATMAN
DEAD TO RIGHTS

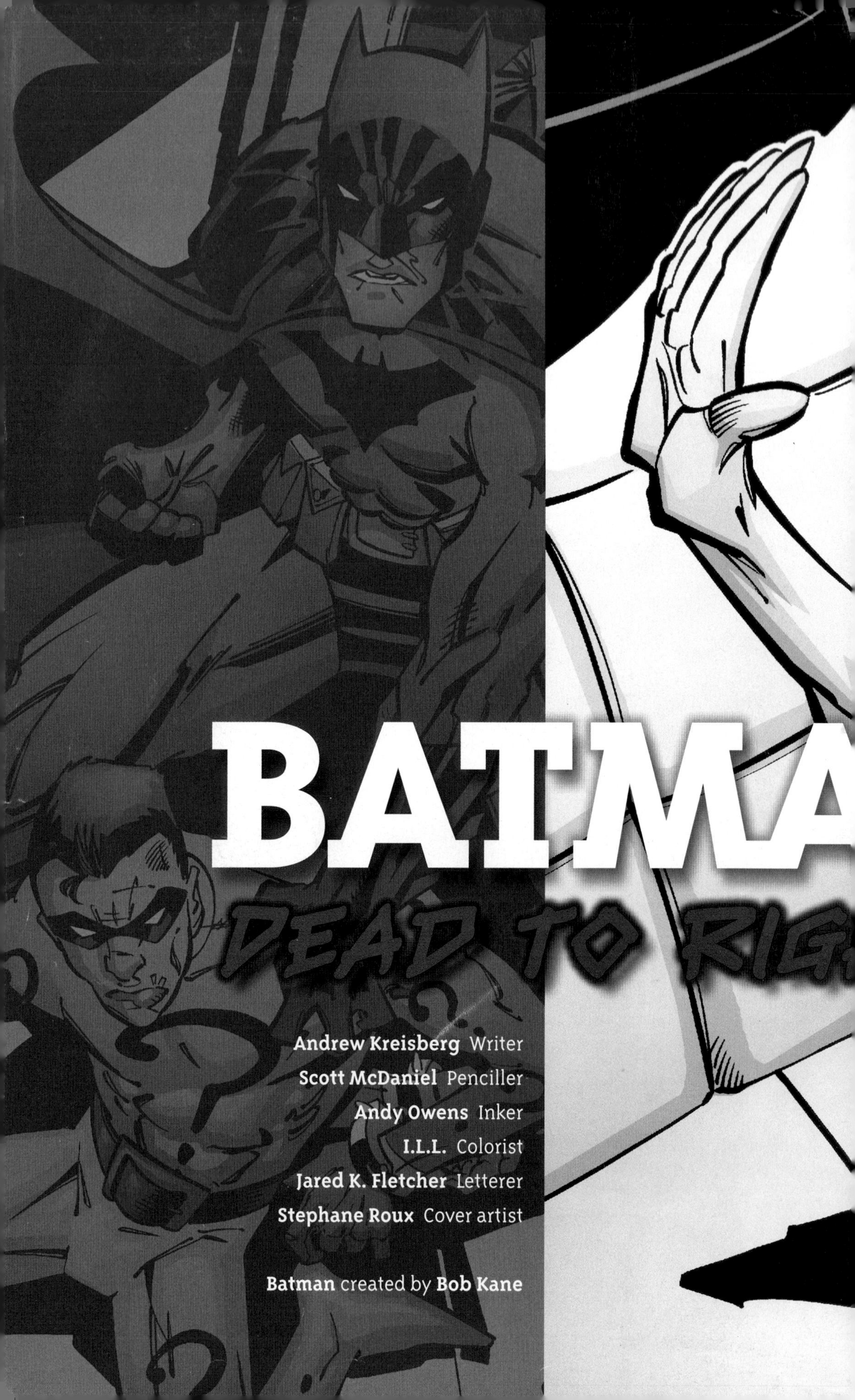

BATMA

DEAD TO RIG

Andrew Kreisberg Writer
Scott McDaniel Penciller
Andy Owens Inker
I.L.L. Colorist
Jared K. Fletcher Letterer
Stephane Roux Cover artist

Batman created by **Bob Kane**

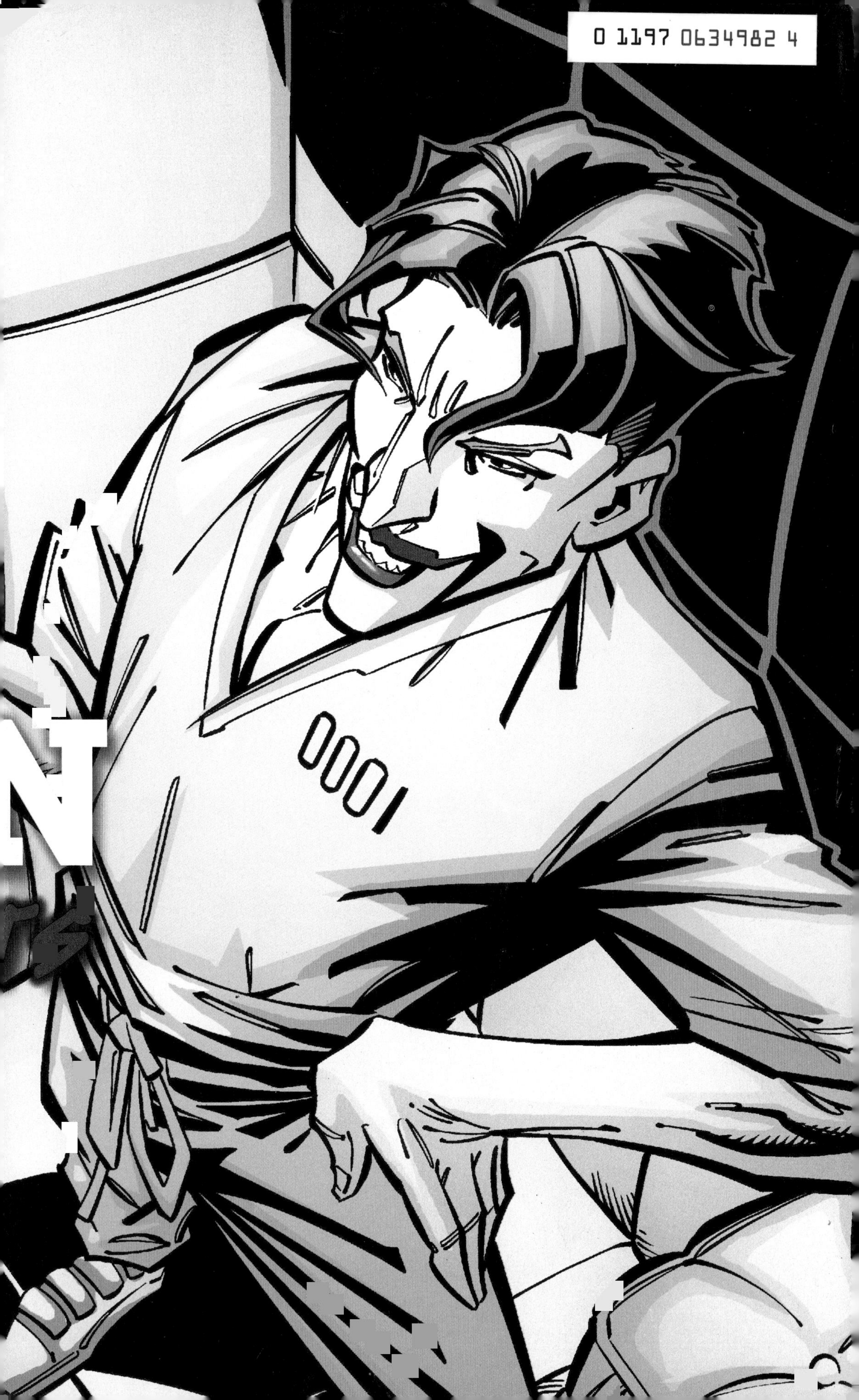
0001

BATMAN: DEAD TO RIGHTS

DC Comics, 1700 Broadway, New York, NY 10019
A Warner Bros. Entertainment Company
Printed by Quad/Graphics, Inc., Dubuque, IA, USA. 11/3/10. First printing.
ISBN: 978-1-4012-2925-2

SUSTAINABLE FORESTRY INITIATIVE
Certified Chain of Custody
Promoting Sustainable Forest Management

Fiber used in this product line meets the sourcing requirements of the SFI program. www.sfiprogram.org PWC-SFICOC-260

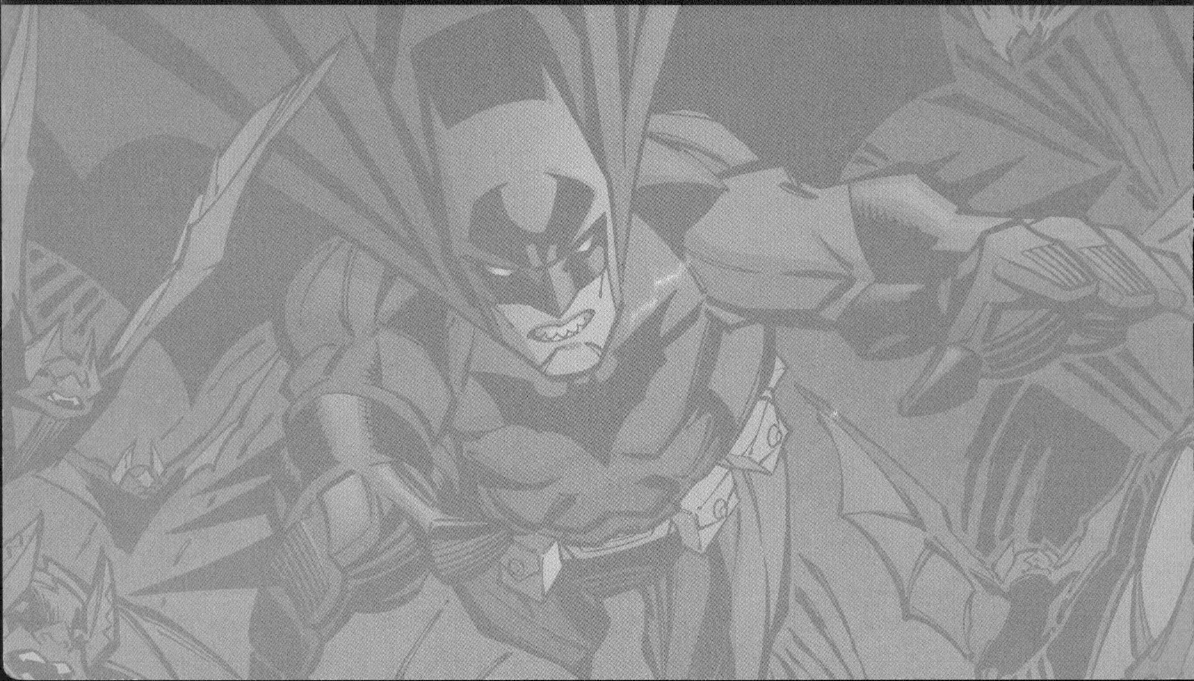

DO YOU UNDERSTAND THESE RIGHTS? PART ONE

YOU HAVE THE RIGHT TO REMAIN SILENT

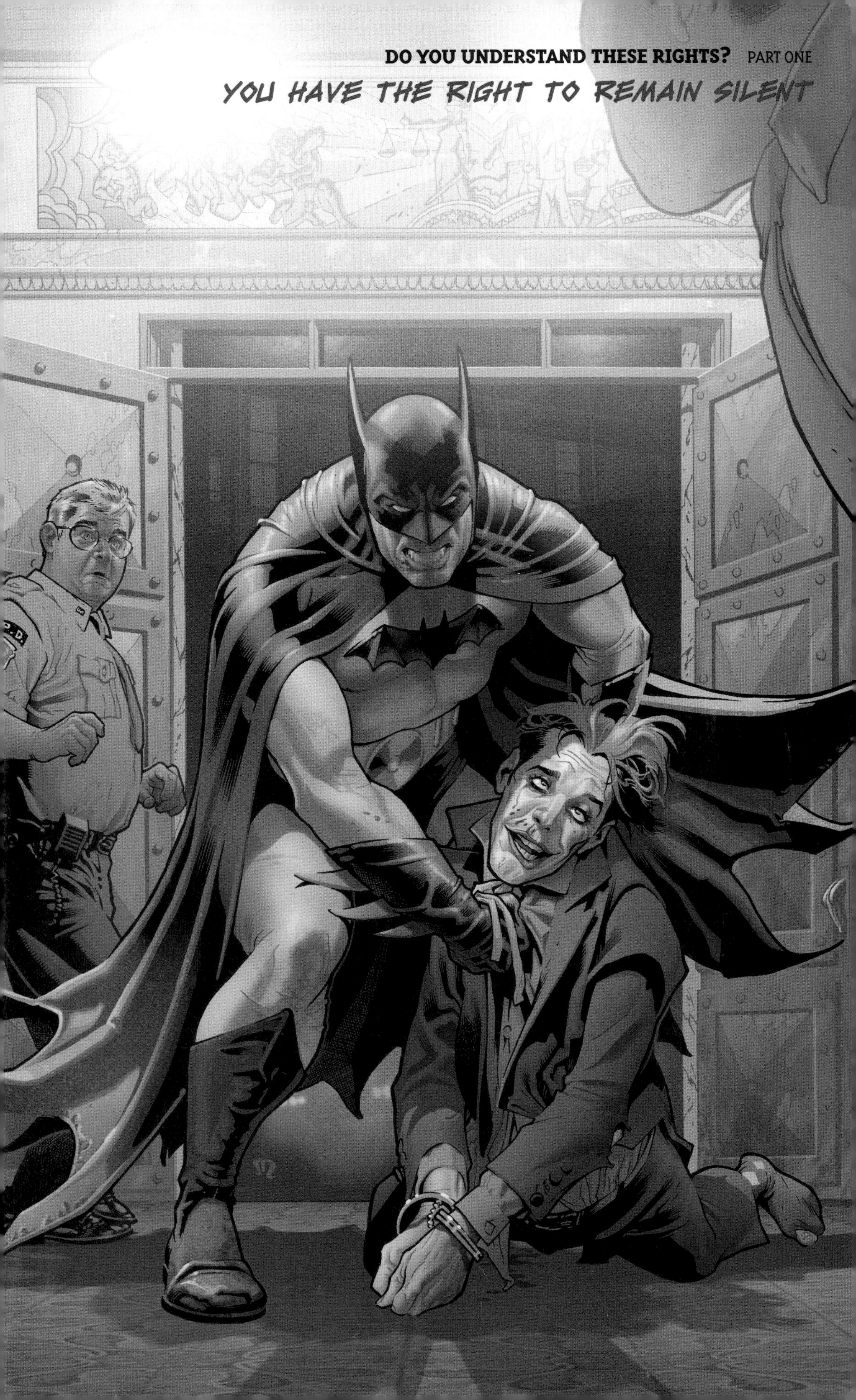

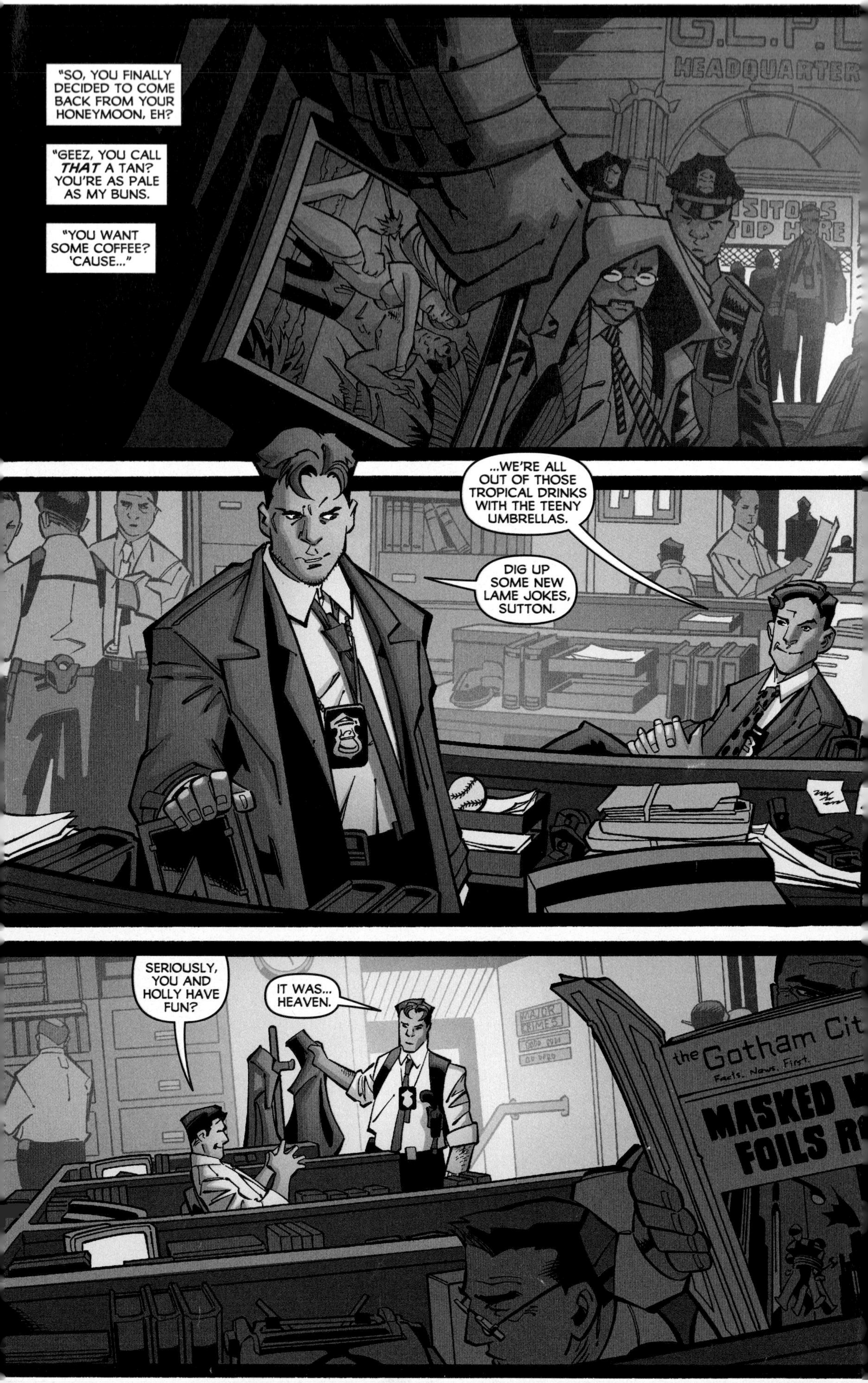
"SO, YOU FINALLY DECIDED TO COME BACK FROM YOUR HONEYMOON, EH?
"GEEZ, YOU CALL *THAT* A TAN? YOU'RE AS PALE AS MY BUNS.
"YOU WANT SOME COFFEE? 'CAUSE..."
...WE'RE ALL OUT OF THOSE TROPICAL DRINKS WITH THE TEENY UMBRELLAS.
DIG UP SOME NEW LAME JOKES, SUTTON.
SERIOUSLY, YOU AND HOLLY HAVE FUN?
IT WAS... HEAVEN.
MAJOR CRIMES
Facts. News. First.
MASKED
FOILS

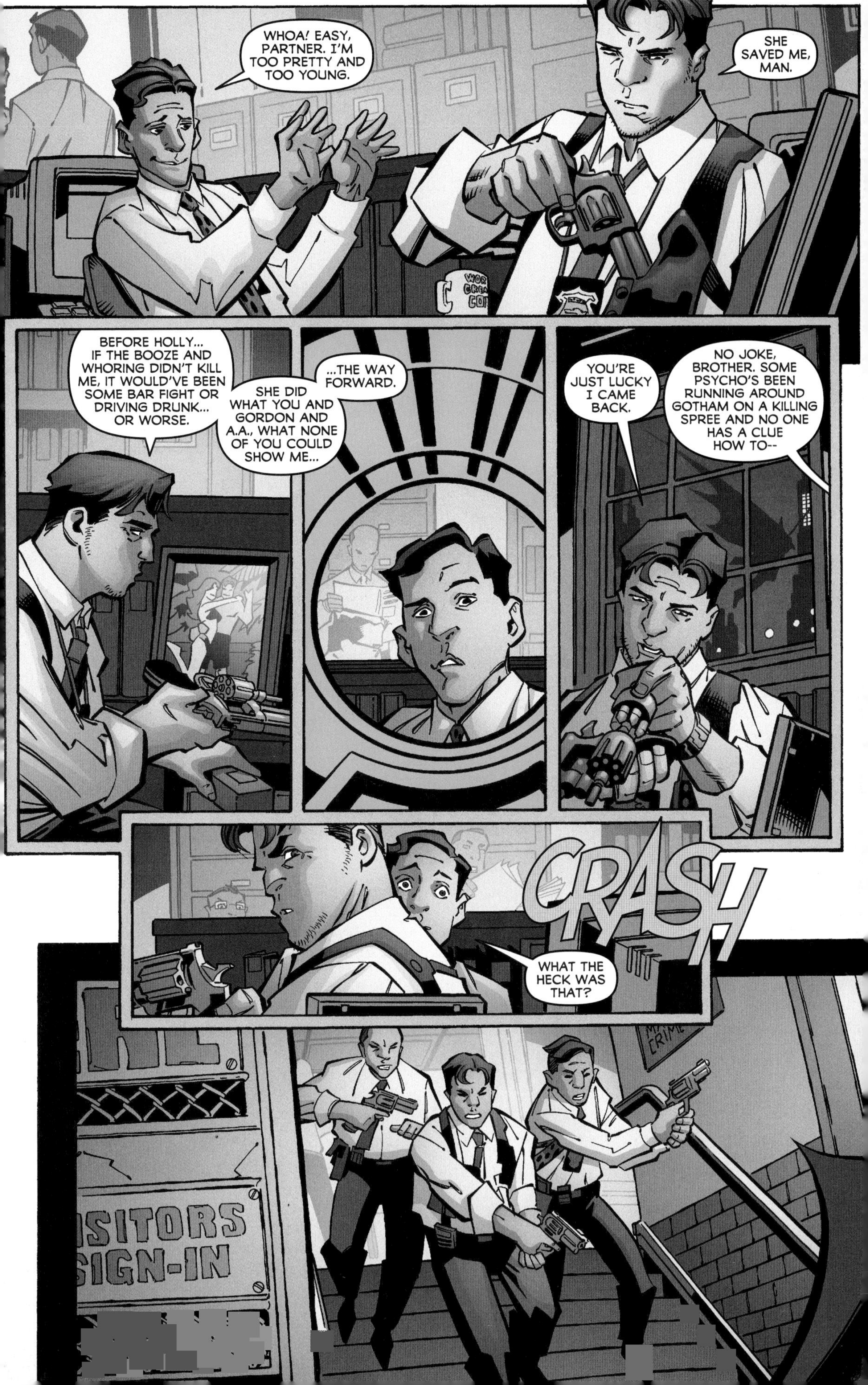
WHOA! EASY, PARTNER. I'M TOO PRETTY AND TOO YOUNG.
SHE SAVED ME, MAN.
BEFORE HOLLY... IF THE BOOZE AND WHORING DIDN'T KILL ME, IT WOULD'VE BEEN SOME BAR FIGHT OR DRIVING DRUNK... OR WORSE.
SHE DID WHAT YOU AND GORDON AND A.A., WHAT NONE OF YOU COULD SHOW ME...
...THE WAY FORWARD.
YOU'RE JUST LUCKY I CAME BACK.
NO JOKE, BROTHER. SOME PSYCHO'S BEEN RUNNING AROUND GOTHAM ON A KILLING SPREE AND NO ONE HAS A CLUE HOW TO--
CRASH
WHAT THE HECK WAS THAT?

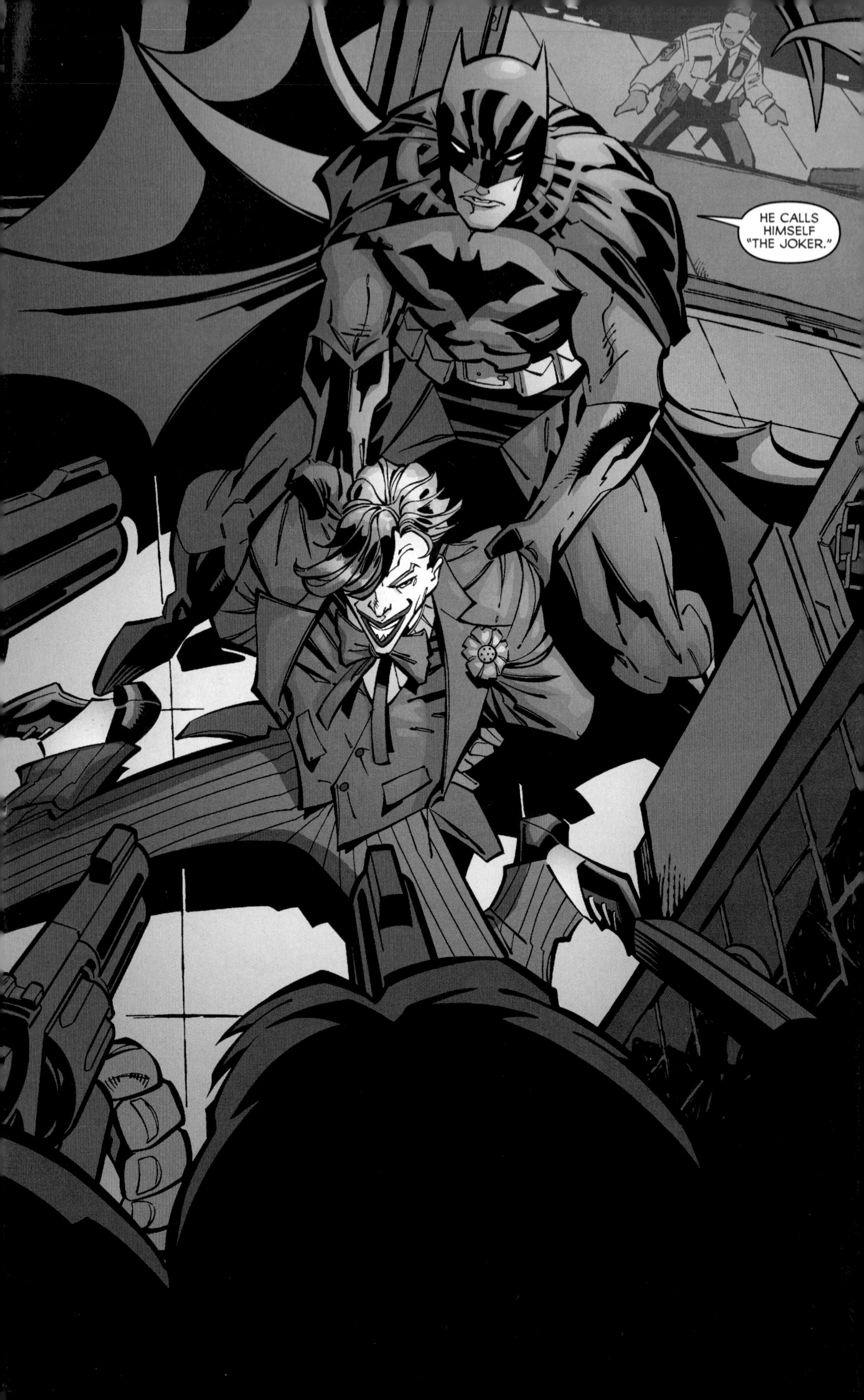
HE CALLS HIMSELF "THE JOKER."

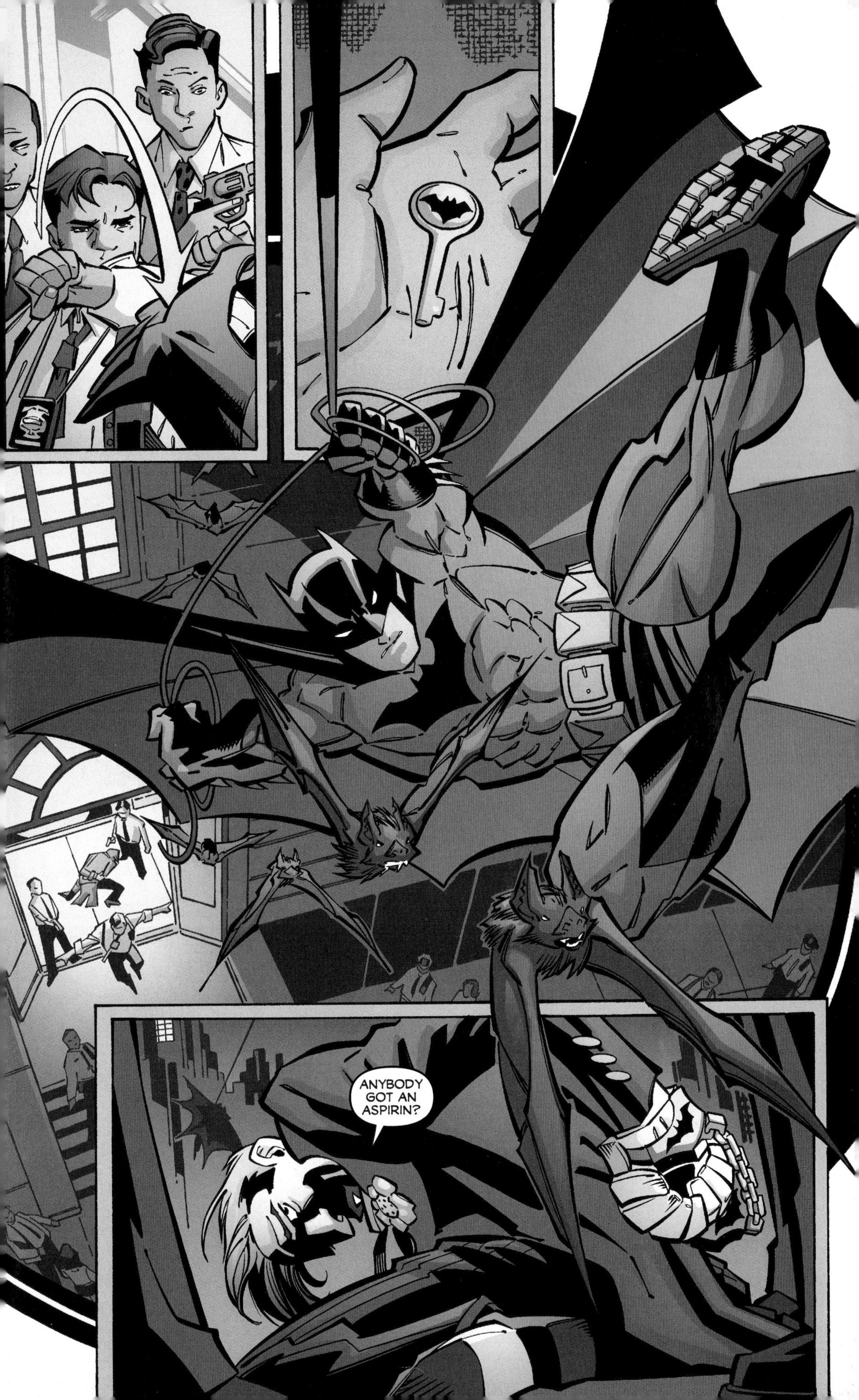
ANYBODY GOT AN ASPIRIN?

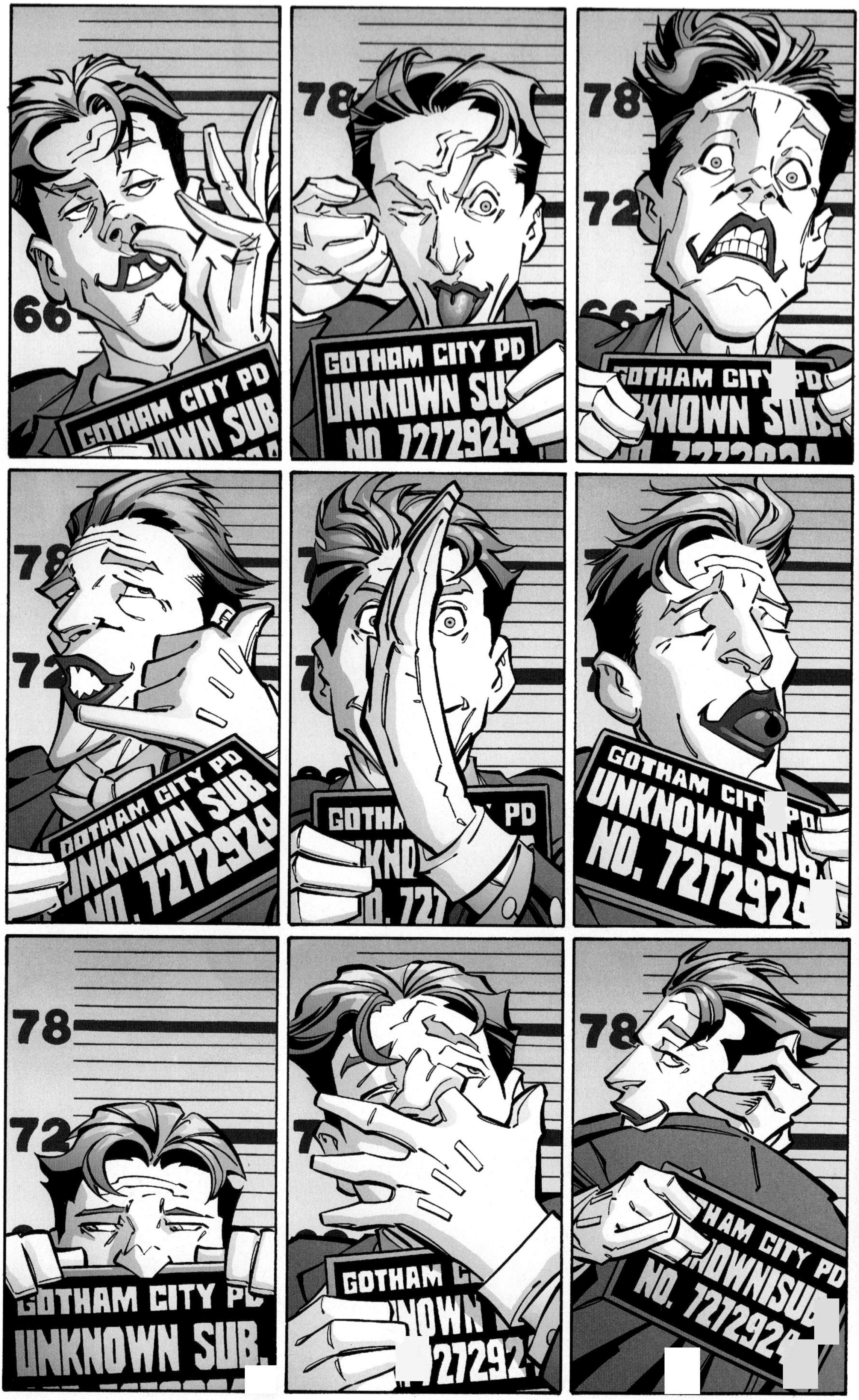
66
GOTHAM CITY PD
78
GOTHAM CITY PD
UNKNOWN SUB
NO. 7272924
78
72
78
72
GOTHAM CITY PD
UNKNOWN SUB.
GOTHAM CITY PD
UNKNOWN SUB
NO. 7272924
78
72
GOTHAM CITY PD
UNKNOWN SUB.
78
NO. 7272924

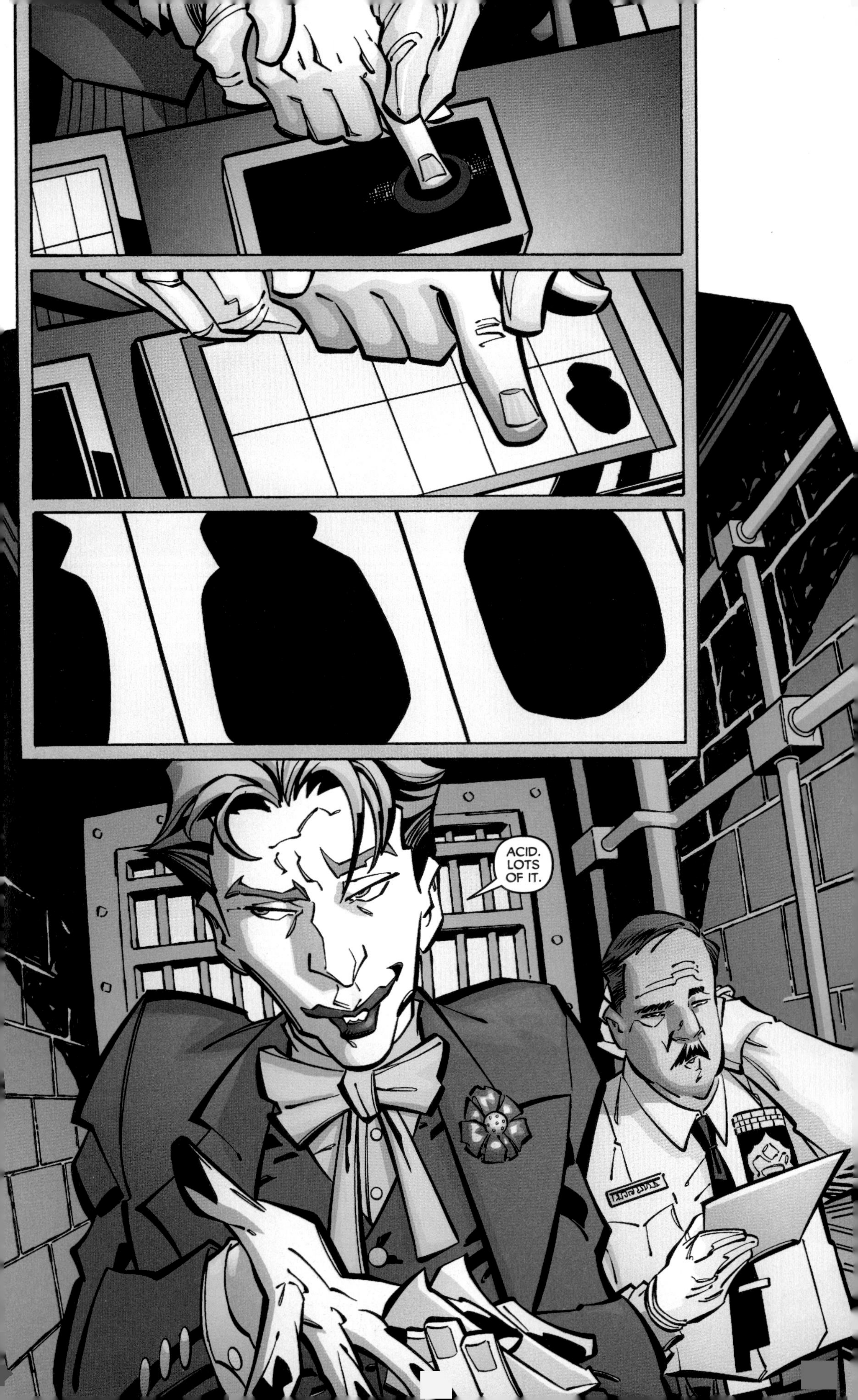
ACID. LOTS OF IT.

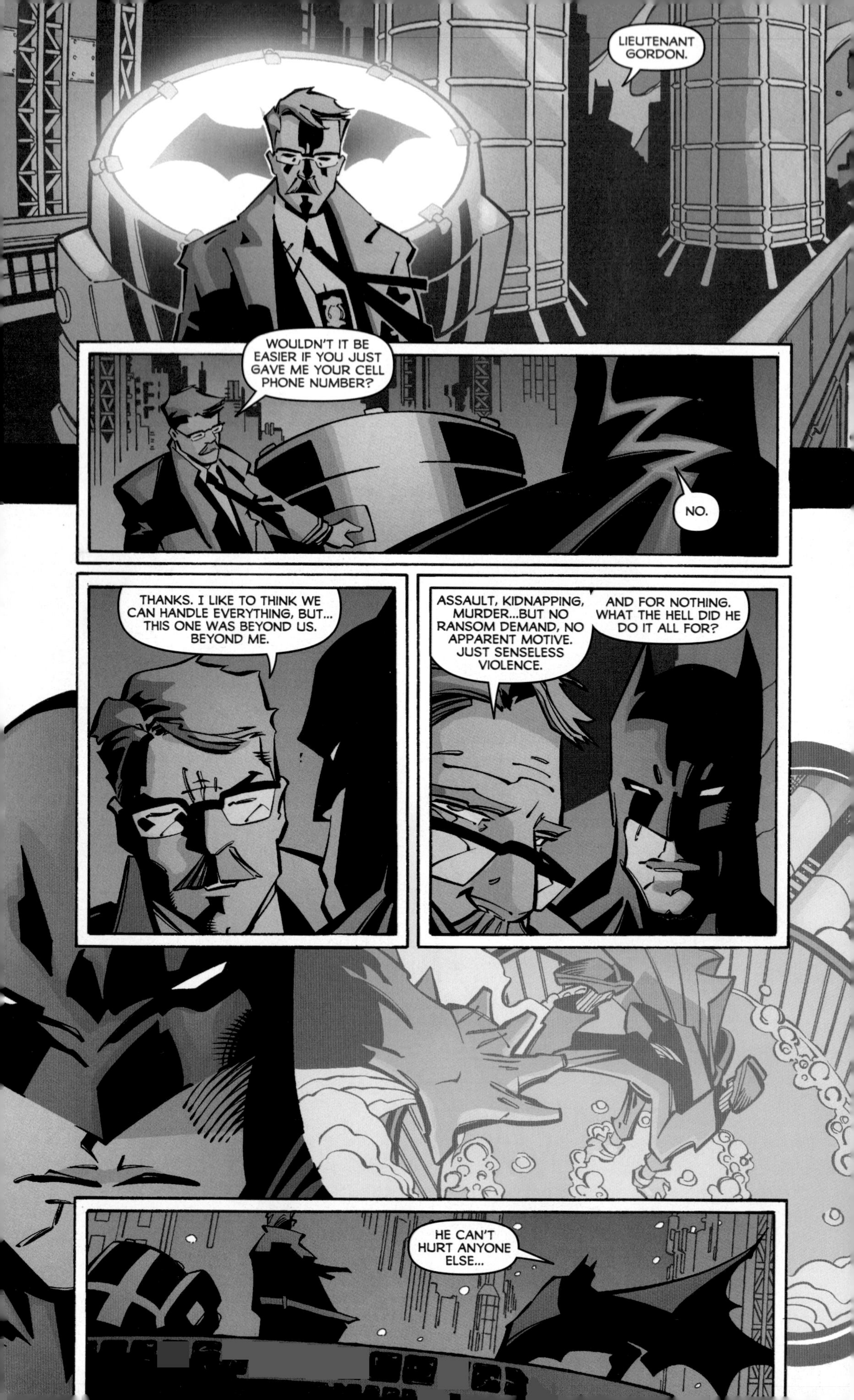
LIEUTENANT GORDON.
WOULDN'T IT BE EASIER IF YOU JUST GAVE ME YOUR CELL PHONE NUMBER?
NO.
THANKS. I LIKE TO THINK WE CAN HANDLE EVERYTHING, BUT... THIS ONE WAS BEYOND US. BEYOND ME.
ASSAULT, KIDNAPPING, MURDER...BUT NO RANSOM DEMAND, NO APPARENT MOTIVE. JUST SENSELESS VIOLENCE.
AND FOR NOTHING. WHAT THE HELL DID HE DO IT ALL FOR?
HE CAN'T HURT ANYONE ELSE...

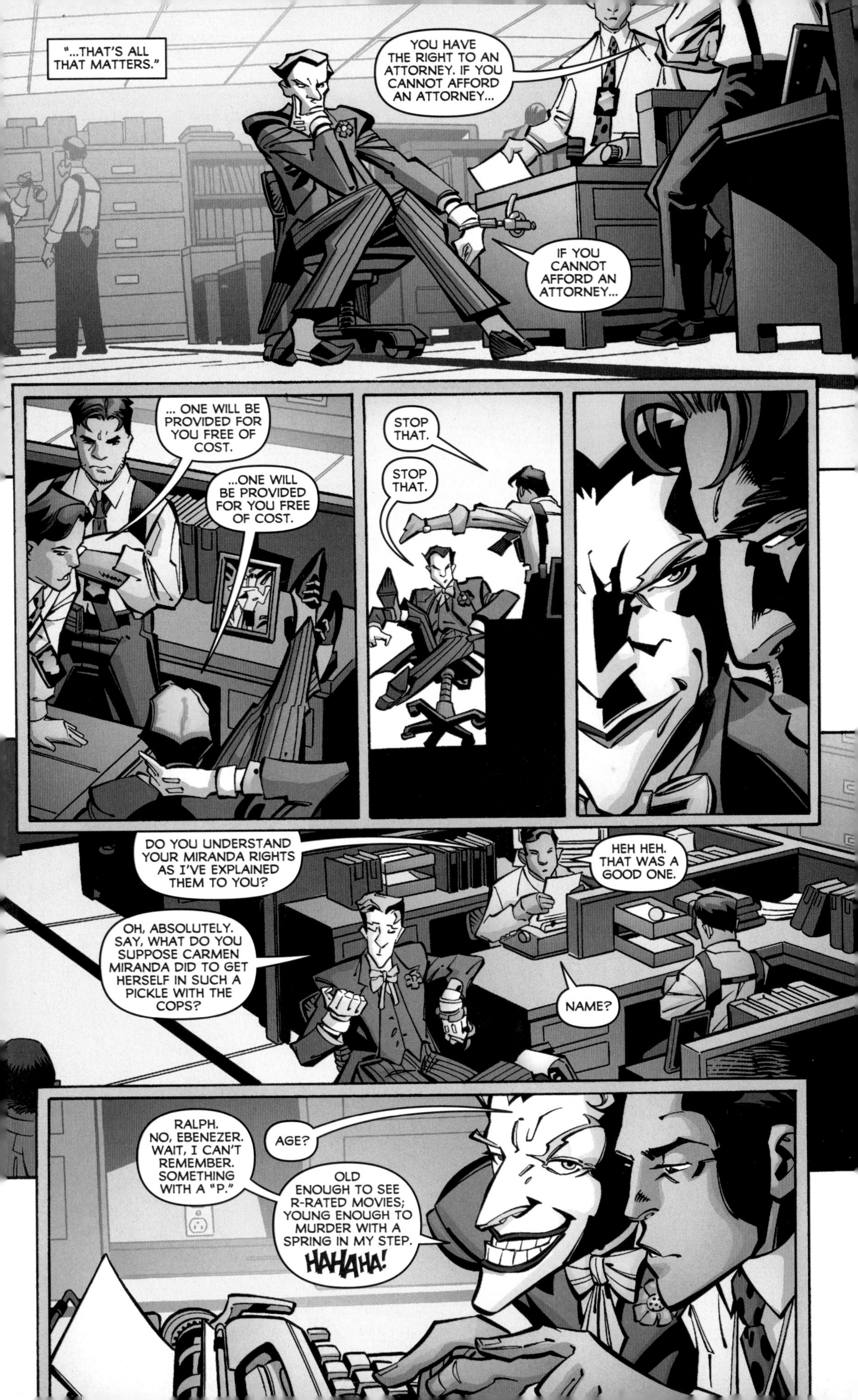
"...THAT'S ALL THAT MATTERS."
YOU HAVE THE RIGHT TO AN ATTORNEY. IF YOU CANNOT AFFORD AN ATTORNEY...
IF YOU CANNOT AFFORD AN ATTORNEY...
... ONE WILL BE PROVIDED FOR YOU FREE OF COST.
...ONE WILL BE PROVIDED FOR YOU FREE OF COST.
STOP THAT.
STOP THAT.
DO YOU UNDERSTAND YOUR MIRANDA RIGHTS AS I'VE EXPLAINED THEM TO YOU?
HEH HEH. THAT WAS A GOOD ONE.
OH, ABSOLUTELY. SAY, WHAT DO YOU SUPPOSE CARMEN MIRANDA DID TO GET HERSELF IN SUCH A PICKLE WITH THE COPS?
NAME?
RALPH. NO, EBENEZER. WAIT, I CAN'T REMEMBER. SOMETHING WITH A "P."
AGE?
OLD ENOUGH TO SEE R-RATED MOVIES; YOUNG ENOUGH TO MURDER WITH A SPRING IN MY STEP.
HAHAHA!

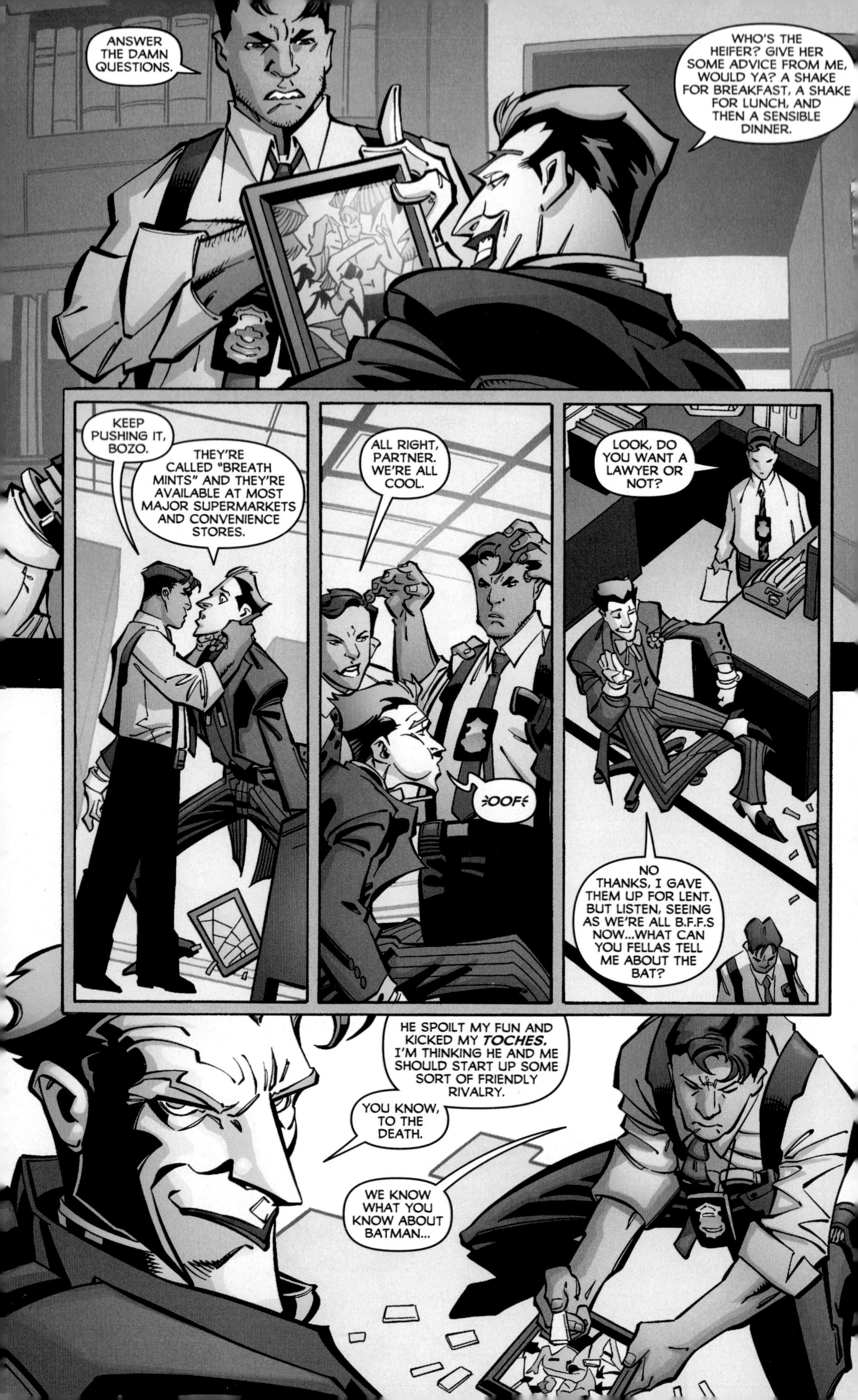
ANSWER THE DAMN QUESTIONS.
WHO'S THE HEIFER? GIVE HER SOME ADVICE FROM ME, WOULD YA? A SHAKE FOR BREAKFAST, A SHAKE FOR LUNCH, AND THEN A SENSIBLE DINNER.
KEEP PUSHING IT, BOZO.
THEY'RE CALLED "BREATH MINTS" AND THEY'RE AVAILABLE AT MOST MAJOR SUPERMARKETS AND CONVENIENCE STORES.
ALL RIGHT, PARTNER. WE'RE ALL COOL.
OOF
LOOK, DO YOU WANT A LAWYER OR NOT?
NO THANKS, I GAVE THEM UP FOR LENT. BUT LISTEN, SEEING AS WE'RE ALL B.F.F.S NOW...WHAT CAN YOU FELLAS TELL ME ABOUT THE BAT?
HE SPOILT MY FUN AND KICKED MY *TOCHES.* I'M THINKING HE AND ME SHOULD START UP SOME SORT OF FRIENDLY RIVALRY.
YOU KNOW, TO THE DEATH.
WE KNOW WHAT YOU KNOW ABOUT BATMAN...

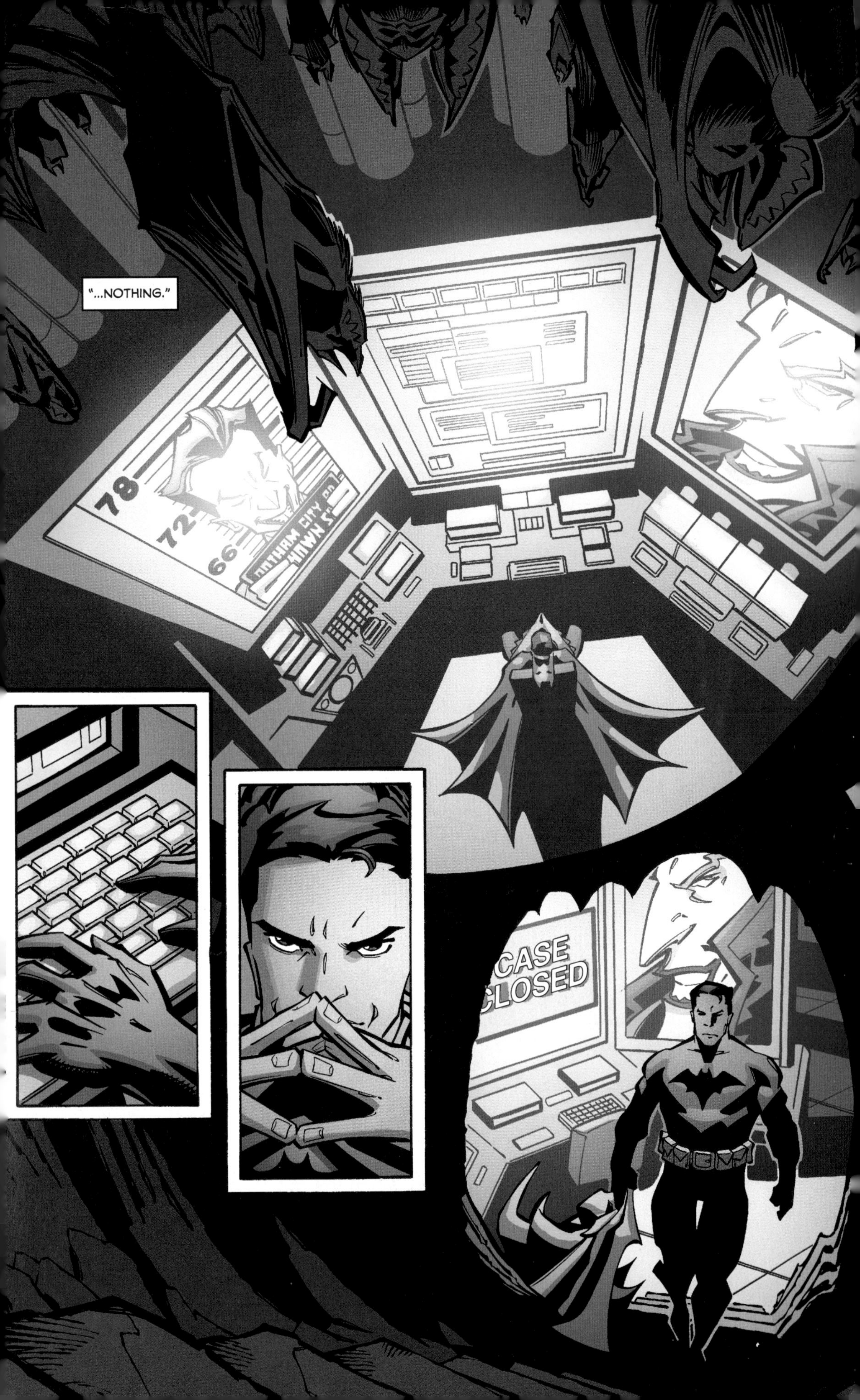
"...NOTHING."
78
72
66
CASE
CLOSED

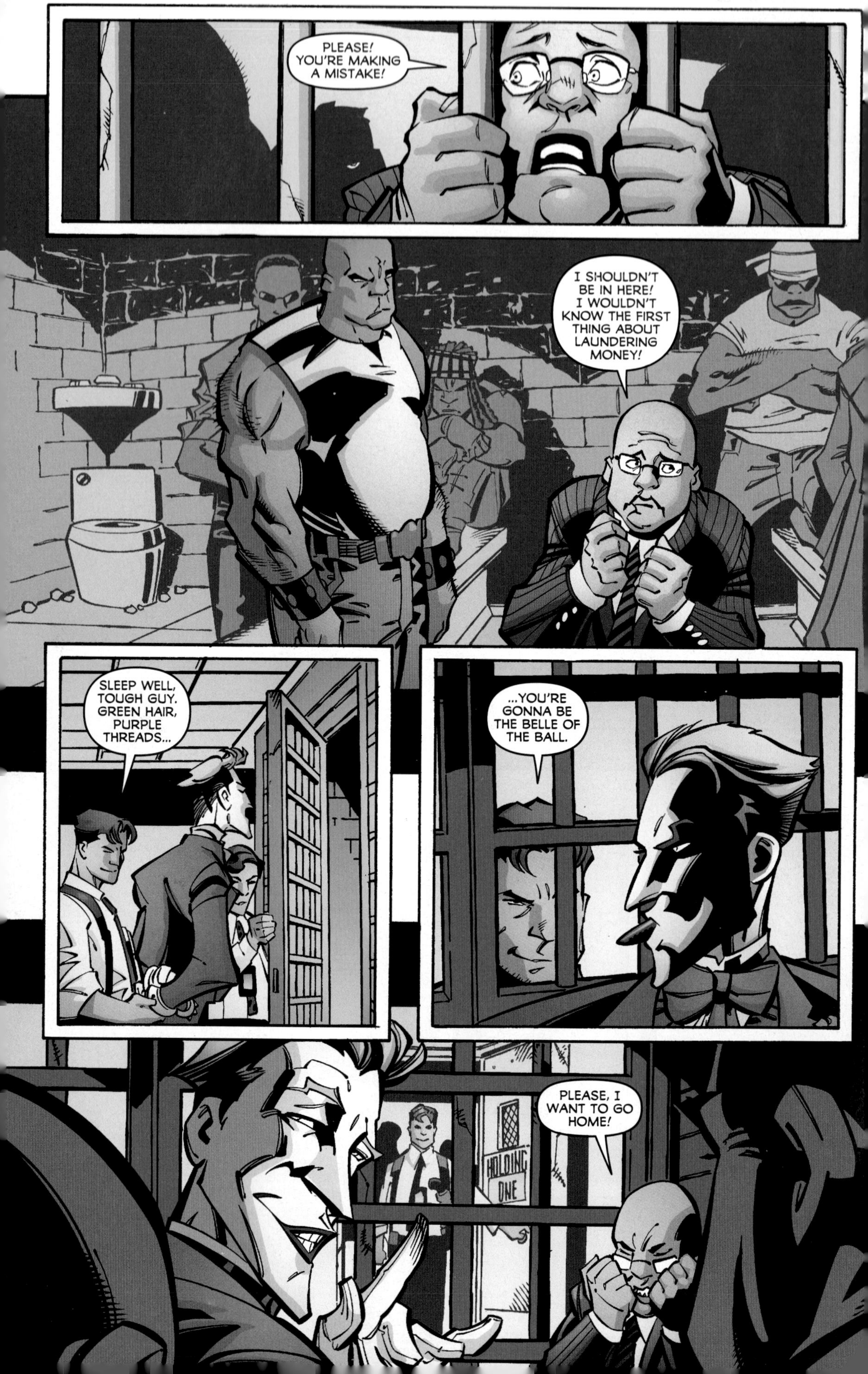
PLEASE! YOU'RE MAKING A MISTAKE!
I SHOULDN'T BE IN HERE! I WOULDN'T KNOW THE FIRST THING ABOUT LAUNDERING MONEY!
SLEEP WELL, TOUGH GUY. GREEN HAIR, PURPLE THREADS...
...YOU'RE GONNA BE THE BELLE OF THE BALL.
PLEASE, I WANT TO GO HOME!
HOLDING ONE

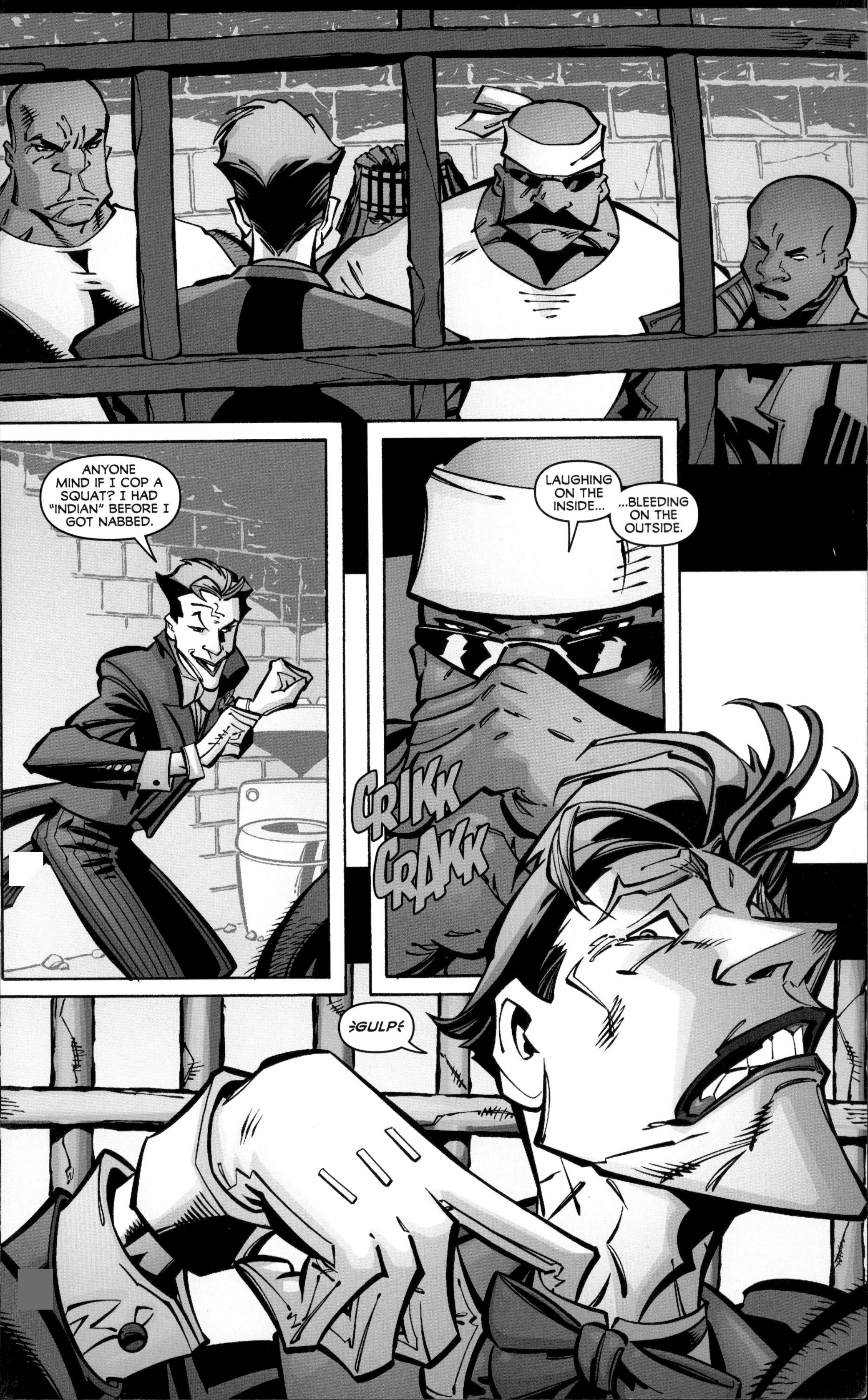
ANYONE MIND IF I COP A SQUAT? I HAD "INDIAN" BEFORE I GOT NABBED.
LAUGHING ON THE INSIDE...
...BLEEDING ON THE OUTSIDE.
CRIKK CRAKK
GULP

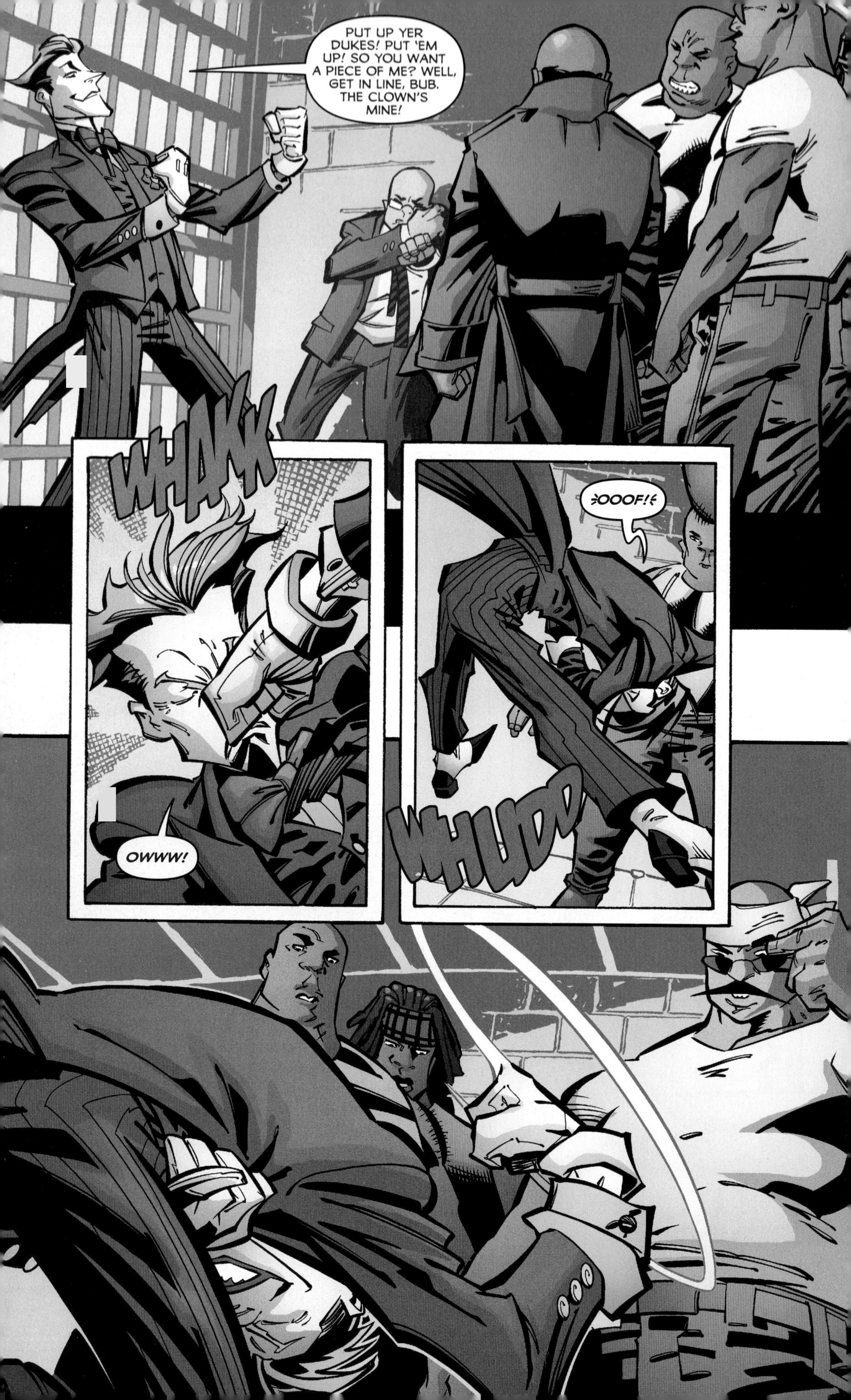
PUT UP YER DUKES! PUT 'EM UP! SO YOU WANT A PIECE OF ME? WELL, GET IN LINE, BUB. THE CLOWN'S MINE!
WHAKK
OWWW!
OOOF!
WHUDD

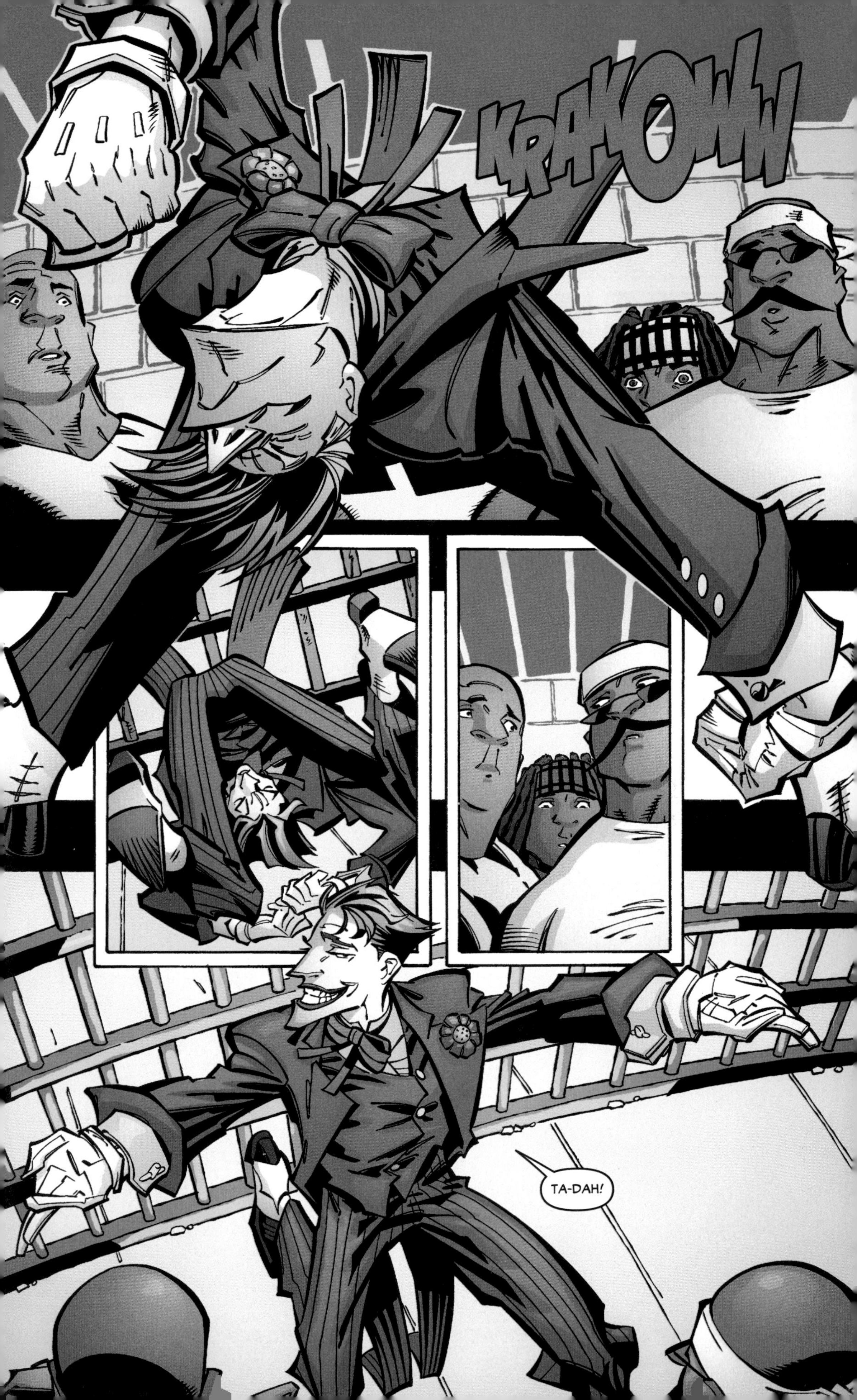
KRAKOWW
TA-DAH!

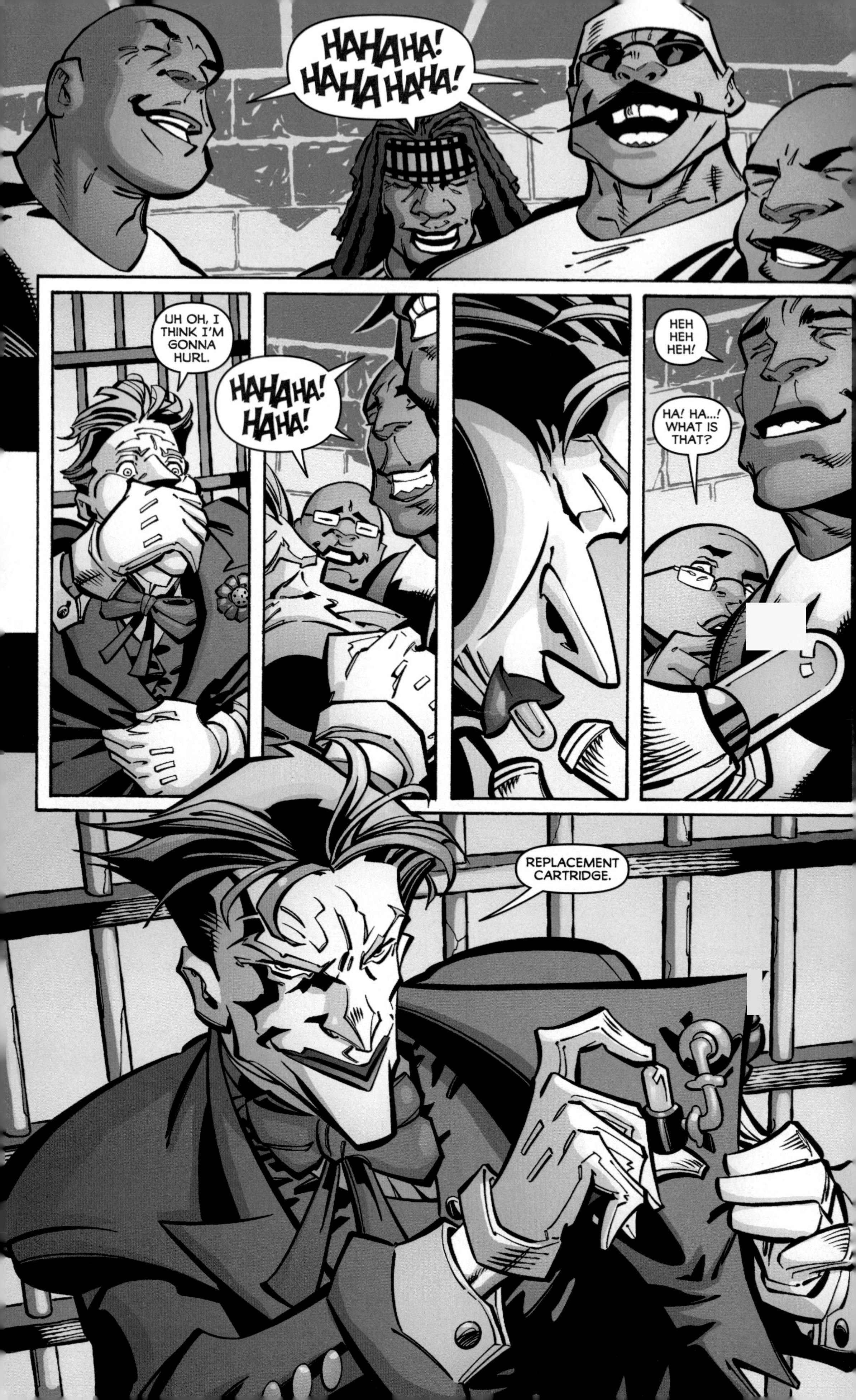
HAHAHA! HAHAHAHA!
UH OH, I THINK I'M GONNA HURL.
HAHAHA! HAHA!
HEH HEH HEH!
HA! HA...! WHAT IS THAT?
REPLACEMENT CARTRIDGE.

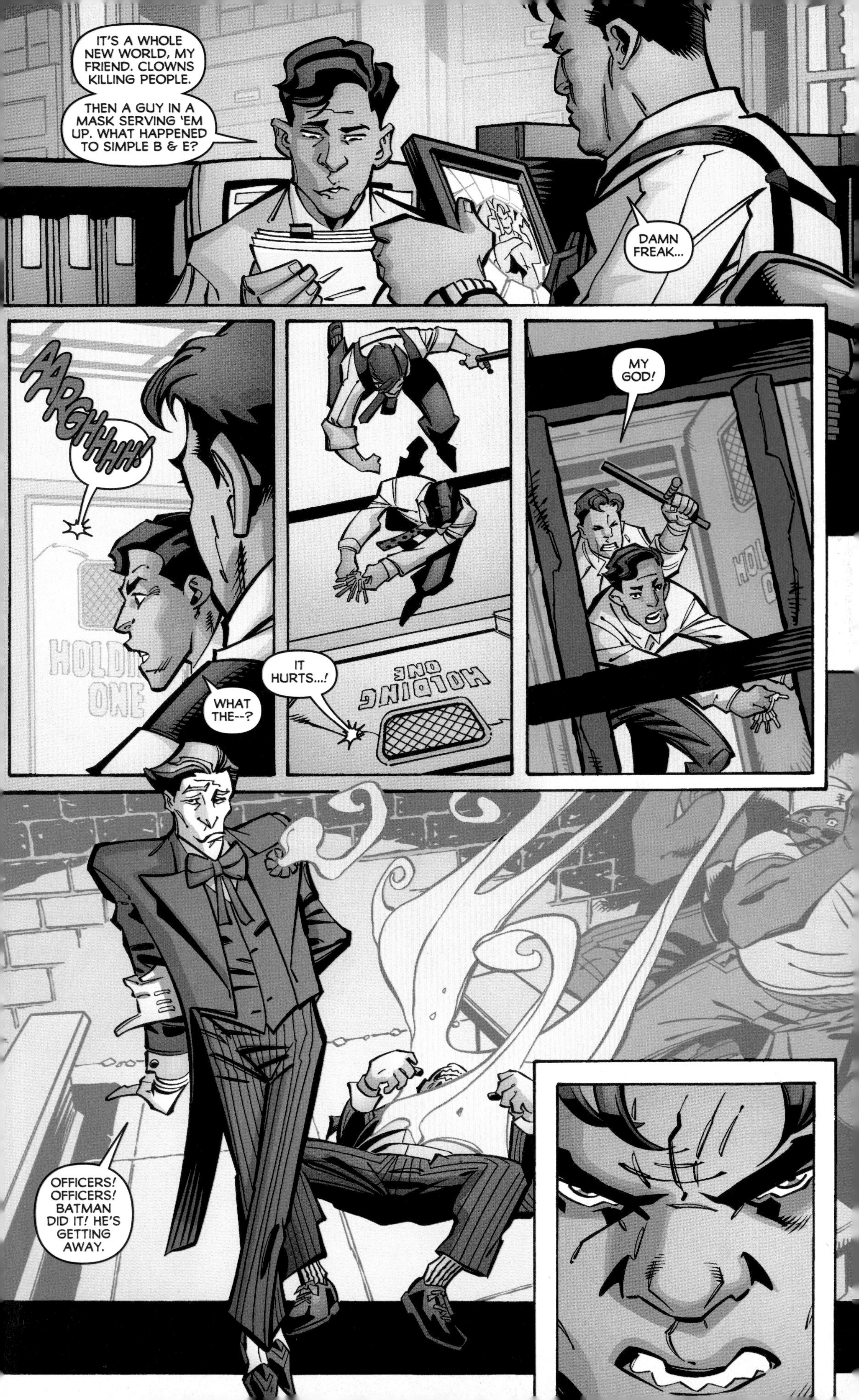

IT'S A WHOLE NEW WORLD, MY FRIEND. CLOWNS KILLING PEOPLE.
THEN A GUY IN A MASK SERVING 'EM UP. WHAT HAPPENED TO SIMPLE B & E?
DAMN FREAK...
AARGHHHH!
HOLDING ONE
WHAT THE--?
IT HURTS...!
HOLDING ONE
MY GOD!
OFFICERS! OFFICERS! BATMAN DID IT! HE'S GETTING AWAY.

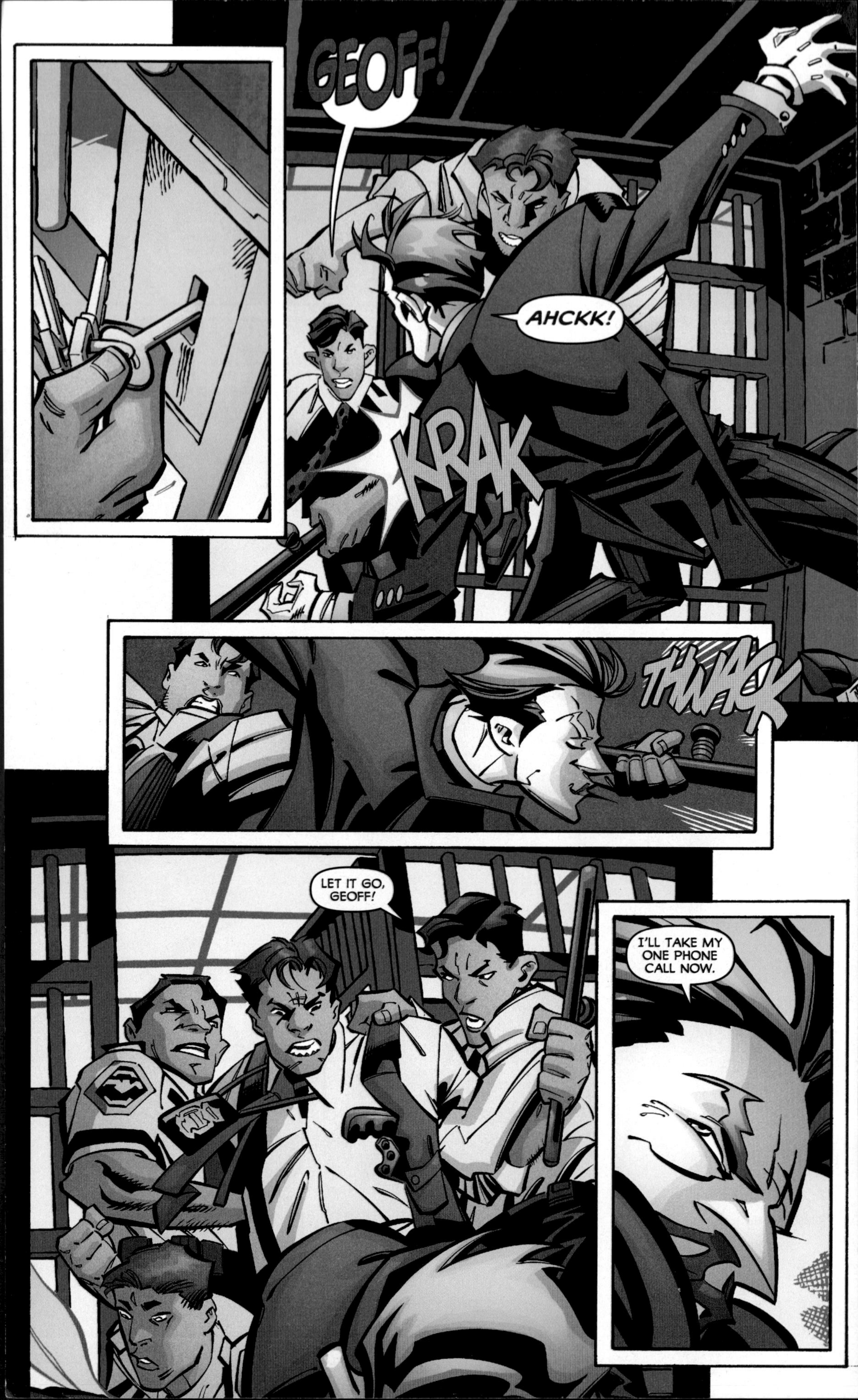
GEOFF!
AHCKK!
KRAK
THWACK
LET IT GO, GEOFF!
I'LL TAKE MY ONE PHONE CALL NOW.

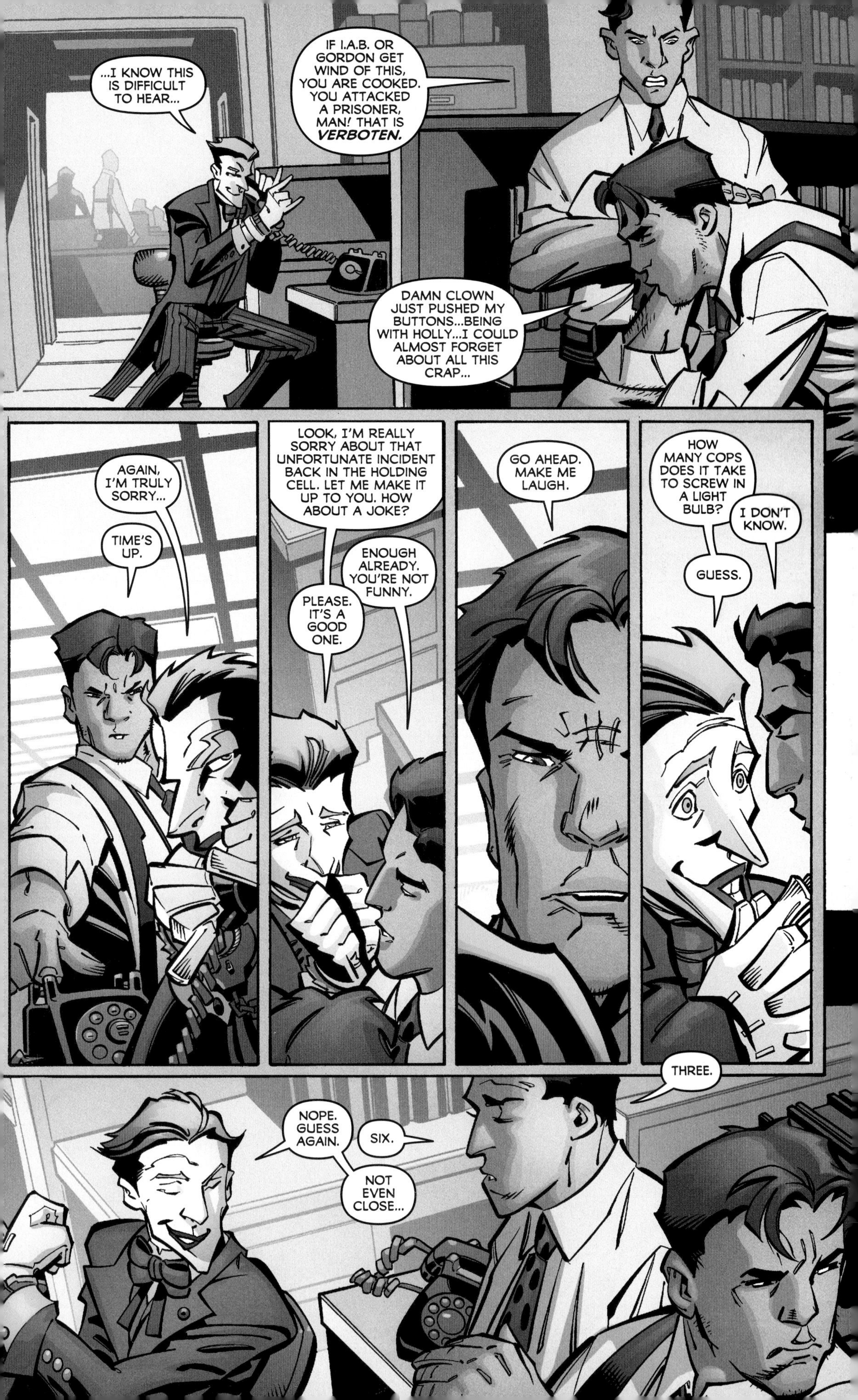
...I KNOW THIS IS DIFFICULT TO HEAR...
IF I.A.B. OR GORDON GET WIND OF THIS, YOU ARE COOKED. YOU ATTACKED A PRISONER, MAN! THAT IS *VERBOTEN.*
DAMN CLOWN JUST PUSHED MY BUTTONS...BEING WITH HOLLY...I COULD ALMOST FORGET ABOUT ALL THIS CRAP...
AGAIN, I'M TRULY SORRY...
TIME'S UP.
LOOK, I'M REALLY SORRY ABOUT THAT UNFORTUNATE INCIDENT BACK IN THE HOLDING CELL. LET ME MAKE IT UP TO YOU. HOW ABOUT A JOKE?
ENOUGH ALREADY. YOU'RE NOT FUNNY.
PLEASE. IT'S A GOOD ONE.
GO AHEAD. MAKE ME LAUGH.
HOW MANY COPS DOES IT TAKE TO SCREW IN A LIGHT BULB?
I DON'T KNOW.
GUESS.
THREE.
NOPE. GUESS AGAIN.
SIX.
NOT EVEN CLOSE...

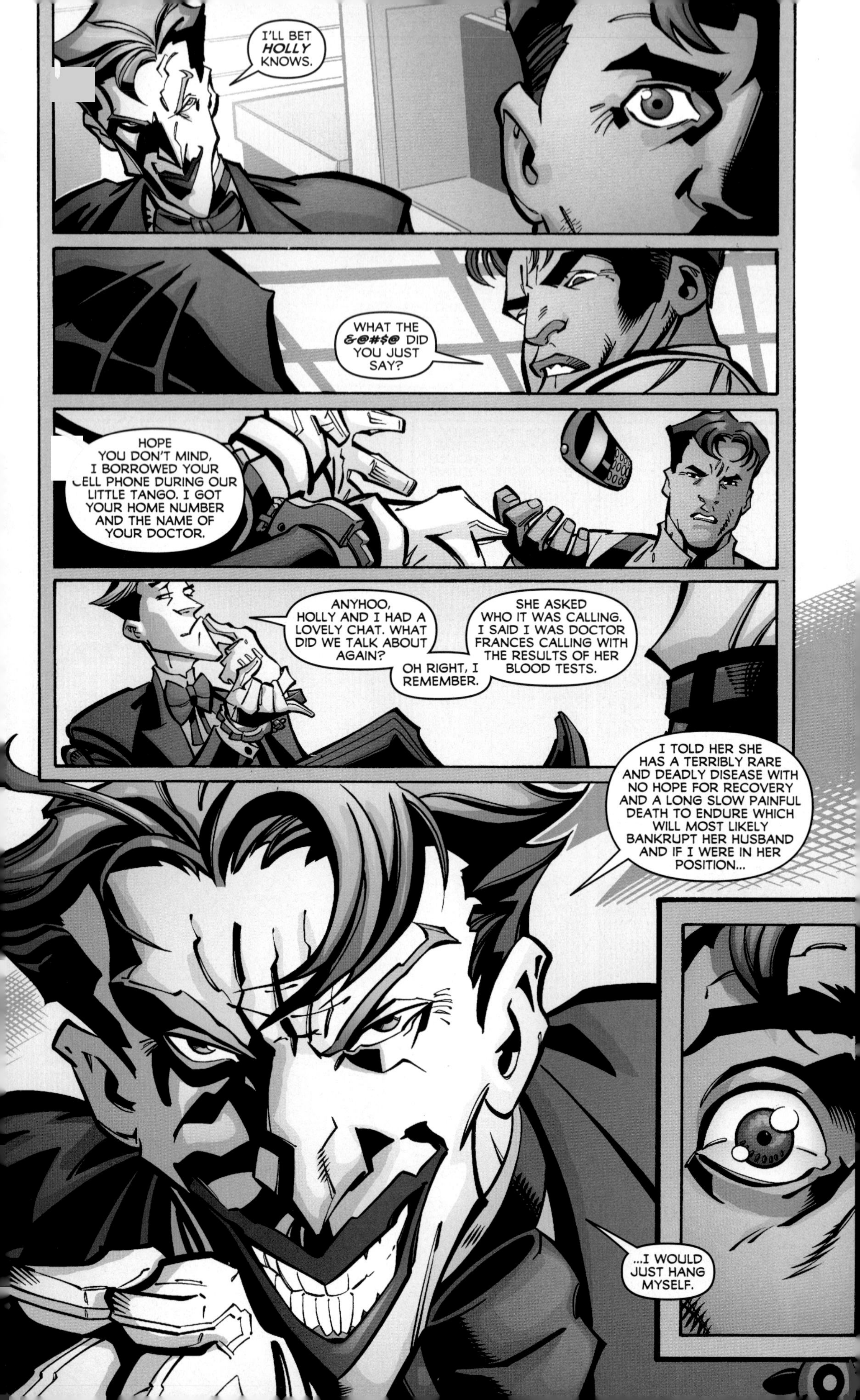
I'LL BET HOLLY KNOWS.
WHAT THE &@#$@ DID YOU JUST SAY?
HOPE YOU DON'T MIND, I BORROWED YOUR CELL PHONE DURING OUR LITTLE TANGO. I GOT YOUR HOME NUMBER AND THE NAME OF YOUR DOCTOR.
ANYHOO, HOLLY AND I HAD A LOVELY CHAT. WHAT DID WE TALK ABOUT AGAIN?
OH RIGHT, I REMEMBER.
SHE ASKED WHO IT WAS CALLING. I SAID I WAS DOCTOR FRANCES CALLING WITH THE RESULTS OF HER BLOOD TESTS.
I TOLD HER SHE HAS A TERRIBLY RARE AND DEADLY DISEASE WITH NO HOPE FOR RECOVERY AND A LONG SLOW PAINFUL DEATH TO ENDURE WHICH WILL MOST LIKELY BANKRUPT HER HUSBAND AND IF I WERE IN HER POSITION...
...I WOULD JUST HANG MYSELF.

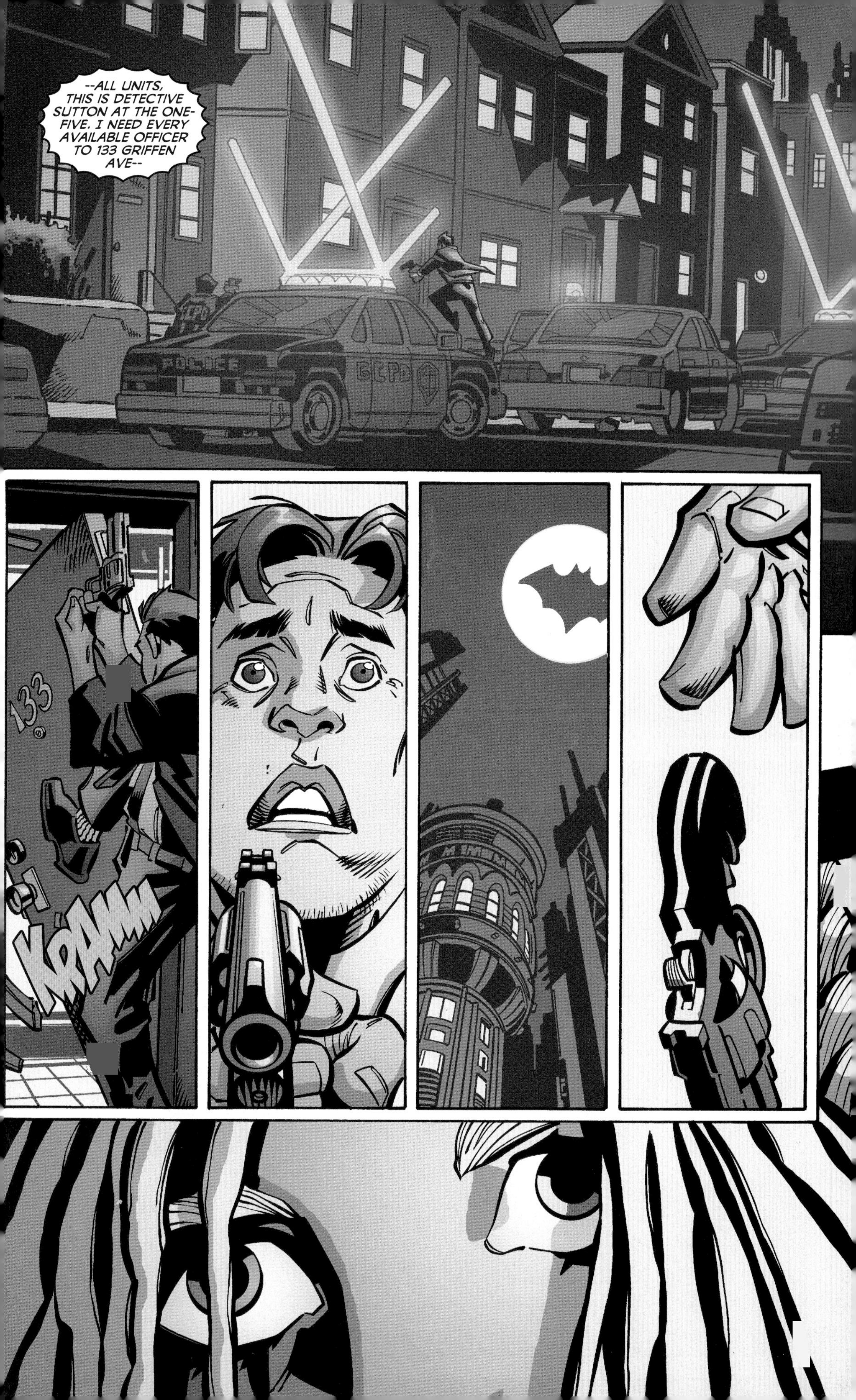
--ALL UNITS, THIS IS DETECTIVE SUTTON AT THE ONE-FIVE. I NEED EVERY AVAILABLE OFFICER TO 133 GRIFFEN AVE--
POLICE
GCPD
133
KRAMM

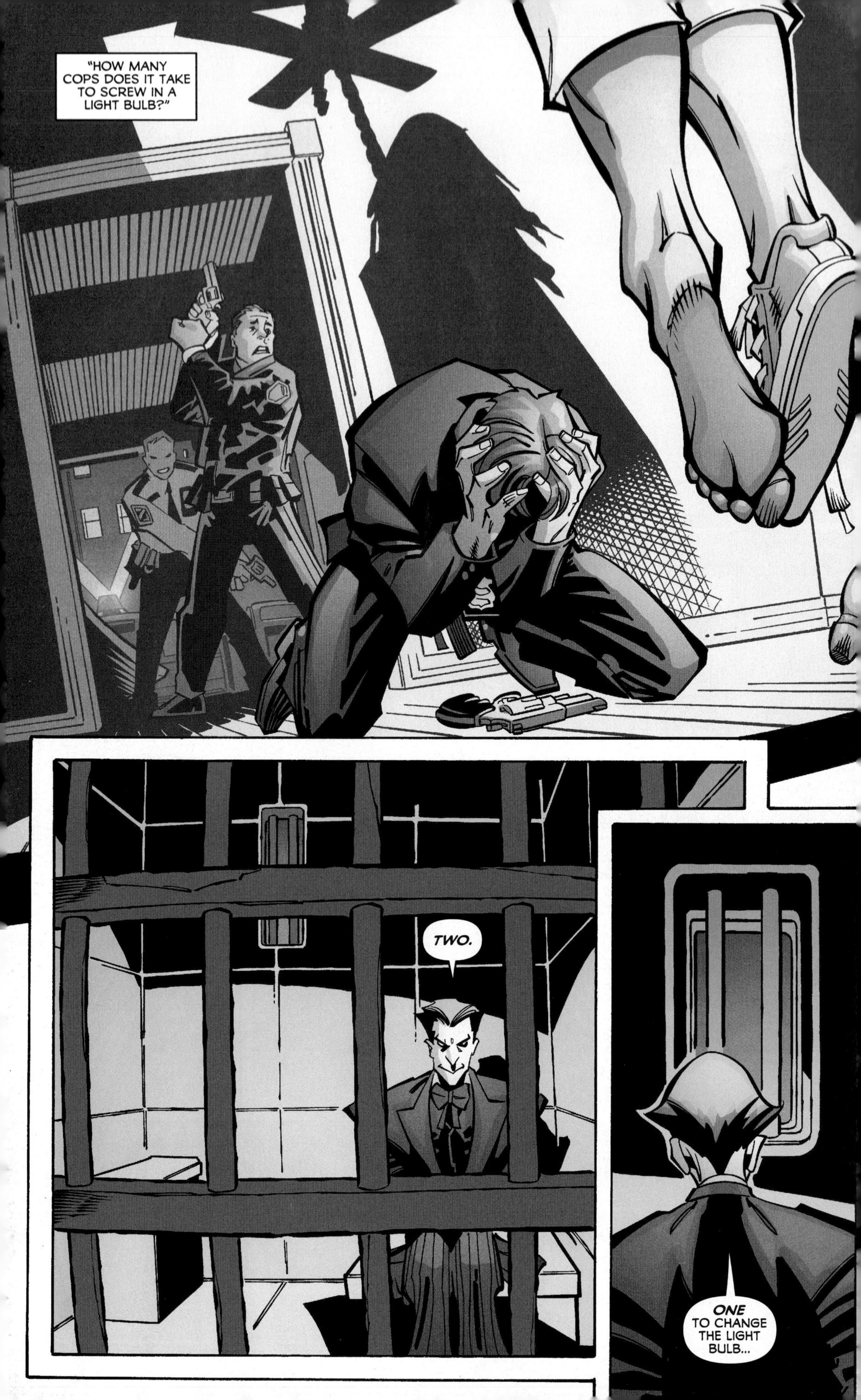
"HOW MANY COPS DOES IT TAKE TO SCREW IN A LIGHT BULB?"
TWO.
ONE TO CHANGE THE LIGHT BULB...

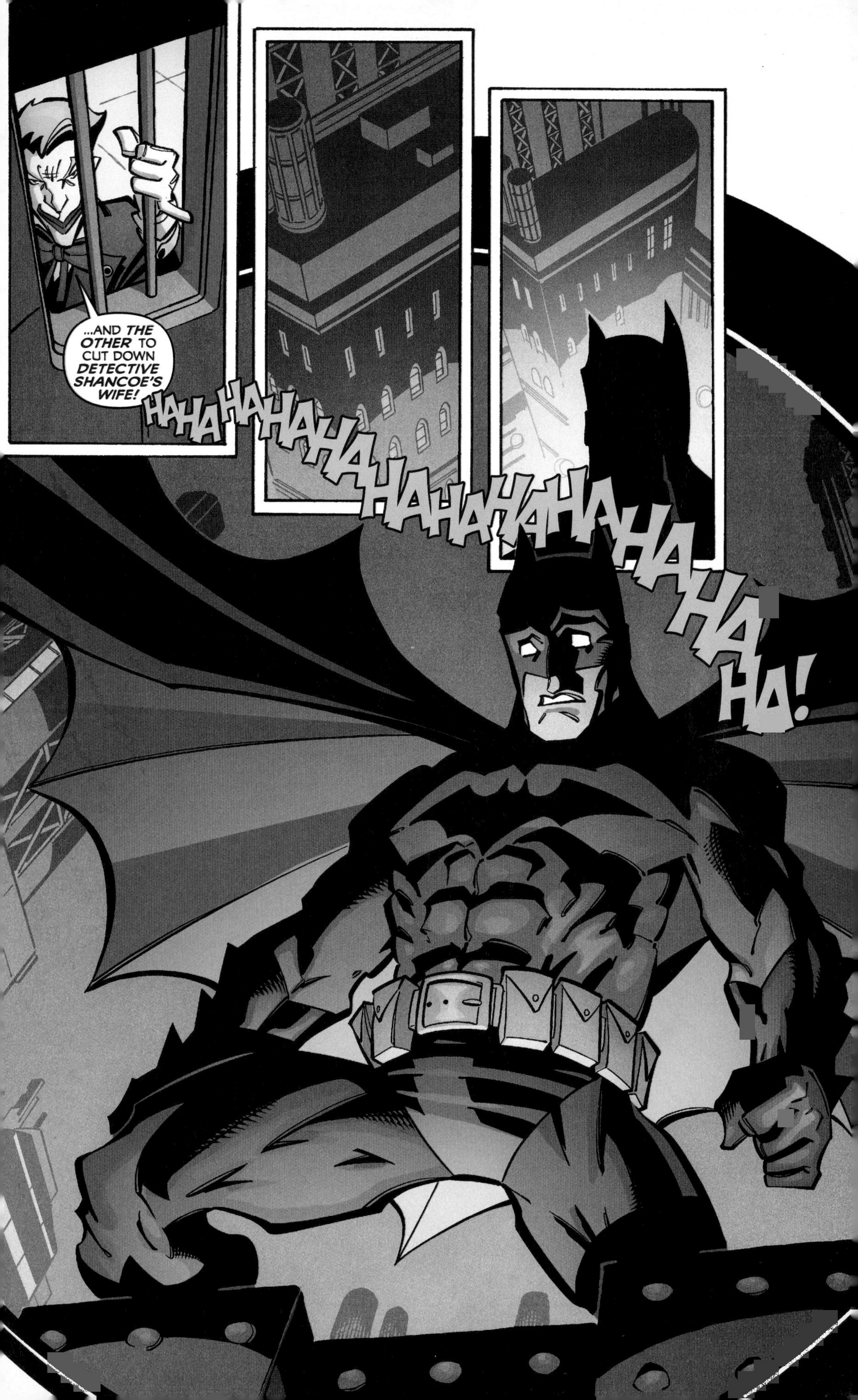
...AND THE OTHER TO CUT DOWN DETECTIVE SHANCOE'S WIFE!
HAHAHAHAHAHAHAHAHAHAHAHAHAHAHAHA!

DO YOU UNDERSTAND THESE RIGHTS? PART TWO

ANYTHING YOU SAY...

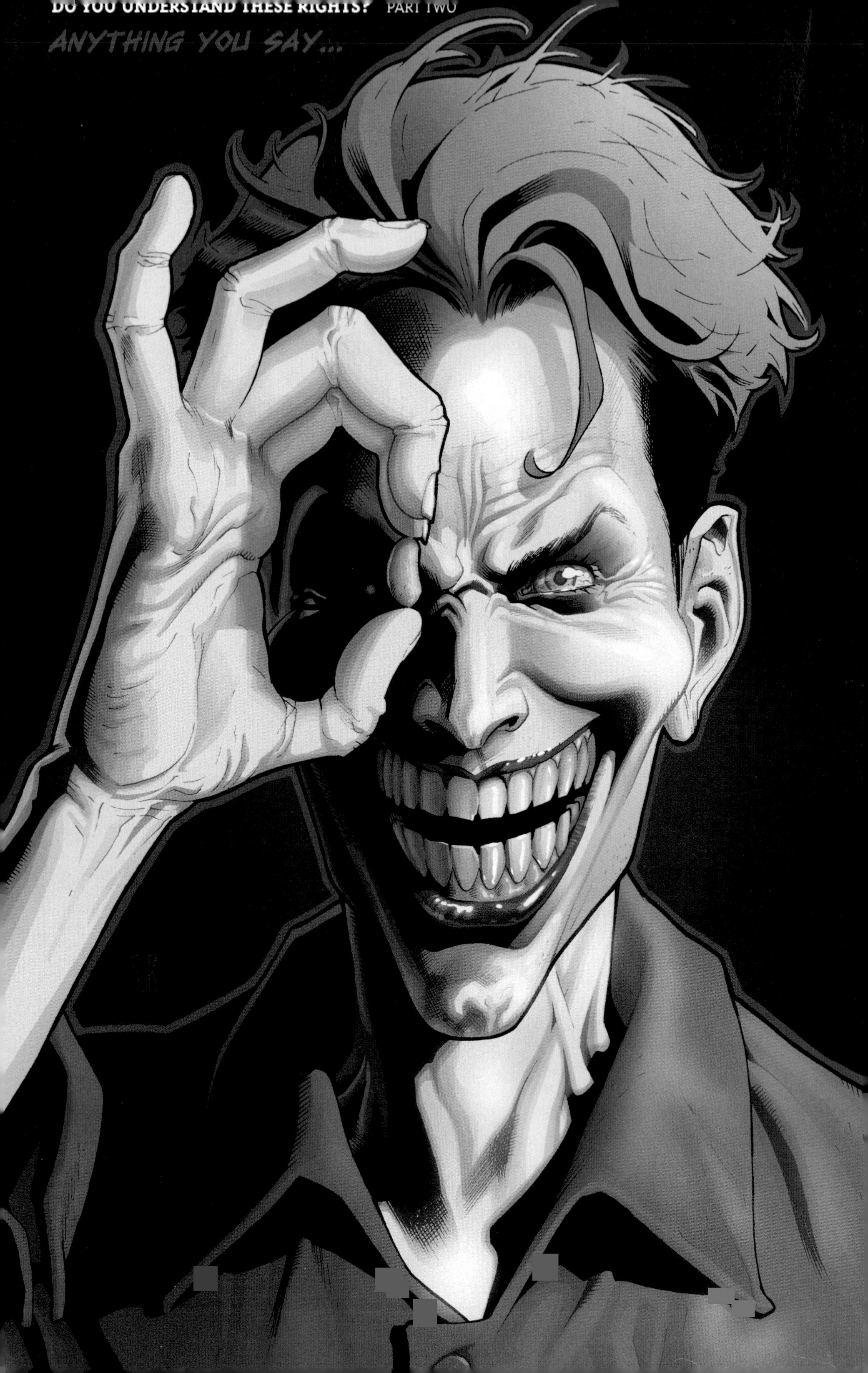

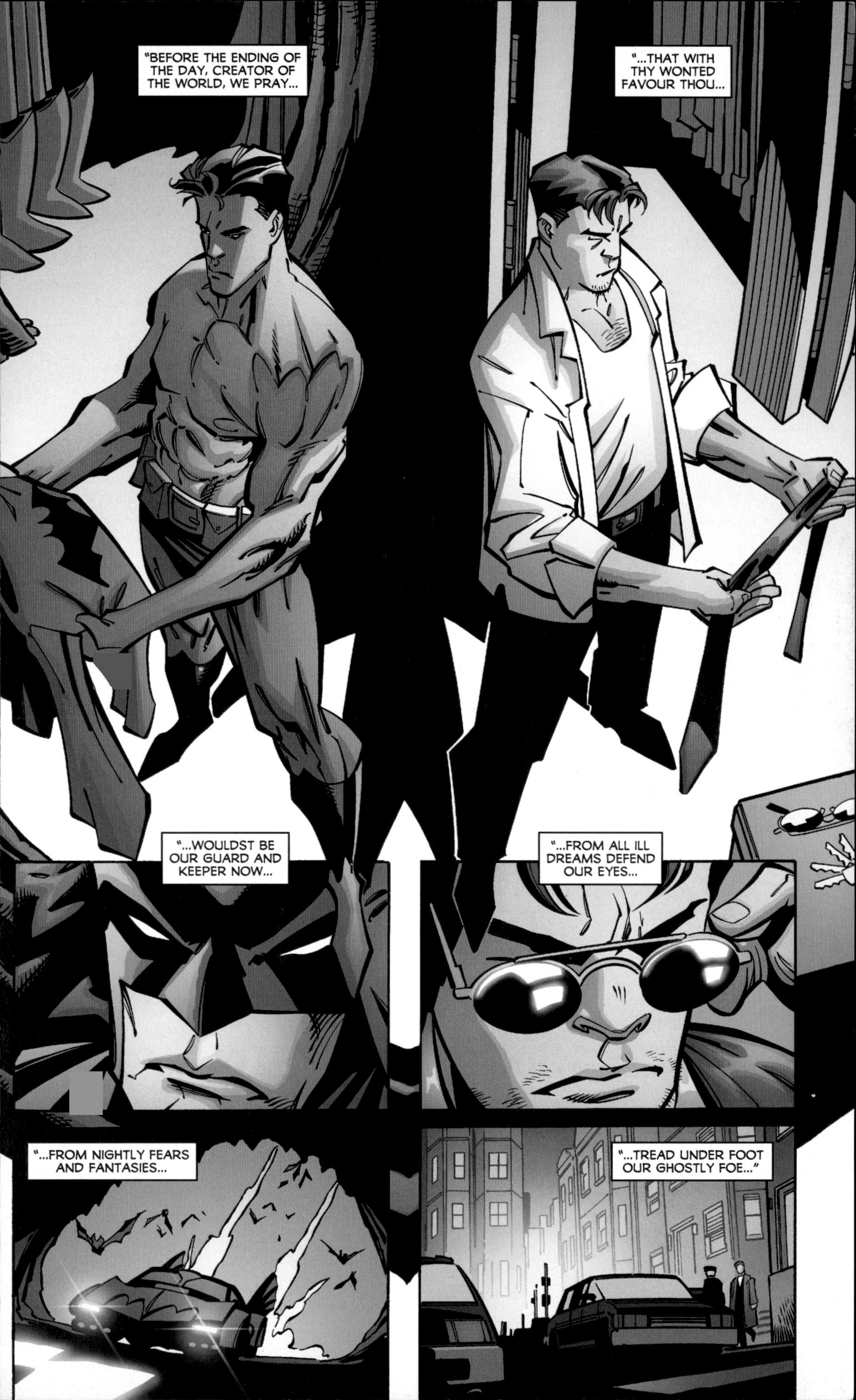
"BEFORE THE ENDING OF THE DAY, CREATOR OF THE WORLD, WE PRAY...
"...THAT WITH THY WONTED FAVOUR THOU...
"...WOULDST BE OUR GUARD AND KEEPER NOW...
"...FROM ALL ILL DREAMS DEFEND OUR EYES...
"...FROM NIGHTLY FEARS AND FANTASIES...
"...TREAD UNDER FOOT OUR GHOSTLY FOE..."

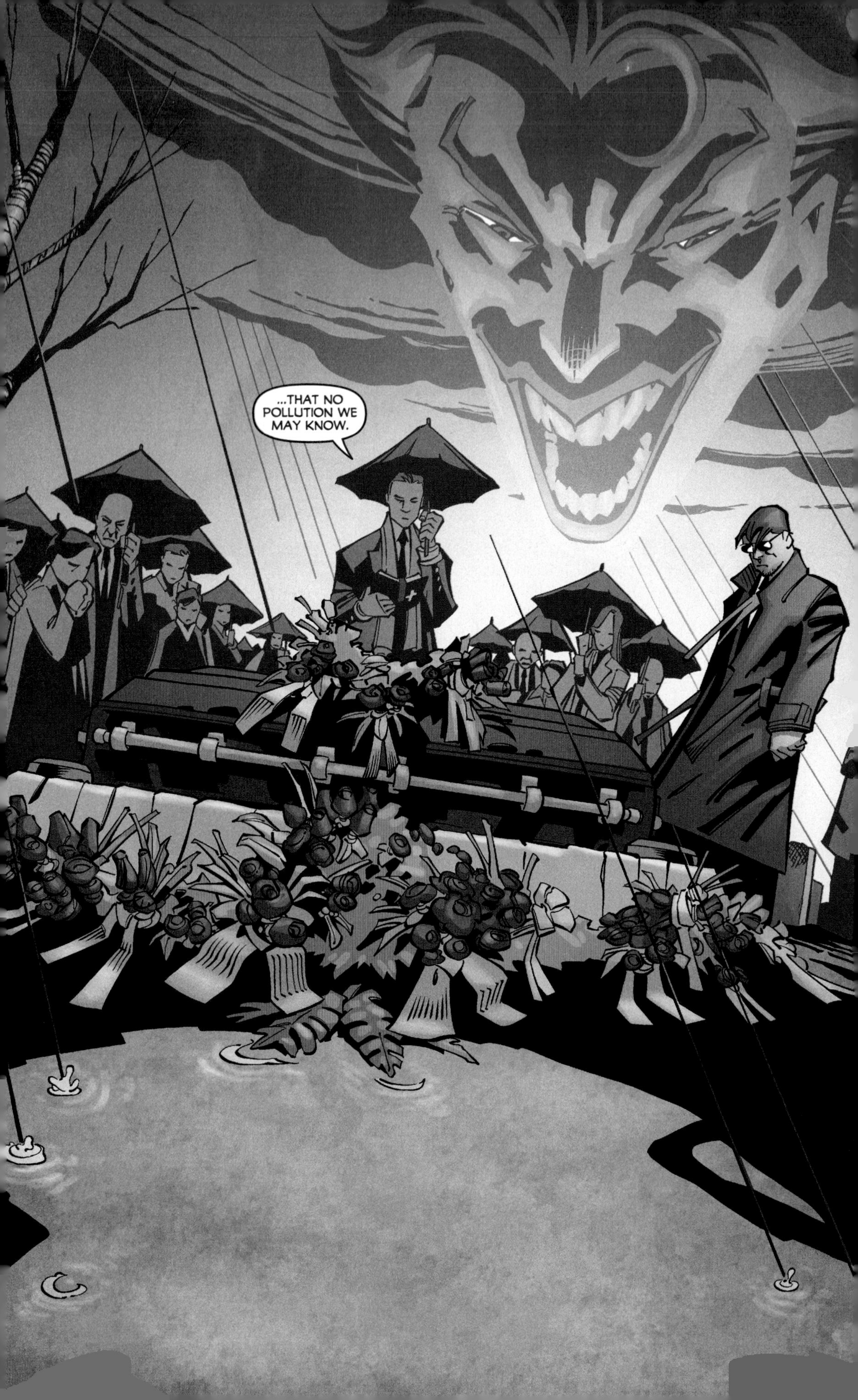
...THAT NO POLLUTION WE MAY KNOW.

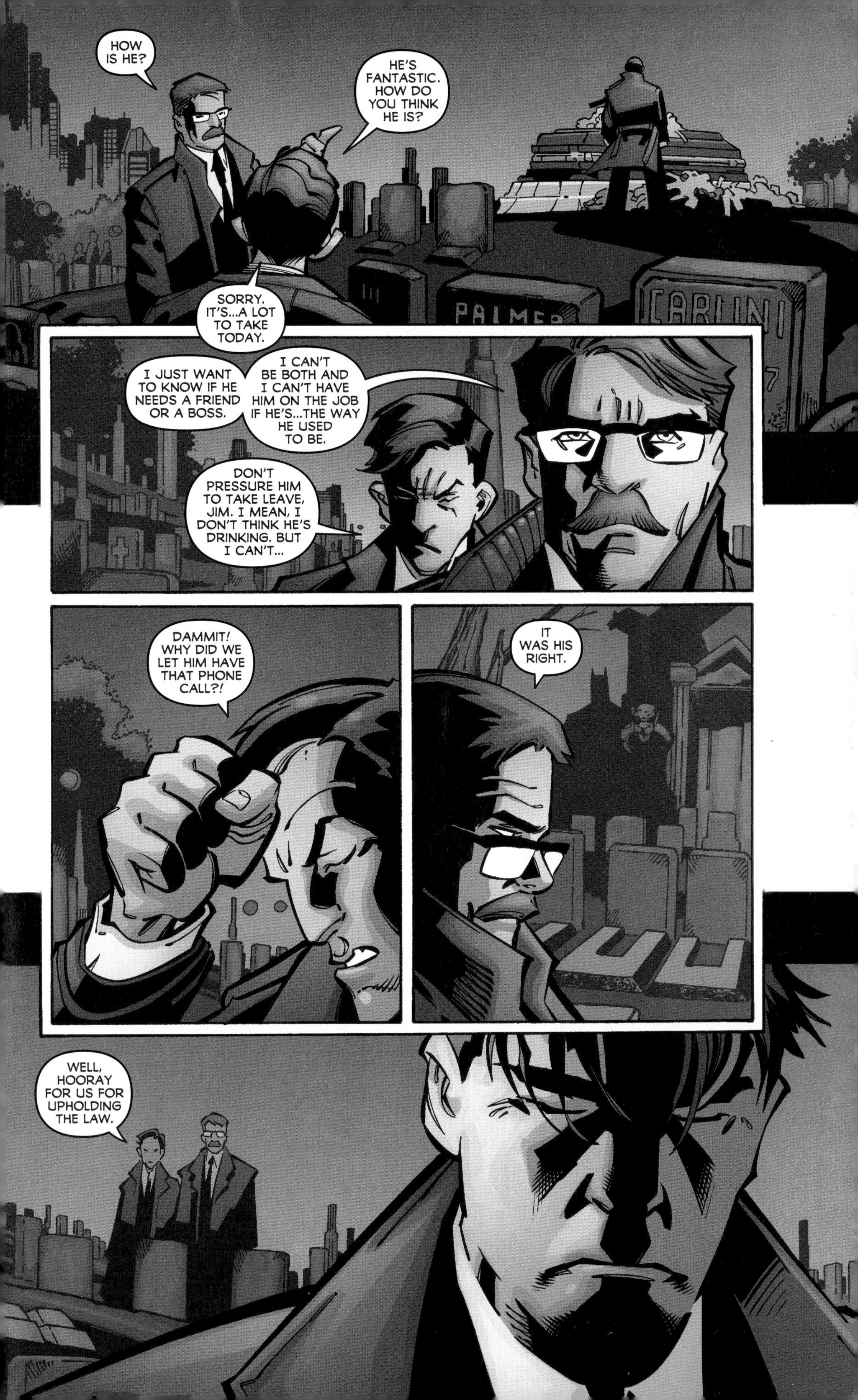
HOW IS HE?
HE'S FANTASTIC. HOW DO YOU THINK HE IS?
SORRY. IT'S...A LOT TO TAKE TODAY.
PALMER
CARLINI
I JUST WANT TO KNOW IF HE NEEDS A FRIEND OR A BOSS.
I CAN'T BE BOTH AND I CAN'T HAVE HIM ON THE JOB IF HE'S...THE WAY HE USED TO BE.
DON'T PRESSURE HIM TO TAKE LEAVE, JIM. I MEAN, I DON'T THINK HE'S DRINKING. BUT I CAN'T...
DAMMIT! WHY DID WE LET HIM HAVE THAT PHONE CALL?!
IT WAS HIS RIGHT.
WELL, HOORAY FOR US FOR UPHOLDING THE LAW.

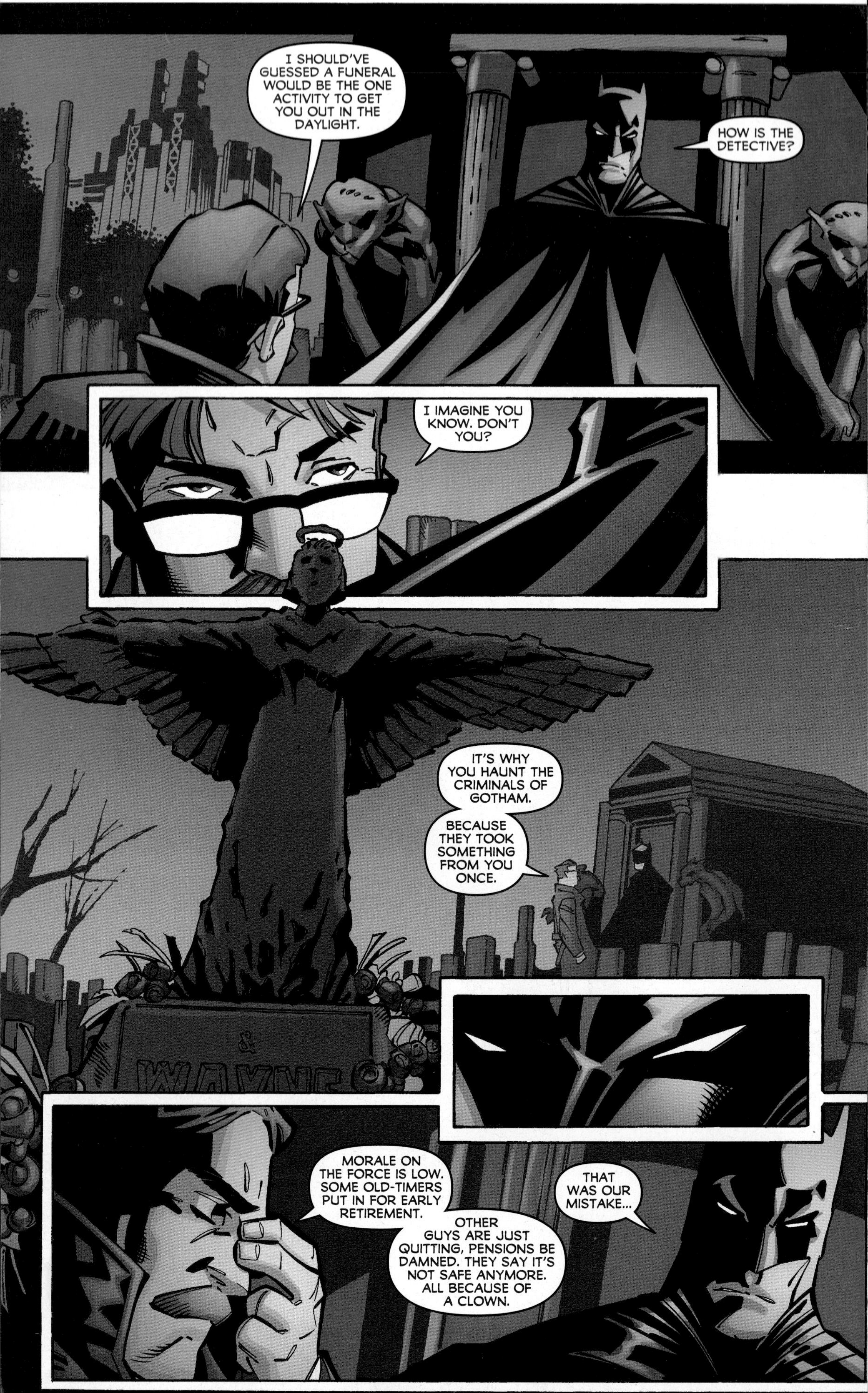
I SHOULD'VE GUESSED A FUNERAL WOULD BE THE ONE ACTIVITY TO GET YOU OUT IN THE DAYLIGHT.
HOW IS THE DETECTIVE?
I IMAGINE YOU KNOW. DON'T YOU?
IT'S WHY YOU HAUNT THE CRIMINALS OF GOTHAM.
BECAUSE THEY TOOK SOMETHING FROM YOU ONCE.
MORALE ON THE FORCE IS LOW. SOME OLD-TIMERS PUT IN FOR EARLY RETIREMENT.
OTHER GUYS ARE JUST QUITTING, PENSIONS BE DAMNED. THEY SAY IT'S NOT SAFE ANYMORE. ALL BECAUSE OF A CLOWN.
THAT WAS OUR MISTAKE...

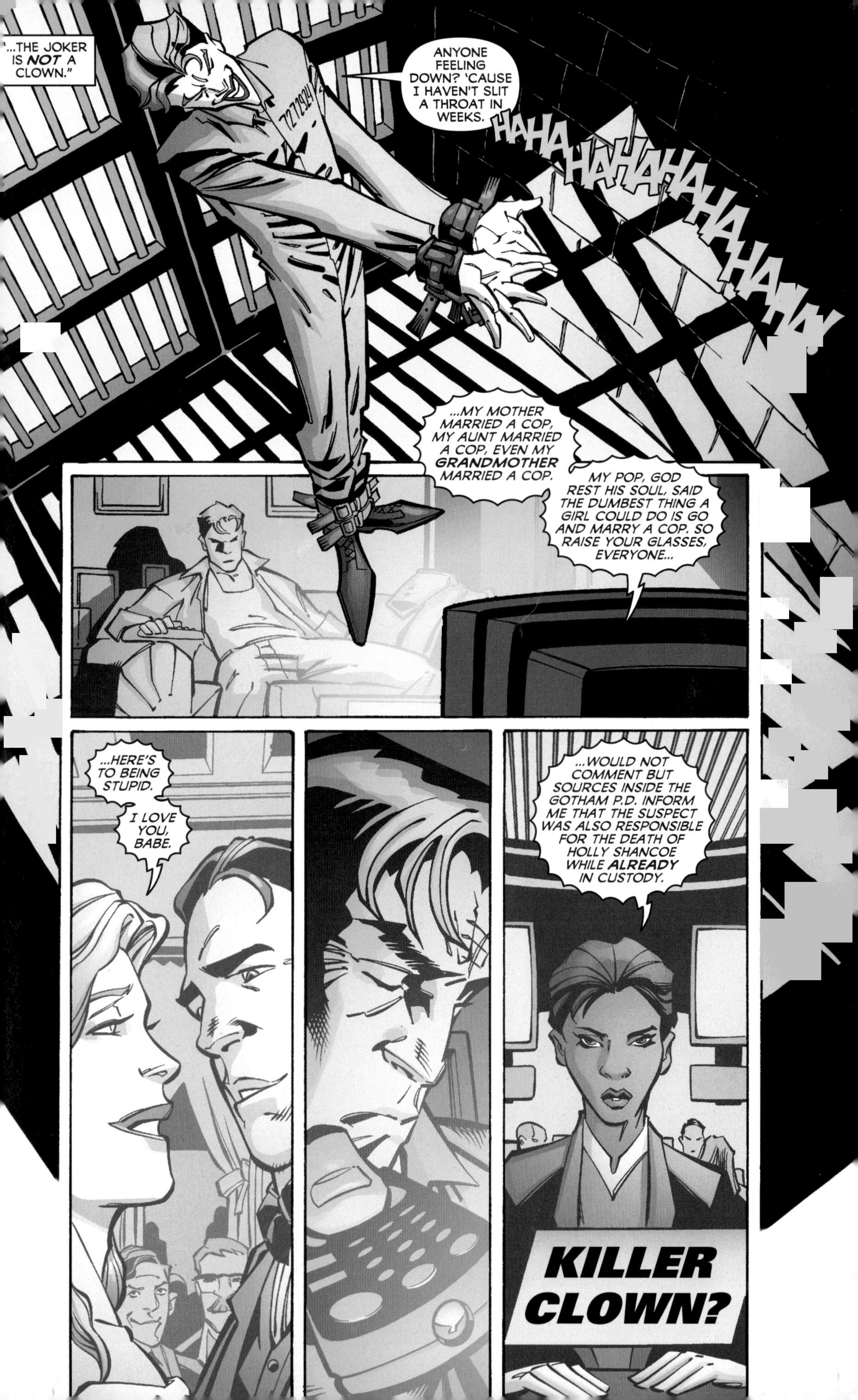
"...THE JOKER IS NOT A CLOWN."
ANYONE FEELING DOWN? 'CAUSE I HAVEN'T SLIT A THROAT IN WEEKS.
HAHA HAHAHAHA HAHA HAHAAA!
...MY MOTHER MARRIED A COP, MY AUNT MARRIED A COP, EVEN MY GRANDMOTHER MARRIED A COP.
MY POP, GOD REST HIS SOUL, SAID THE DUMBEST THING A GIRL COULD DO IS GO AND MARRY A COP. SO RAISE YOUR GLASSES, EVERYONE...
...HERE'S TO BEING STUPID.
I LOVE YOU, BABE.
...WOULD NOT COMMENT BUT SOURCES INSIDE THE GOTHAM P.D. INFORM ME THAT THE SUSPECT WAS ALSO RESPONSIBLE FOR THE DEATH OF HOLLY SHANCOE WHILE ALREADY IN CUSTODY.
KILLER CLOWN?

THERE IS NO WORD YET ON WHY THE SUSPECT WHO IS YET TO BE IDENTIFIED TARGETED DETECTIVE SHANCOE'S WIFE...

...BUT A CHARGE OF CRIMINALLY NEGLIGENT HOMICIDE IN THE DEATH OF MRS. SHANCOE IS EXPECTED TO BE ADDED BY THE D.A.'S OFFICE.

THE SUSPECT WILL BE TRANSFERRED TO THE COURTHOUSE JAIL LATER TONIGHT...

...FOR HIS ARRAIGNMENT TOMORROW MORNING. REPORTING LIVE, I'M CATHERINE VILLALOBOS.

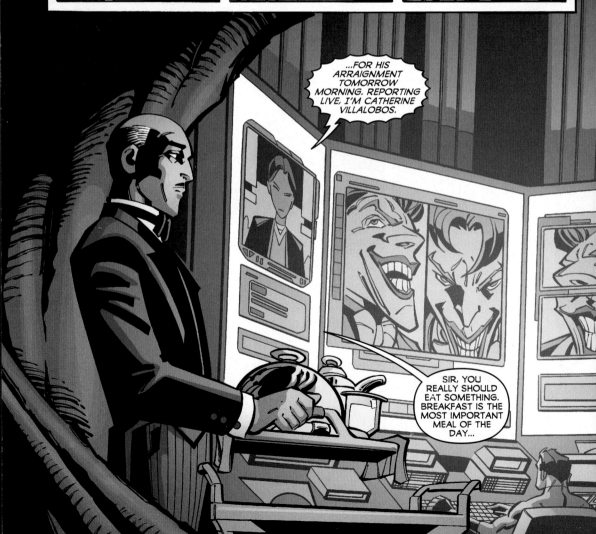

SIR, YOU REALLY SHOULD EAT SOMETHING. BREAKFAST IS THE MOST IMPORTANT MEAL OF THE DAY...

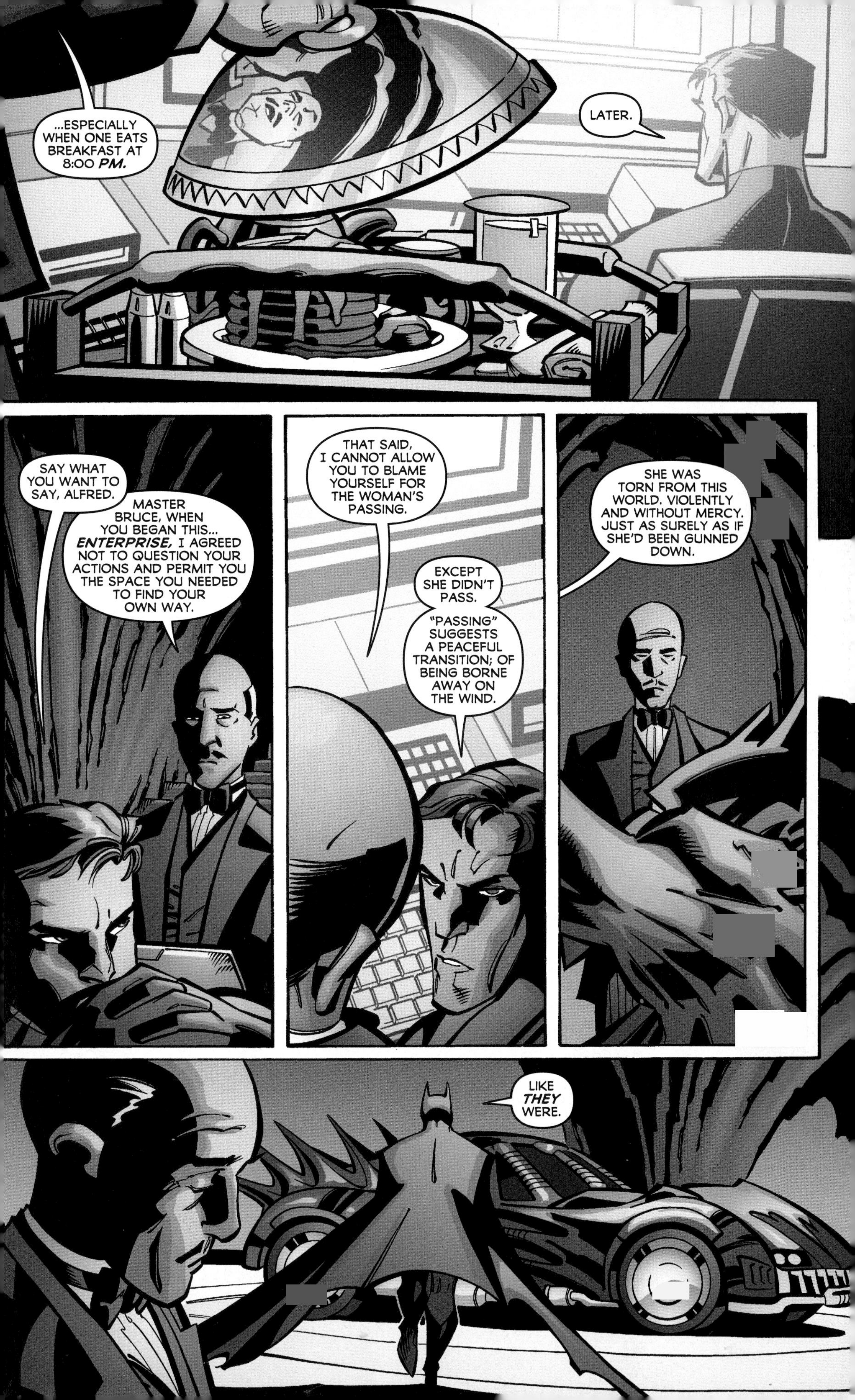
...ESPECIALLY WHEN ONE EATS BREAKFAST AT 8:00 *PM.*
LATER.
SAY WHAT YOU WANT TO SAY, ALFRED.
MASTER BRUCE, WHEN YOU BEGAN THIS... *ENTERPRISE,* I AGREED NOT TO QUESTION YOUR ACTIONS AND PERMIT YOU THE SPACE YOU NEEDED TO FIND YOUR OWN WAY.
THAT SAID, I CANNOT ALLOW YOU TO BLAME YOURSELF FOR THE WOMAN'S PASSING.
EXCEPT SHE DIDN'T PASS.
"PASSING" SUGGESTS A PEACEFUL TRANSITION; OF BEING BORNE AWAY ON THE WIND.
SHE WAS TORN FROM THIS WORLD. VIOLENTLY AND WITHOUT MERCY. JUST AS SURELY AS IF SHE'D BEEN GUNNED DOWN.
LIKE *THEY* WERE.

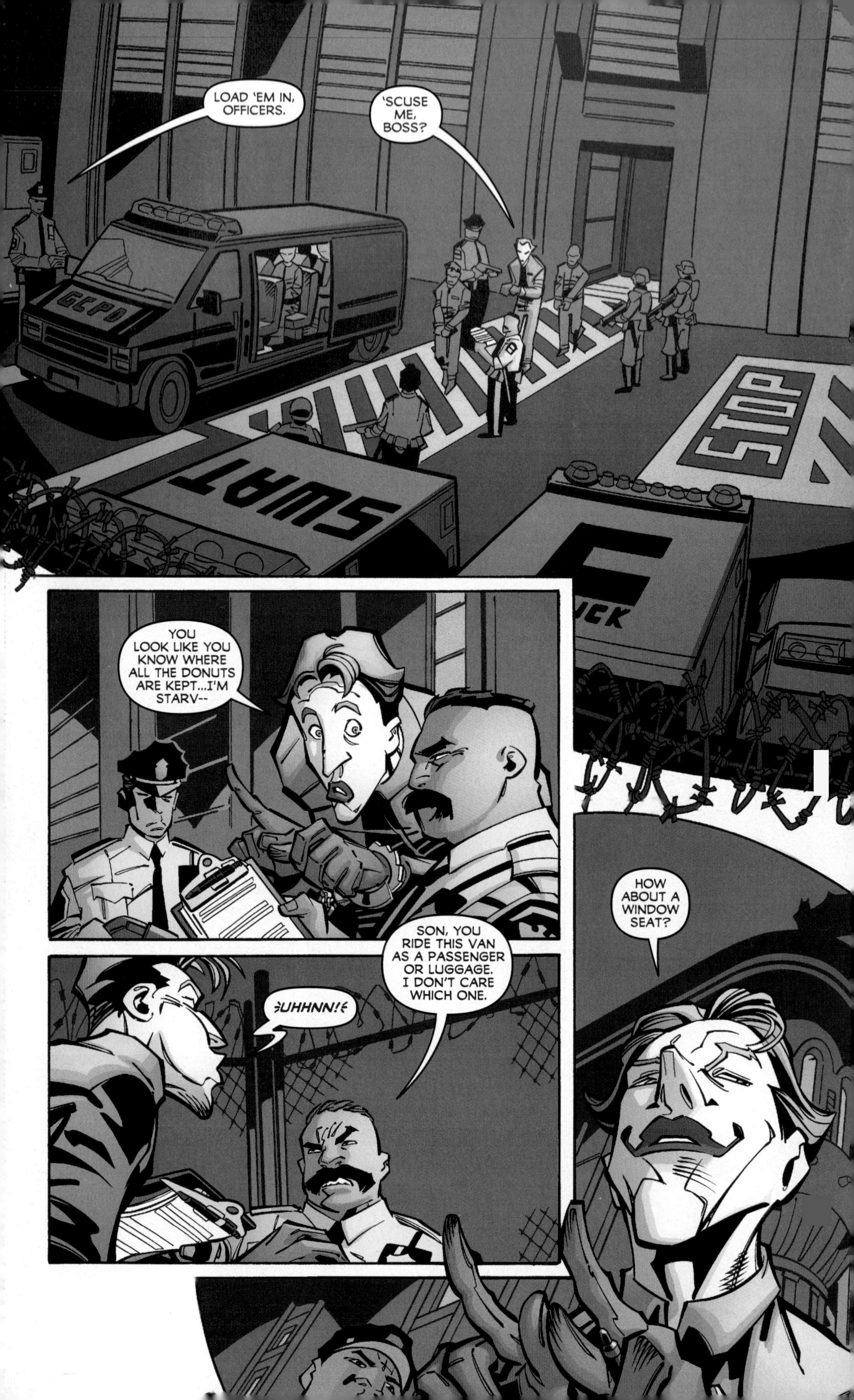
LOAD 'EM IN, OFFICERS.
'SCUSE ME, BOSS?
GCPD
SWAT
STOP
YOU LOOK LIKE YOU KNOW WHERE ALL THE DONUTS ARE KEPT...I'M STARV--
HOW ABOUT A WINDOW SEAT?
SON, YOU RIDE THIS VAN AS A PASSENGER OR LUGGAGE. I DON'T CARE WHICH ONE.
UHHNN!

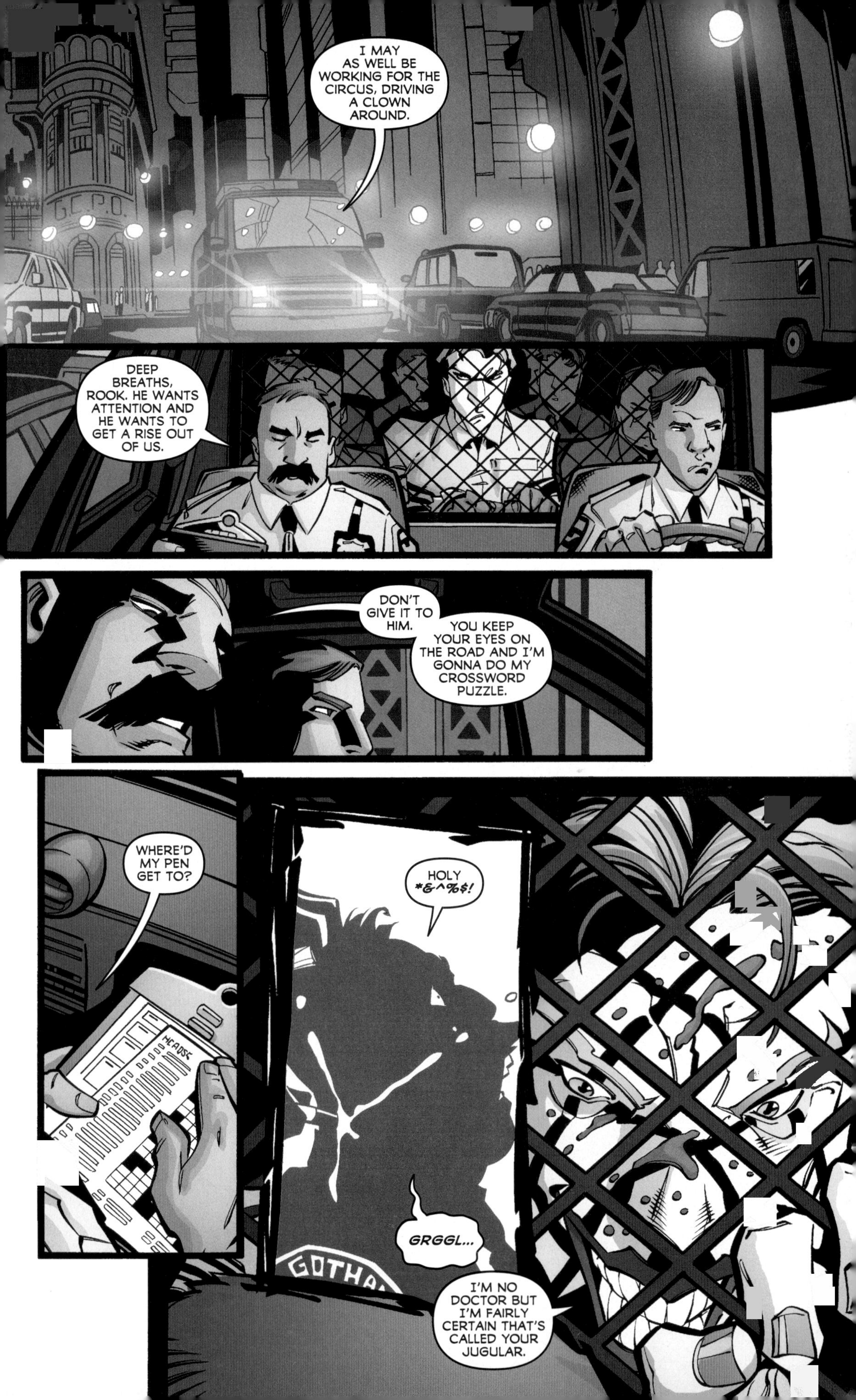
I MAY AS WELL BE WORKING FOR THE CIRCUS, DRIVING A CLOWN AROUND.
DEEP BREATHS, ROOK. HE WANTS ATTENTION AND HE WANTS TO GET A RISE OUT OF US.
DON'T GIVE IT TO HIM.
YOU KEEP YOUR EYES ON THE ROAD AND I'M GONNA DO MY CROSSWORD PUZZLE.
WHERE'D MY PEN GET TO?
HOLY *&^%$!
GRGGL...
I'M NO DOCTOR BUT I'M FAIRLY CERTAIN THAT'S CALLED YOUR JUGULAR.
G.C.P.D.
GOTHA

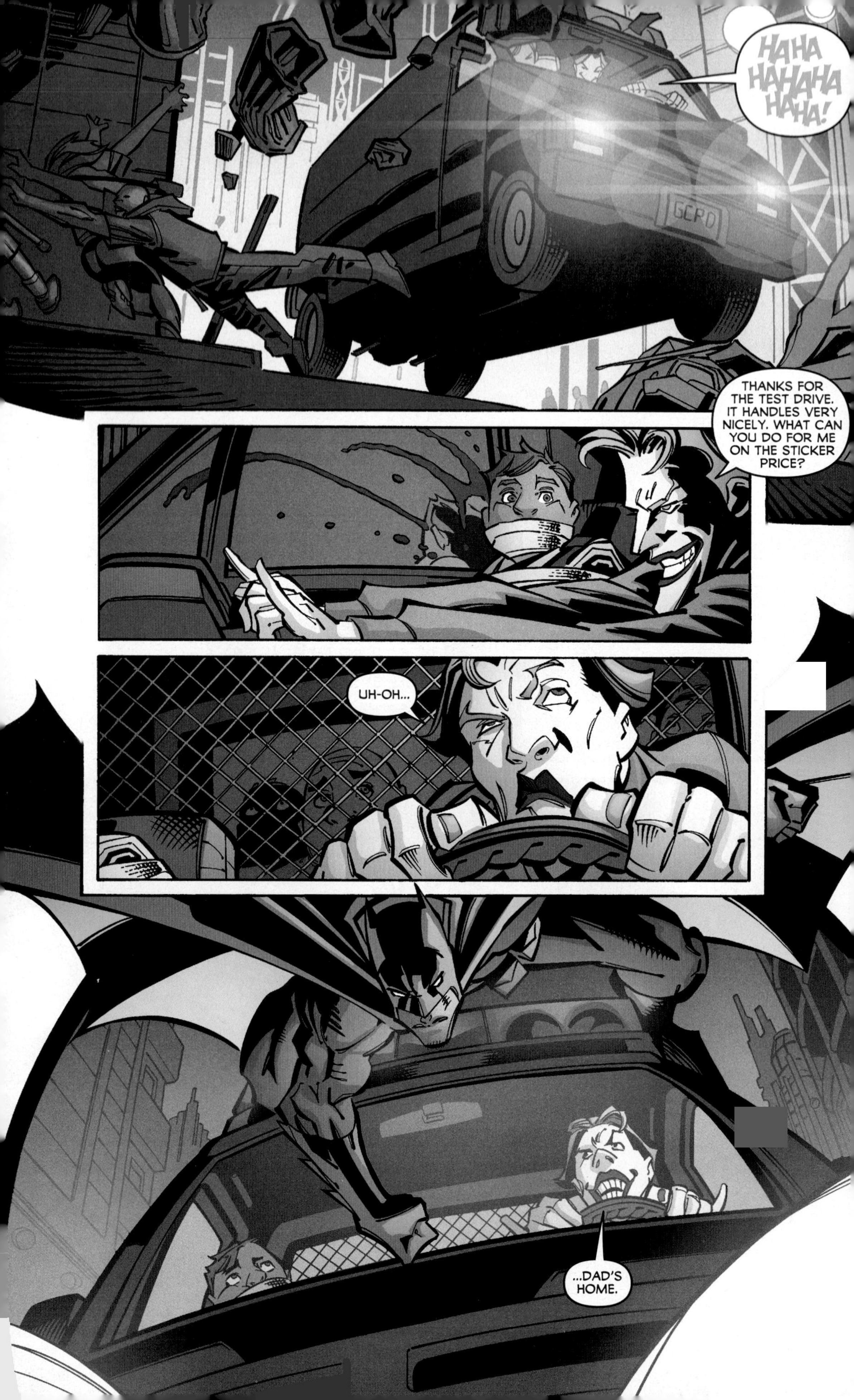
HAHA HAHAHA HAHA!
GCPD
THANKS FOR THE TEST DRIVE. IT HANDLES VERY NICELY. WHAT CAN YOU DO FOR ME ON THE STICKER PRICE?
UH-OH...
...DAD'S HOME.

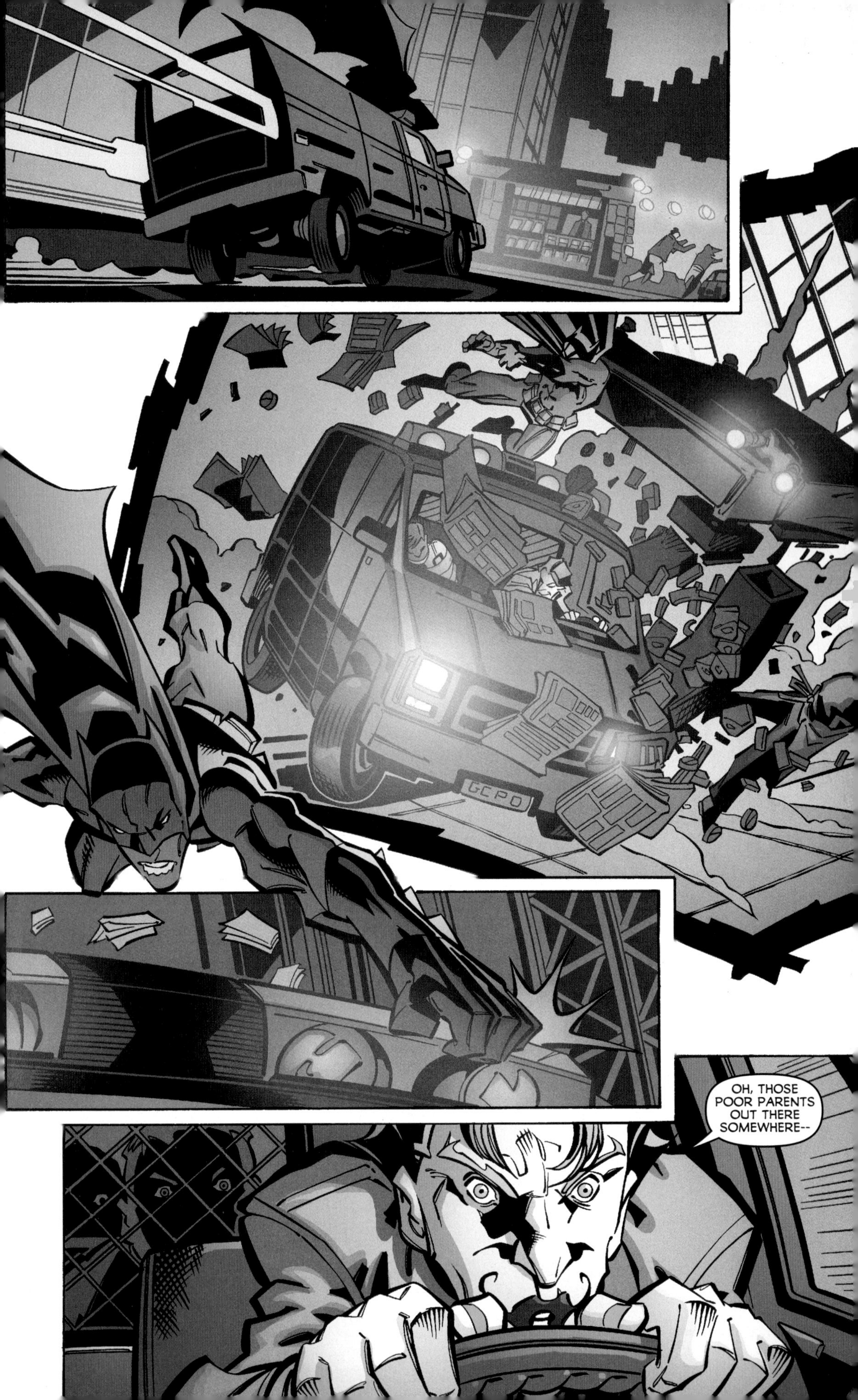
GCPD
OH, THOSE POOR PARENTS OUT THERE SOMEWHERE--

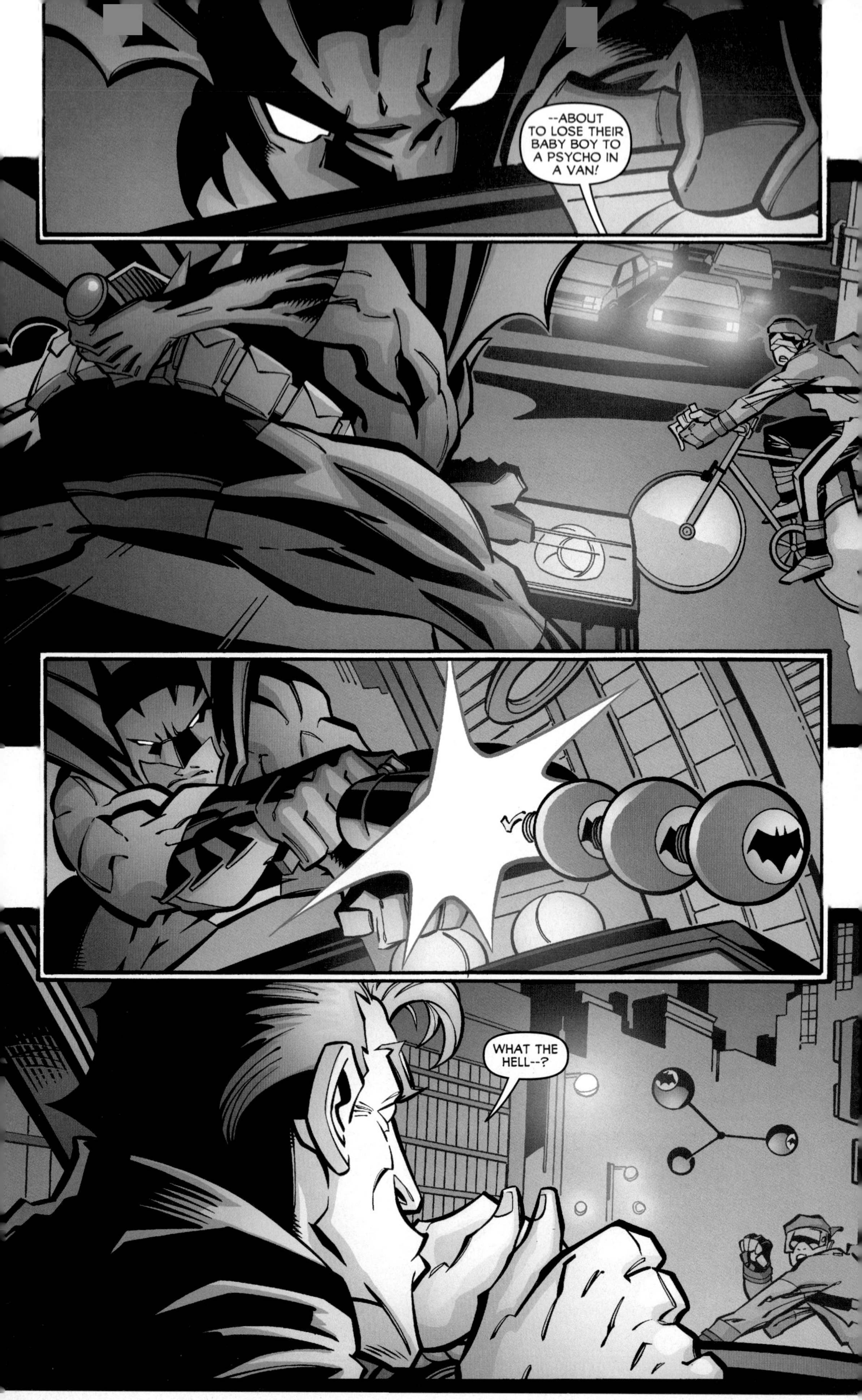
--ABOUT TO LOSE THEIR BABY BOY TO A PSYCHO IN A VAN!
WHAT THE HELL--?

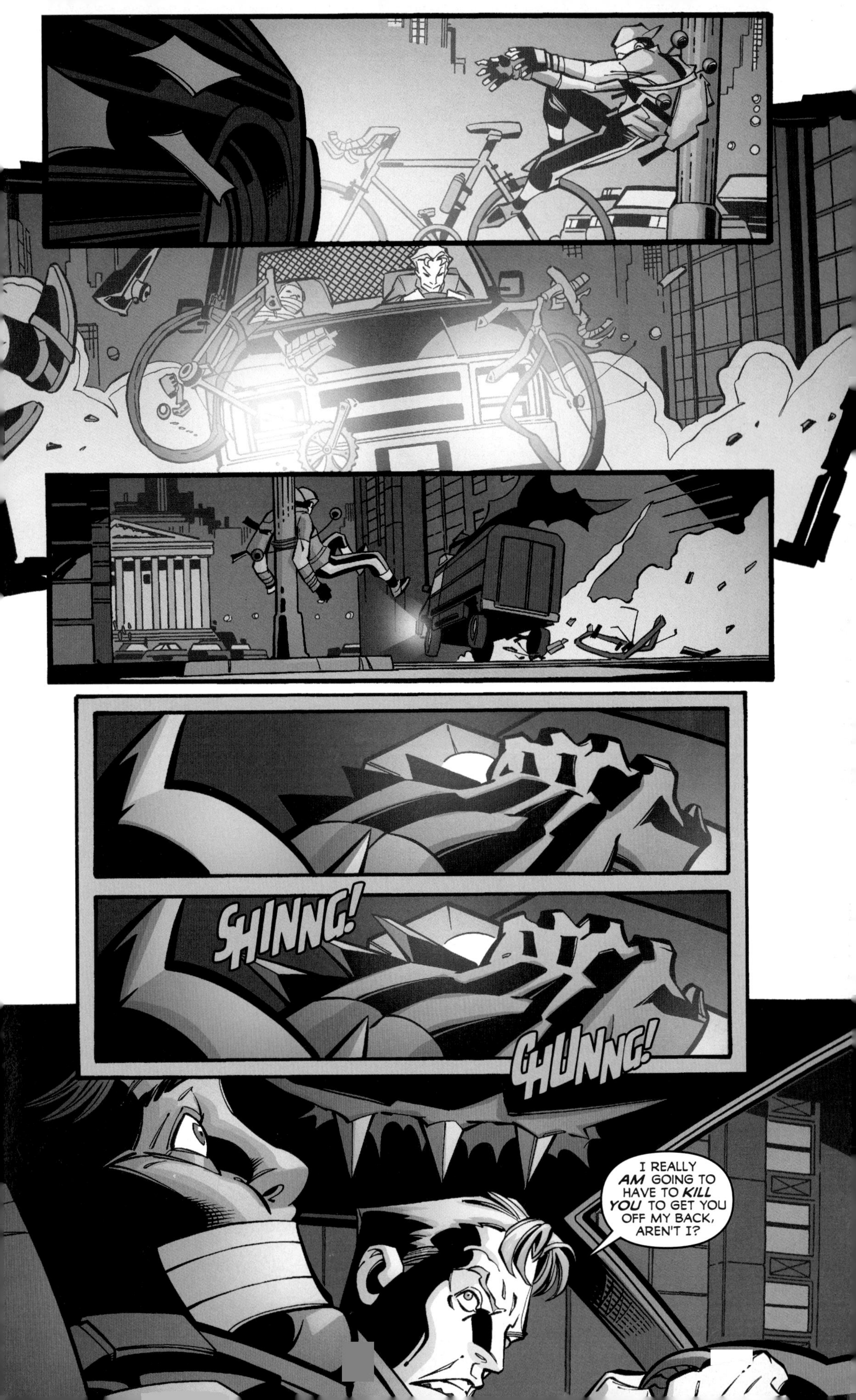
SHINNG!
CHUNNG!
I REALLY AM GOING TO HAVE TO KILL YOU TO GET YOU OFF MY BACK, AREN'T I?

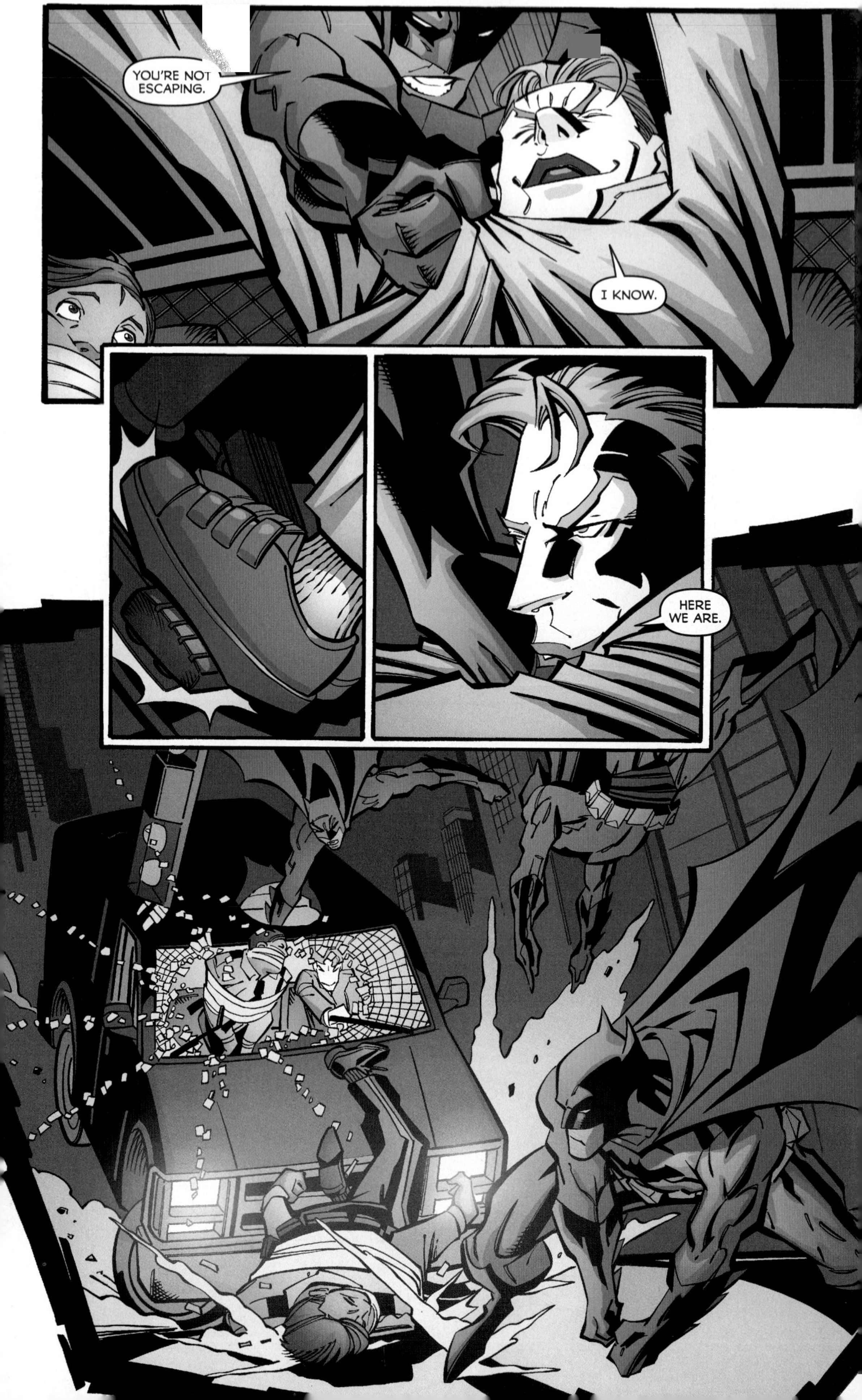
YOU'RE NOT ESCAPING.
I KNOW.
HERE WE ARE.

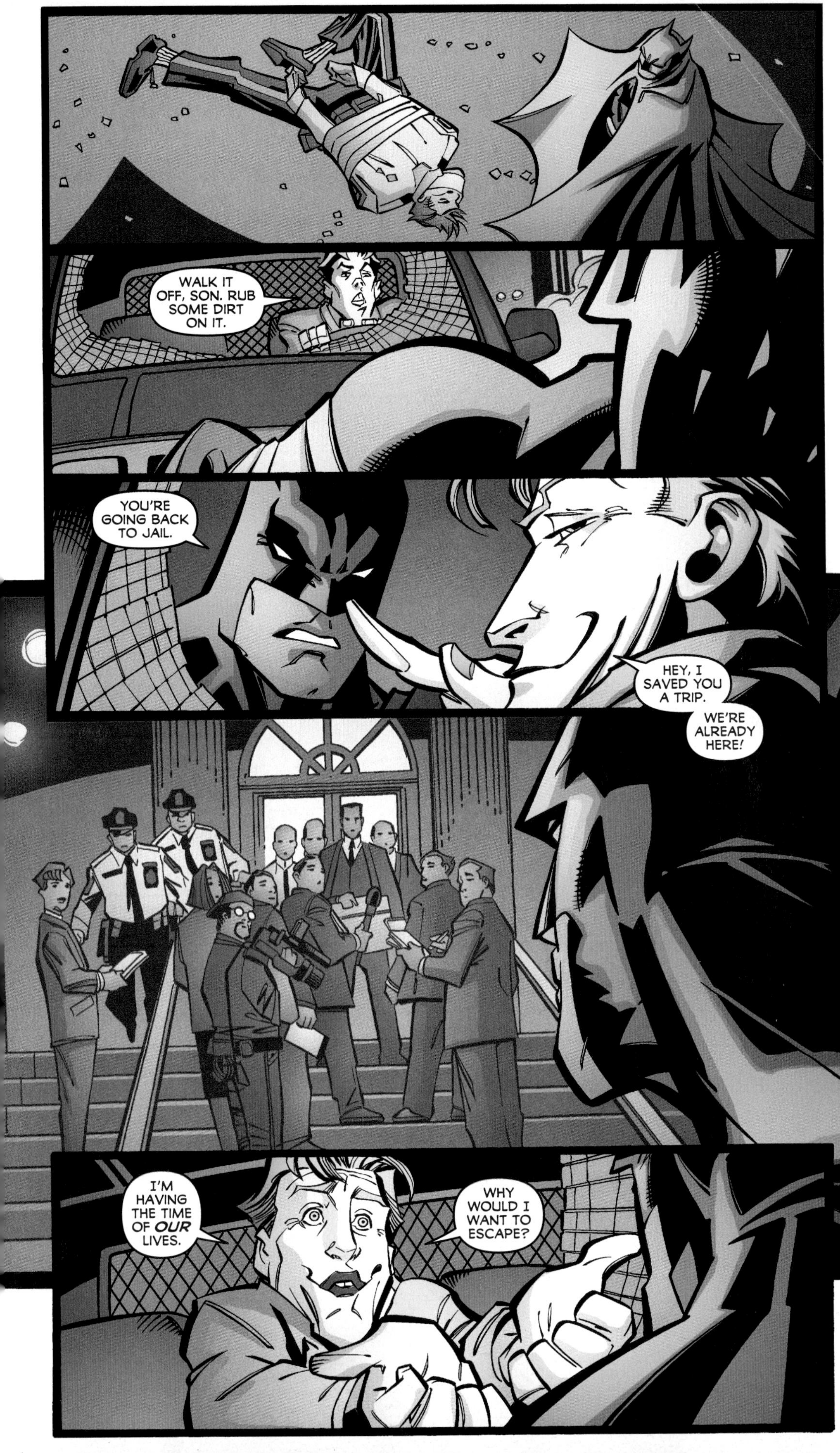
WALK IT OFF, SON. RUB SOME DIRT ON IT.
YOU'RE GOING BACK TO JAIL.
HEY, I SAVED YOU A TRIP.
WE'RE ALREADY HERE!
I'M HAVING THE TIME OF *OUR* LIVES.
WHY WOULD I WANT TO ESCAPE?

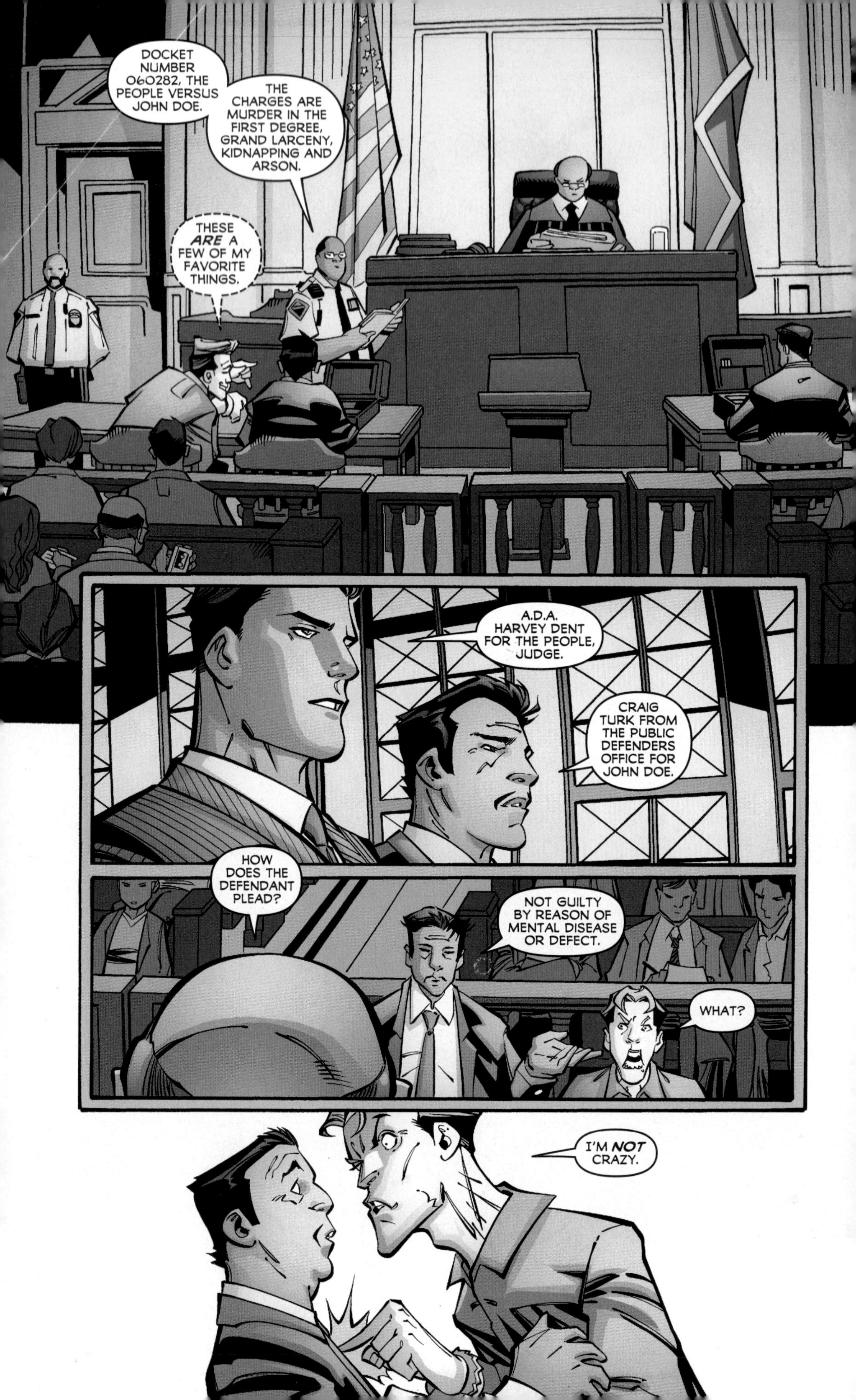
DOCKET NUMBER 060282, THE PEOPLE VERSUS JOHN DOE.
THE CHARGES ARE MURDER IN THE FIRST DEGREE, GRAND LARCENY, KIDNAPPING AND ARSON.
THESE ARE A FEW OF MY FAVORITE THINGS.
A.D.A. HARVEY DENT FOR THE PEOPLE, JUDGE.
CRAIG TURK FROM THE PUBLIC DEFENDERS OFFICE FOR JOHN DOE.
HOW DOES THE DEFENDANT PLEAD?
NOT GUILTY BY REASON OF MENTAL DISEASE OR DEFECT.
WHAT?
I'M NOT CRAZY.

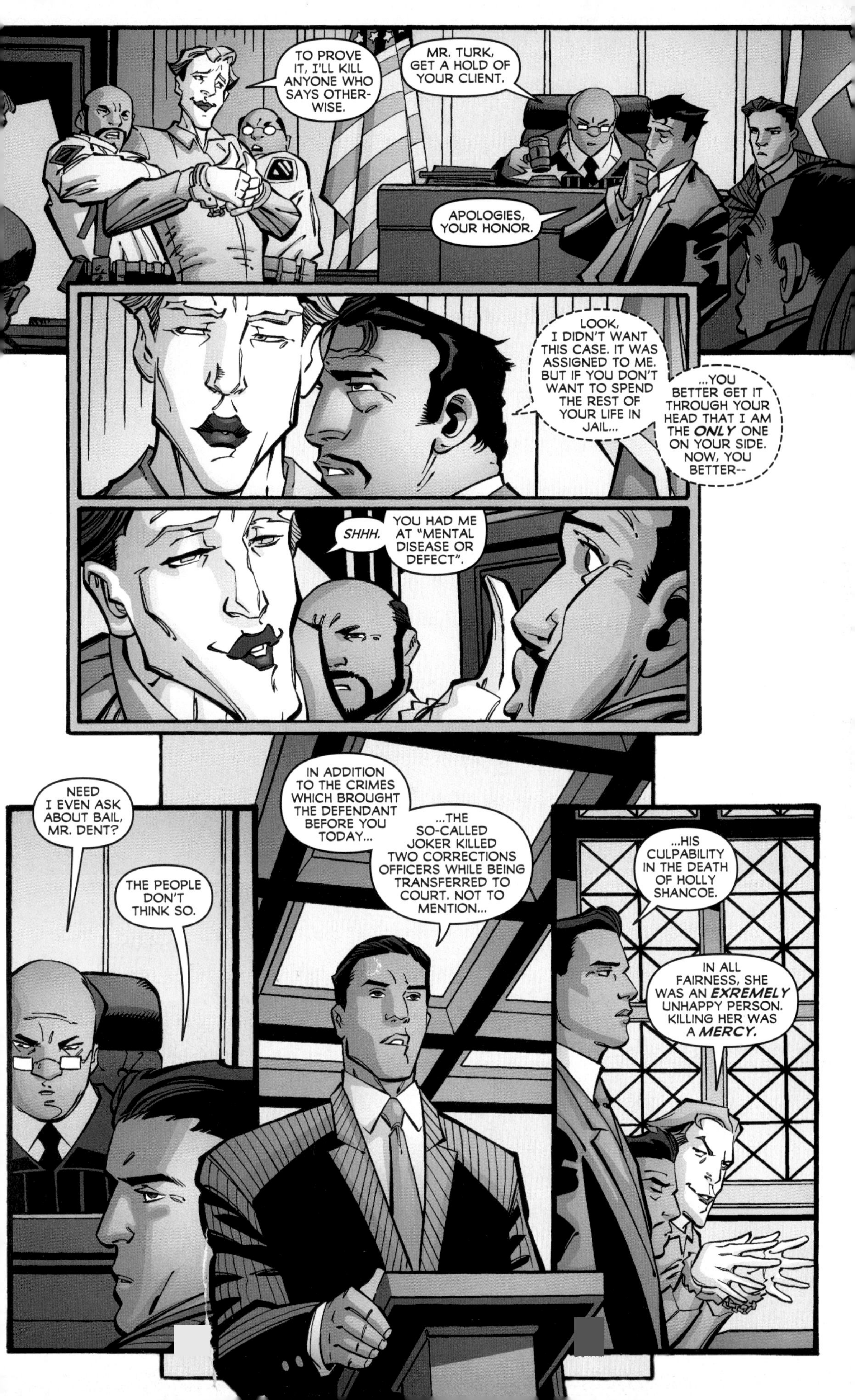
TO PROVE IT, I'LL KILL ANYONE WHO SAYS OTHER-WISE.
MR. TURK, GET A HOLD OF YOUR CLIENT.
APOLOGIES, YOUR HONOR.
LOOK, I DIDN'T WANT THIS CASE. IT WAS ASSIGNED TO ME. BUT IF YOU DON'T WANT TO SPEND THE REST OF YOUR LIFE IN JAIL...
...YOU BETTER GET IT THROUGH YOUR HEAD THAT I AM THE ONLY ONE ON YOUR SIDE. NOW, YOU BETTER--
SHHH.
YOU HAD ME AT "MENTAL DISEASE OR DEFECT".
NEED I EVEN ASK ABOUT BAIL, MR. DENT?
THE PEOPLE DON'T THINK SO.
IN ADDITION TO THE CRIMES WHICH BROUGHT THE DEFENDANT BEFORE YOU TODAY...
...THE SO-CALLED JOKER KILLED TWO CORRECTIONS OFFICERS WHILE BEING TRANSFERRED TO COURT. NOT TO MENTION...
...HIS CULPABILITY IN THE DEATH OF HOLLY SHANCOE.
IN ALL FAIRNESS, SHE WAS AN EXREMELY UNHAPPY PERSON. KILLING HER WAS A MERCY.

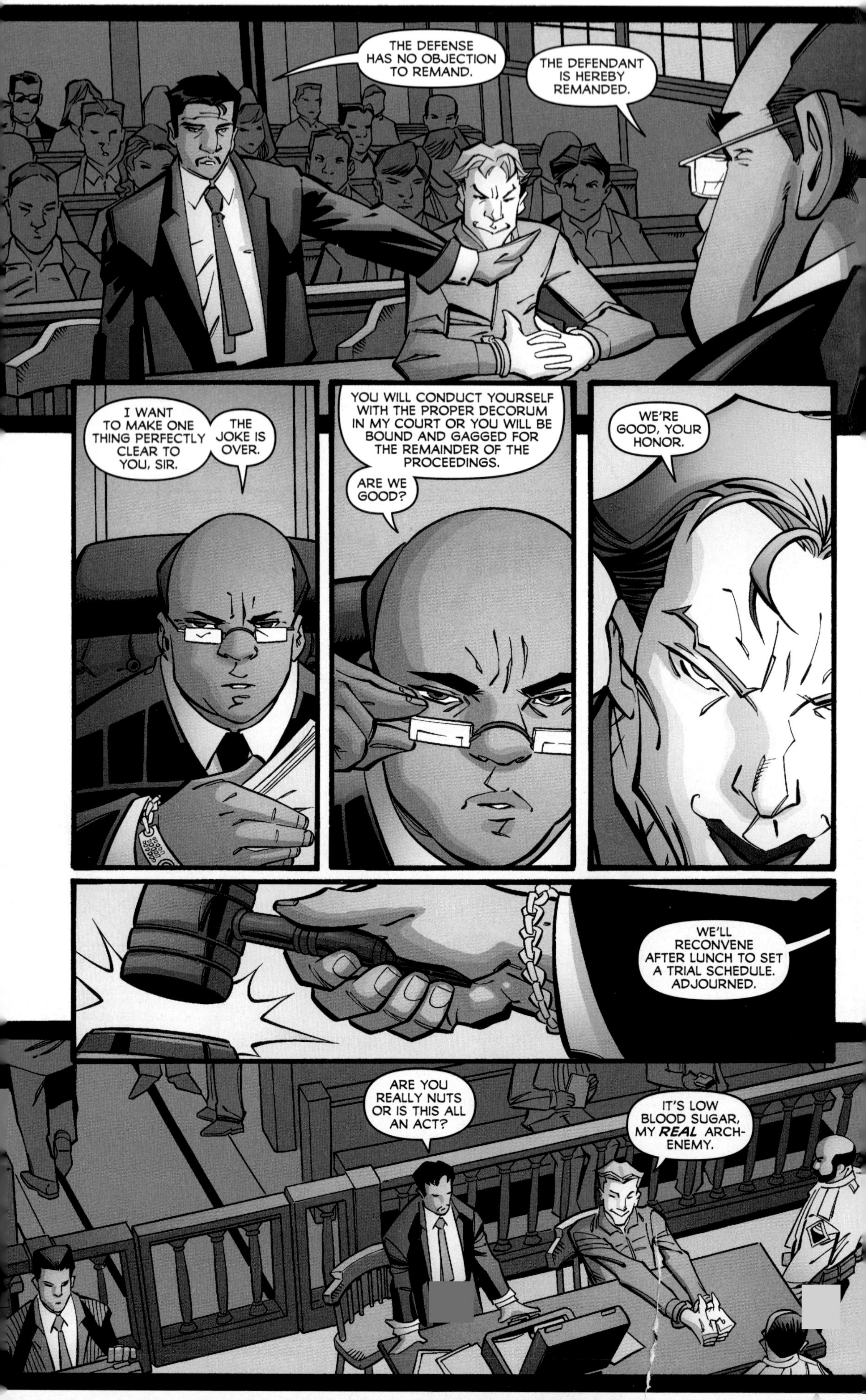
THE DEFENSE HAS NO OBJECTION TO REMAND.
THE DEFENDANT IS HEREBY REMANDED.
I WANT TO MAKE ONE THING PERFECTLY CLEAR TO YOU, SIR.
THE JOKE IS OVER.
YOU WILL CONDUCT YOURSELF WITH THE PROPER DECORUM IN MY COURT OR YOU WILL BE BOUND AND GAGGED FOR THE REMAINDER OF THE PROCEEDINGS.
ARE WE GOOD?
WE'RE GOOD, YOUR HONOR.
WE'LL RECONVENE AFTER LUNCH TO SET A TRIAL SCHEDULE. ADJOURNED.
ARE YOU REALLY NUTS OR IS THIS ALL AN ACT?
IT'S LOW BLOOD SUGAR, MY *REAL* ARCH-ENEMY.

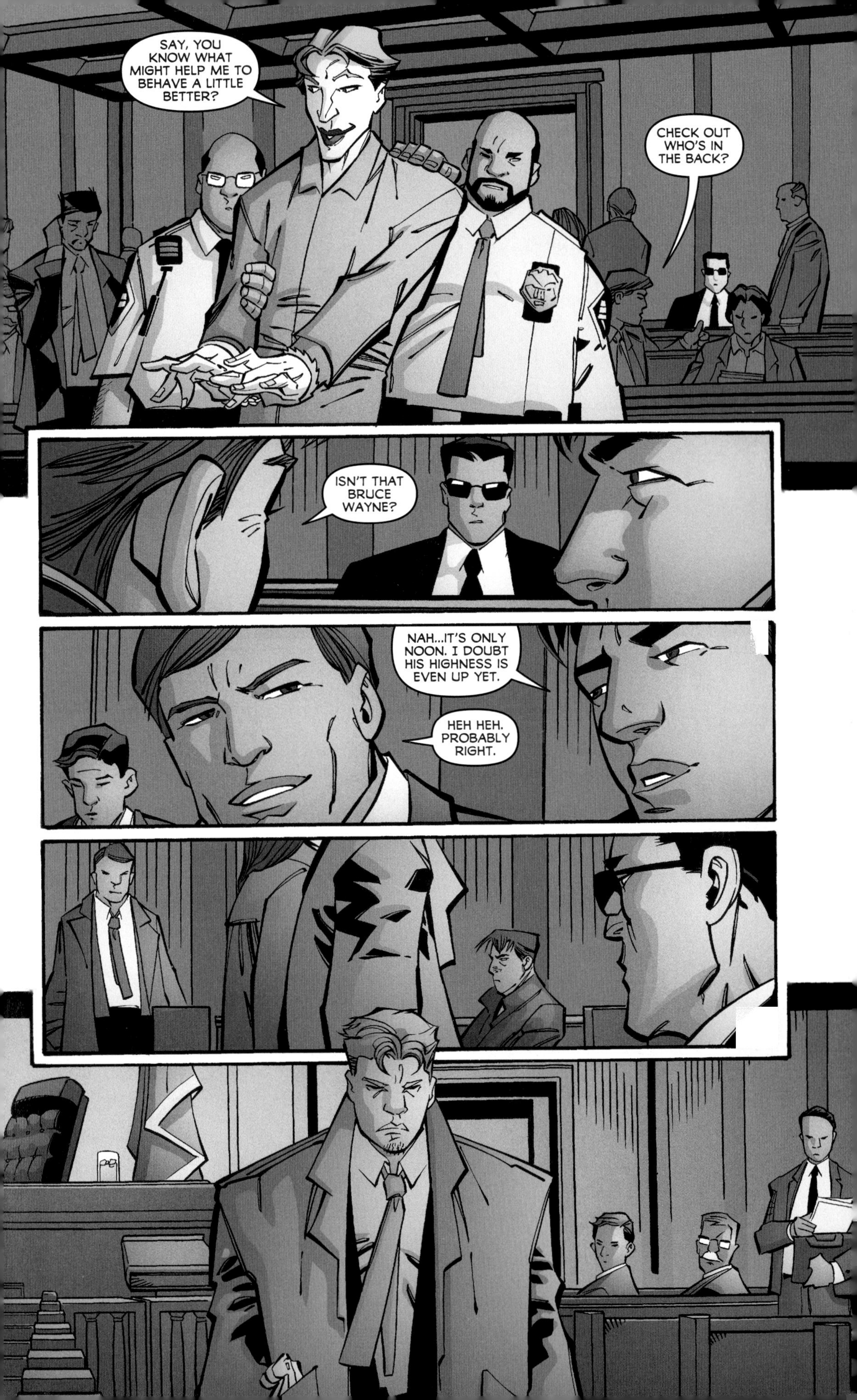
SAY, YOU KNOW WHAT MIGHT HELP ME TO BEHAVE A LITTLE BETTER?
CHECK OUT WHO'S IN THE BACK?
ISN'T THAT BRUCE WAYNE?
NAH...IT'S ONLY NOON. I DOUBT HIS HIGHNESS IS EVEN UP YET.
HEH HEH. PROBABLY RIGHT.

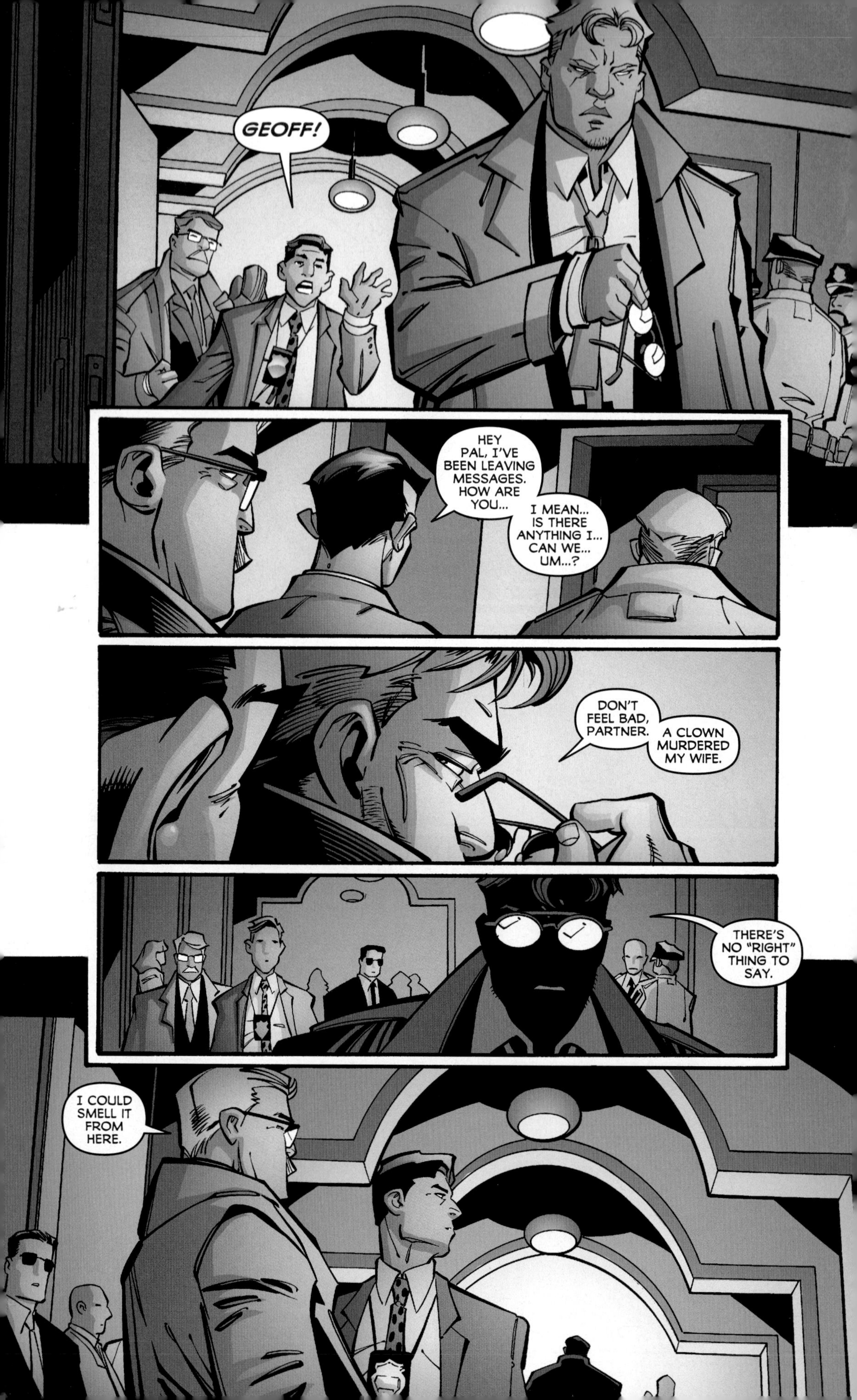
GEOFF!
HEY PAL, I'VE BEEN LEAVING MESSAGES. HOW ARE YOU...
I MEAN... IS THERE ANYTHING I... CAN WE... UM...?
DON'T FEEL BAD, PARTNER.
A CLOWN MURDERED MY WIFE.
THERE'S NO "RIGHT" THING TO SAY.
I COULD SMELL IT FROM HERE.

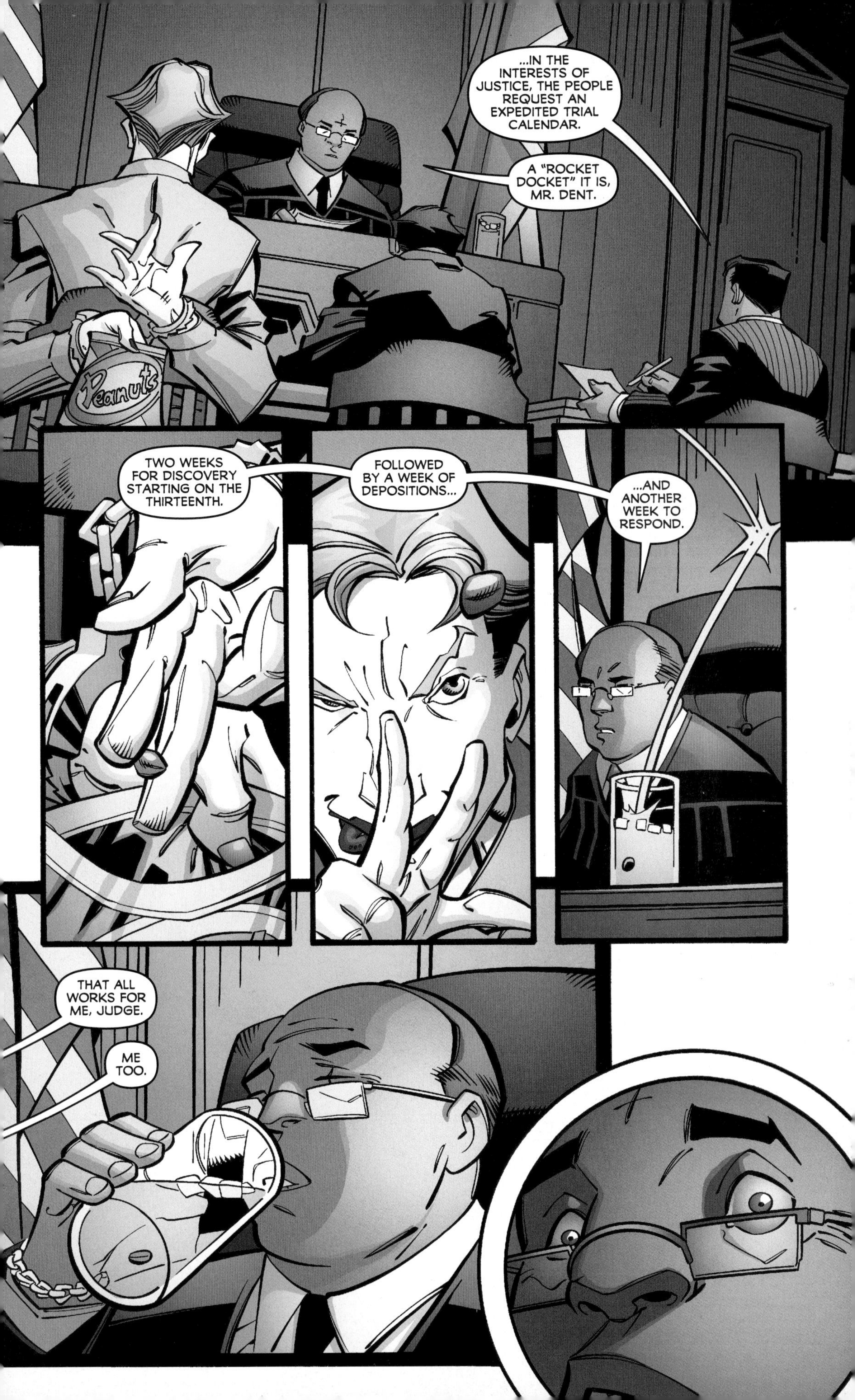
...IN THE INTERESTS OF JUSTICE, THE PEOPLE REQUEST AN EXPEDITED TRIAL CALENDAR.
A "ROCKET DOCKET" IT IS, MR. DENT.
Peanuts
TWO WEEKS FOR DISCOVERY STARTING ON THE THIRTEENTH.
FOLLOWED BY A WEEK OF DEPOSITIONS...
...AND ANOTHER WEEK TO RESPOND.
THAT ALL WORKS FOR ME, JUDGE.
ME TOO.

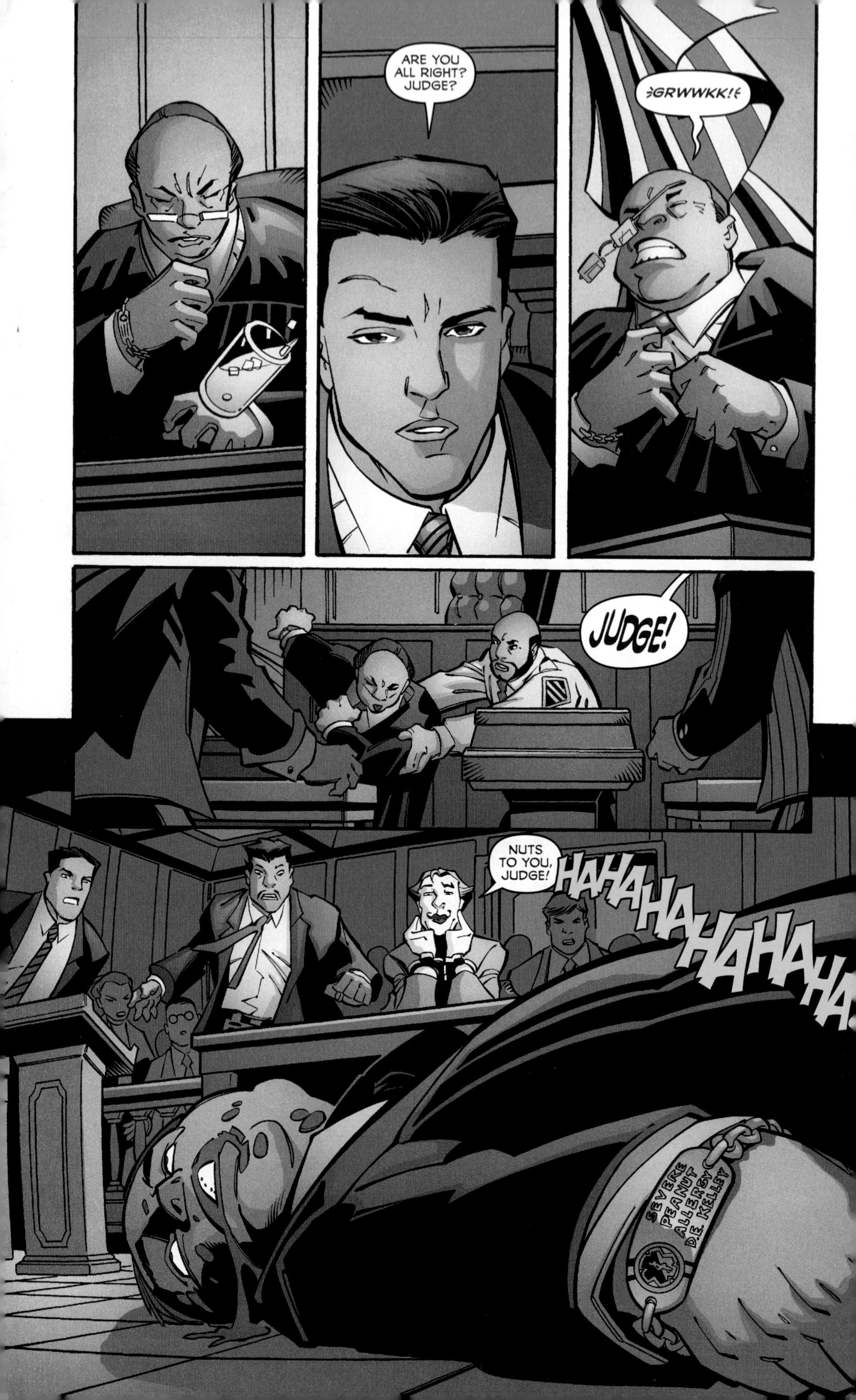
ARE YOU ALL RIGHT? JUDGE?
GRWWKK!
JUDGE!
NUTS TO YOU, JUDGE!
HAHAHAHAHAHAHAHA
SEVERE PEANUT ALLERGY D.E. KELLEY

DO YOU UNDERSTAND THESE RIGHTS? PART THREE

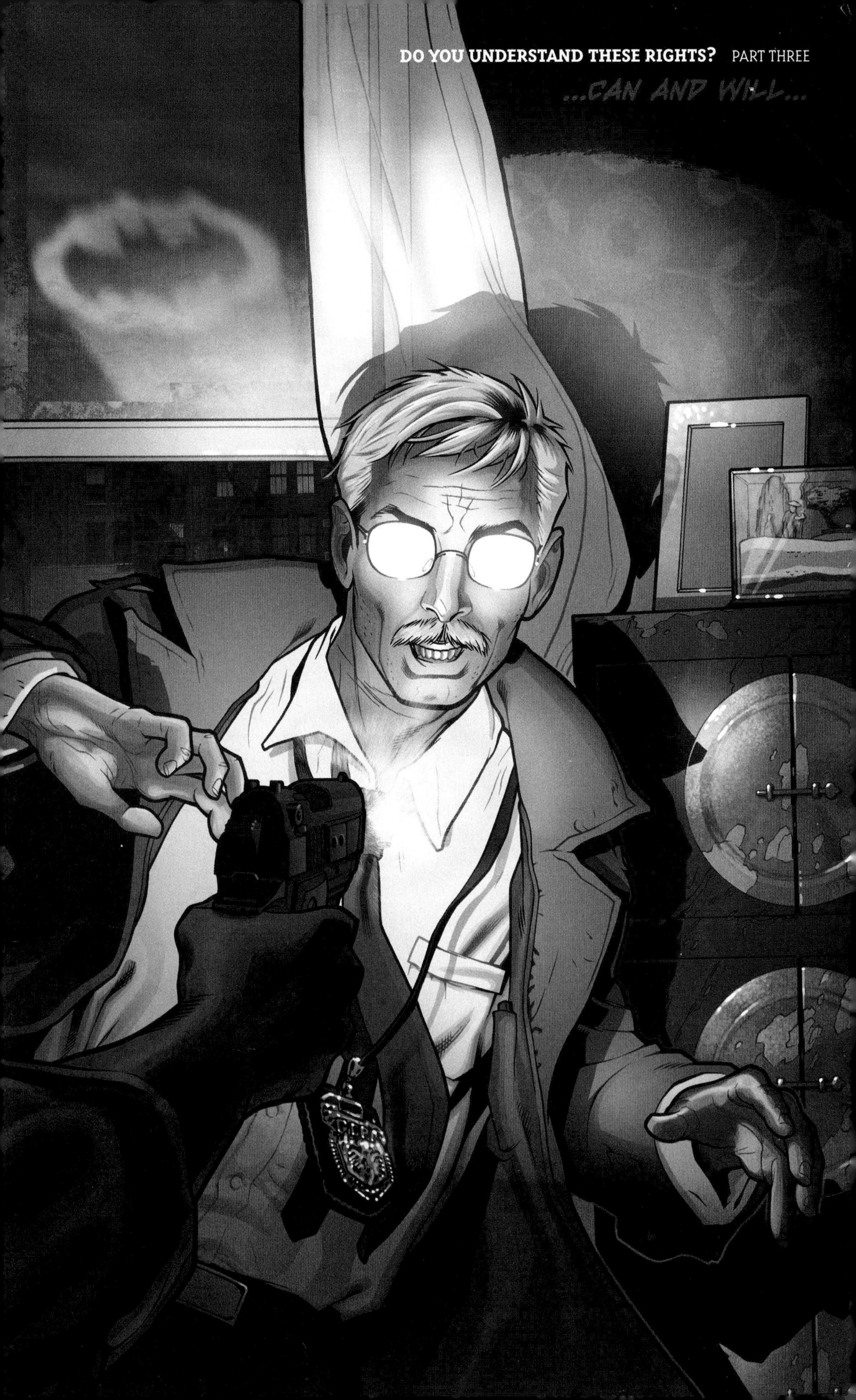
...CAN AND WILL...

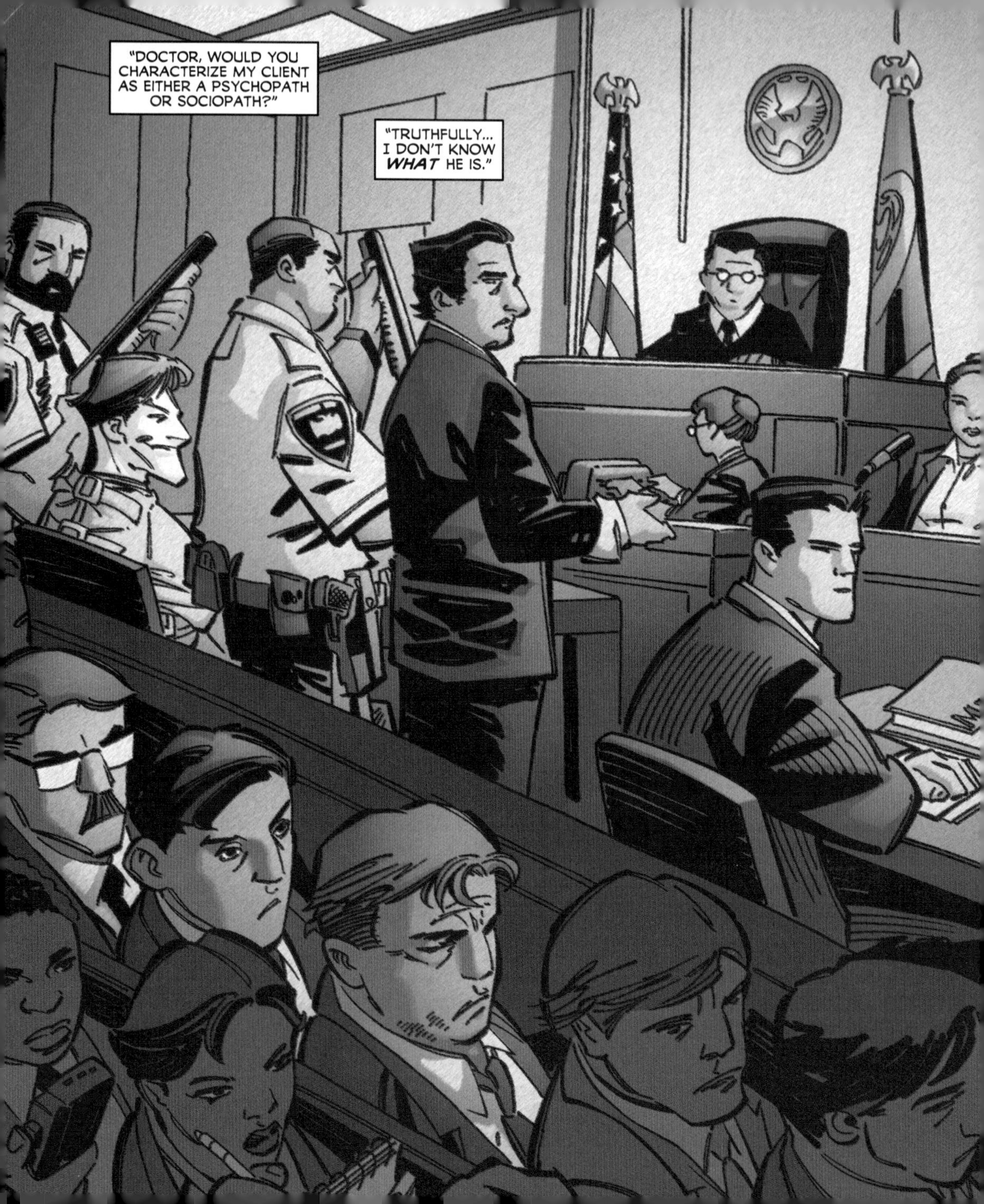
"DOCTOR, WOULD YOU CHARACTERIZE MY CLIENT AS EITHER A PSYCHOPATH OR SOCIOPATH?"
"TRUTHFULLY... I DON'T KNOW *WHAT* HE IS."

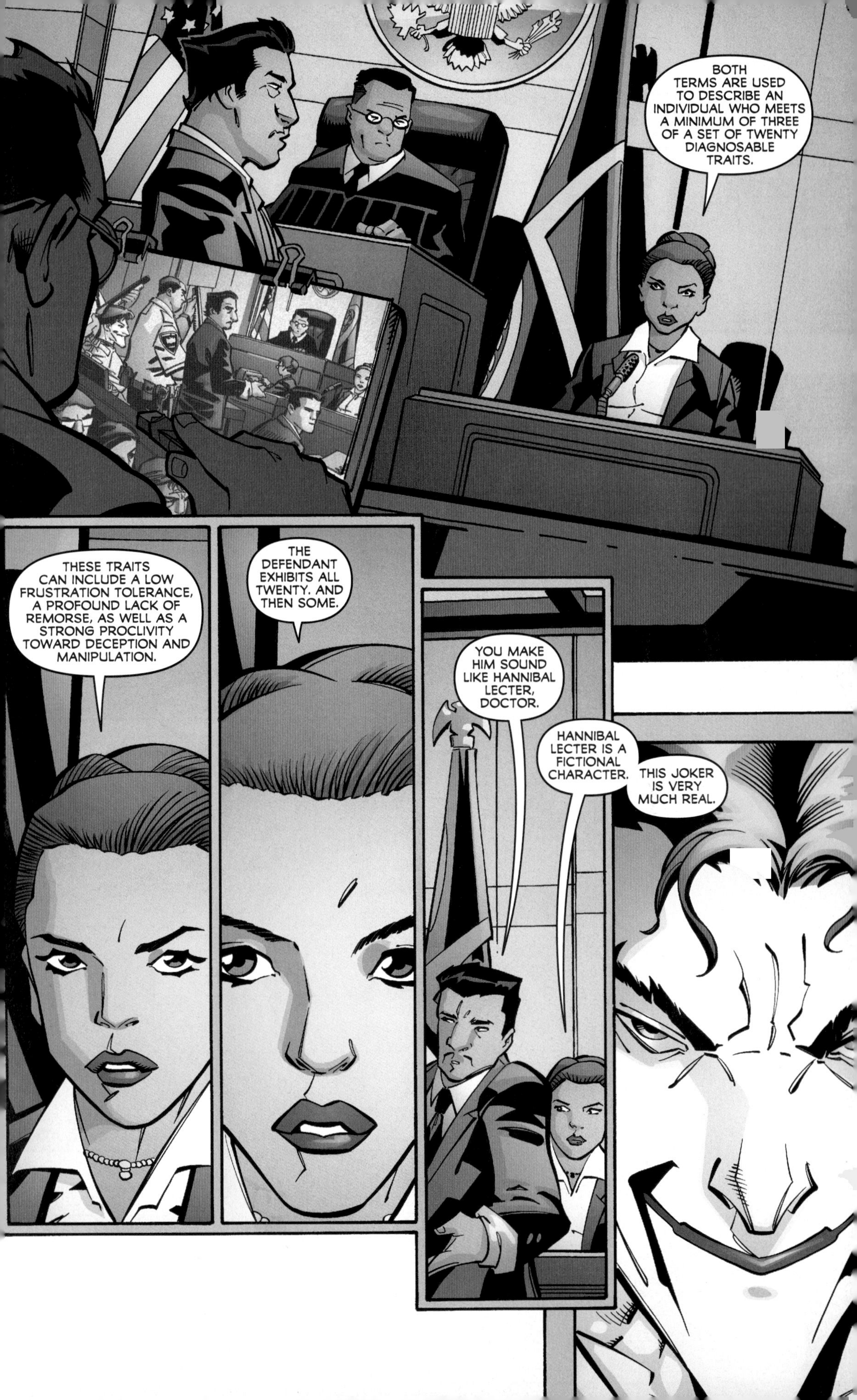
BOTH TERMS ARE USED TO DESCRIBE AN INDIVIDUAL WHO MEETS A MINIMUM OF THREE OF A SET OF TWENTY DIAGNOSABLE TRAITS.
THESE TRAITS CAN INCLUDE A LOW FRUSTRATION TOLERANCE, A PROFOUND LACK OF REMORSE, AS WELL AS A STRONG PROCLIVITY TOWARD DECEPTION AND MANIPULATION.
THE DEFENDANT EXHIBITS ALL TWENTY. AND THEN SOME.
YOU MAKE HIM SOUND LIKE HANNIBAL LECTER, DOCTOR.
HANNIBAL LECTER IS A FICTIONAL CHARACTER.
THIS JOKER IS VERY MUCH REAL.

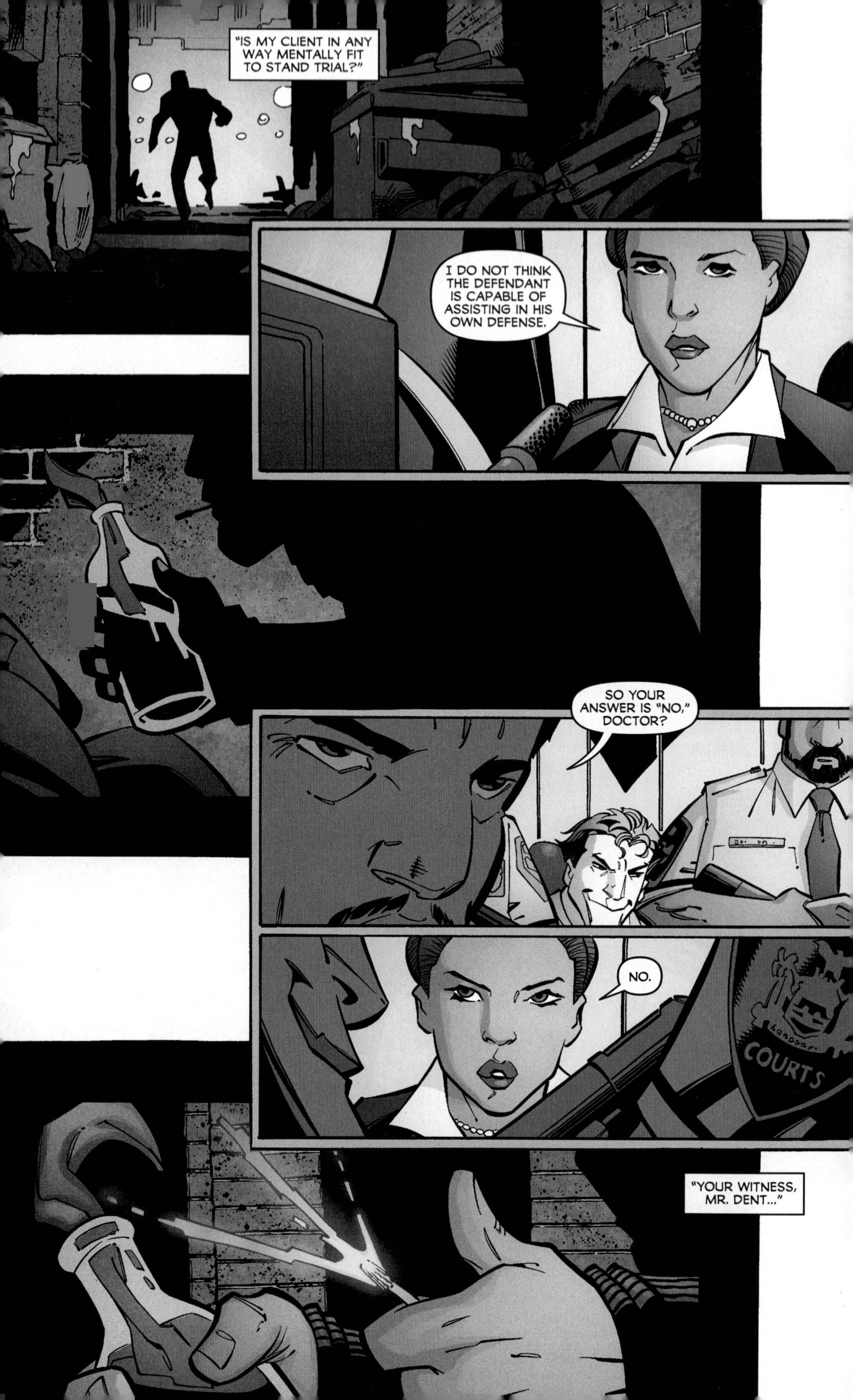
"IS MY CLIENT IN ANY WAY MENTALLY FIT TO STAND TRIAL?"
I DO NOT THINK THE DEFENDANT IS CAPABLE OF ASSISTING IN HIS OWN DEFENSE.
SO YOUR ANSWER IS "NO," DOCTOR?
NO.
COURTS
"YOUR WITNESS, MR. DENT..."

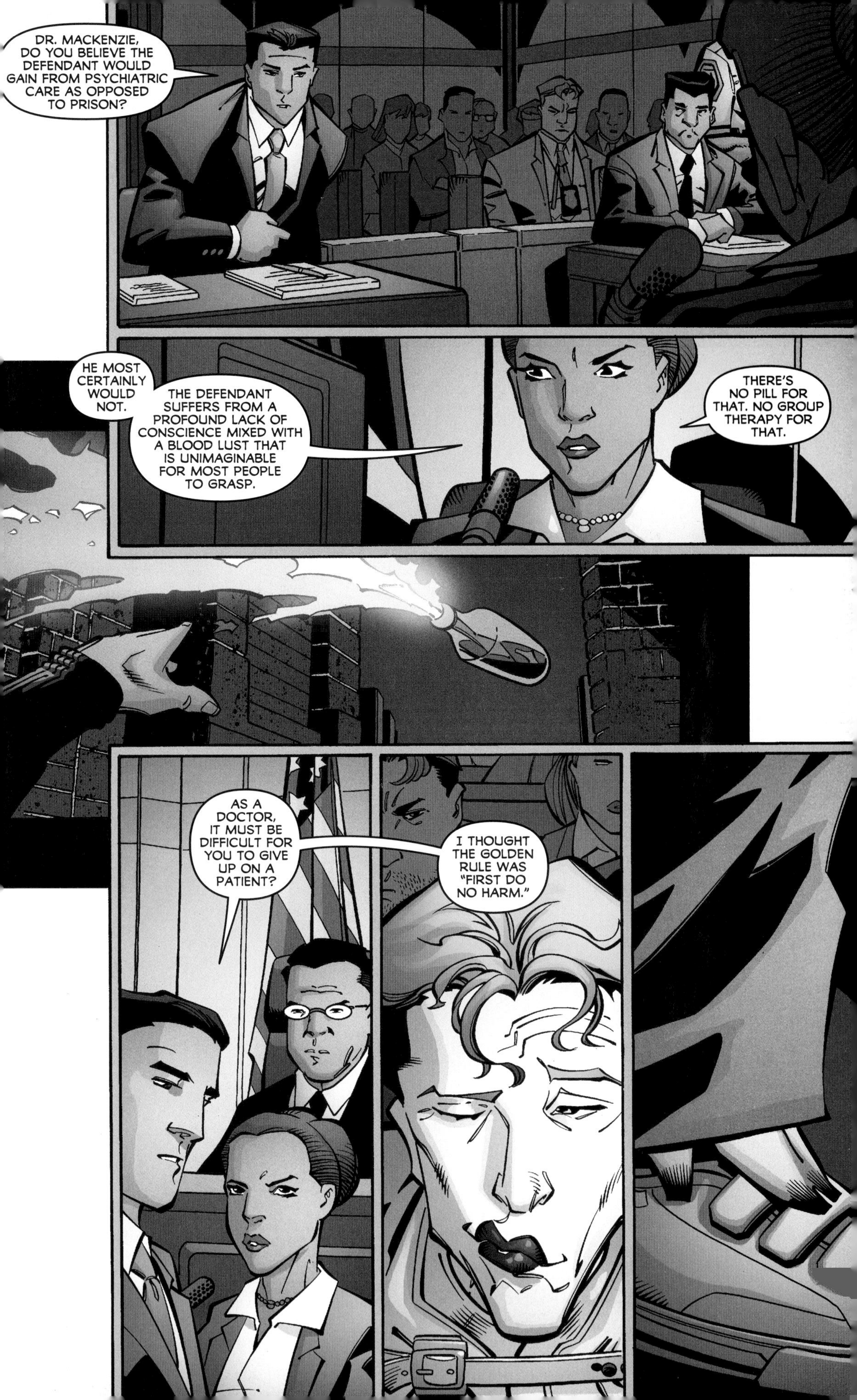
DR. MACKENZIE, DO YOU BELIEVE THE DEFENDANT WOULD GAIN FROM PSYCHIATRIC CARE AS OPPOSED TO PRISON?
HE MOST CERTAINLY WOULD NOT.
THE DEFENDANT SUFFERS FROM A PROFOUND LACK OF CONSCIENCE MIXED WITH A BLOOD LUST THAT IS UNIMAGINABLE FOR MOST PEOPLE TO GRASP.
THERE'S NO PILL FOR THAT. NO GROUP THERAPY FOR THAT.
AS A DOCTOR, IT MUST BE DIFFICULT FOR YOU TO GIVE UP ON A PATIENT?
I THOUGHT THE GOLDEN RULE WAS "FIRST DO NO HARM."

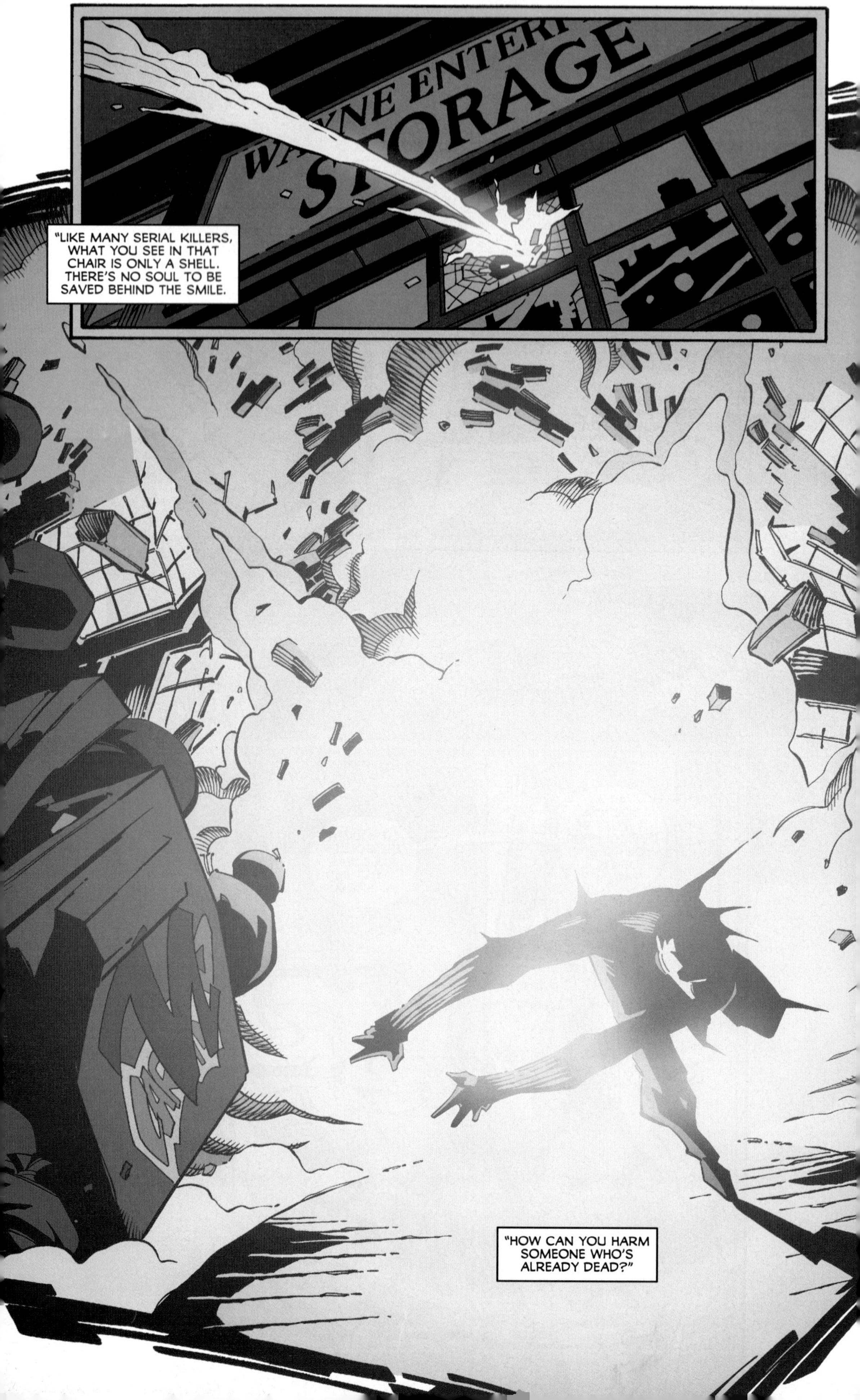
STORAGE
"LIKE MANY SERIAL KILLERS, WHAT YOU SEE IN THAT CHAIR IS ONLY A SHELL. THERE'S NO SOUL TO BE SAVED BEHIND THE SMILE.
"HOW CAN YOU HARM SOMEONE WHO'S ALREADY DEAD?"

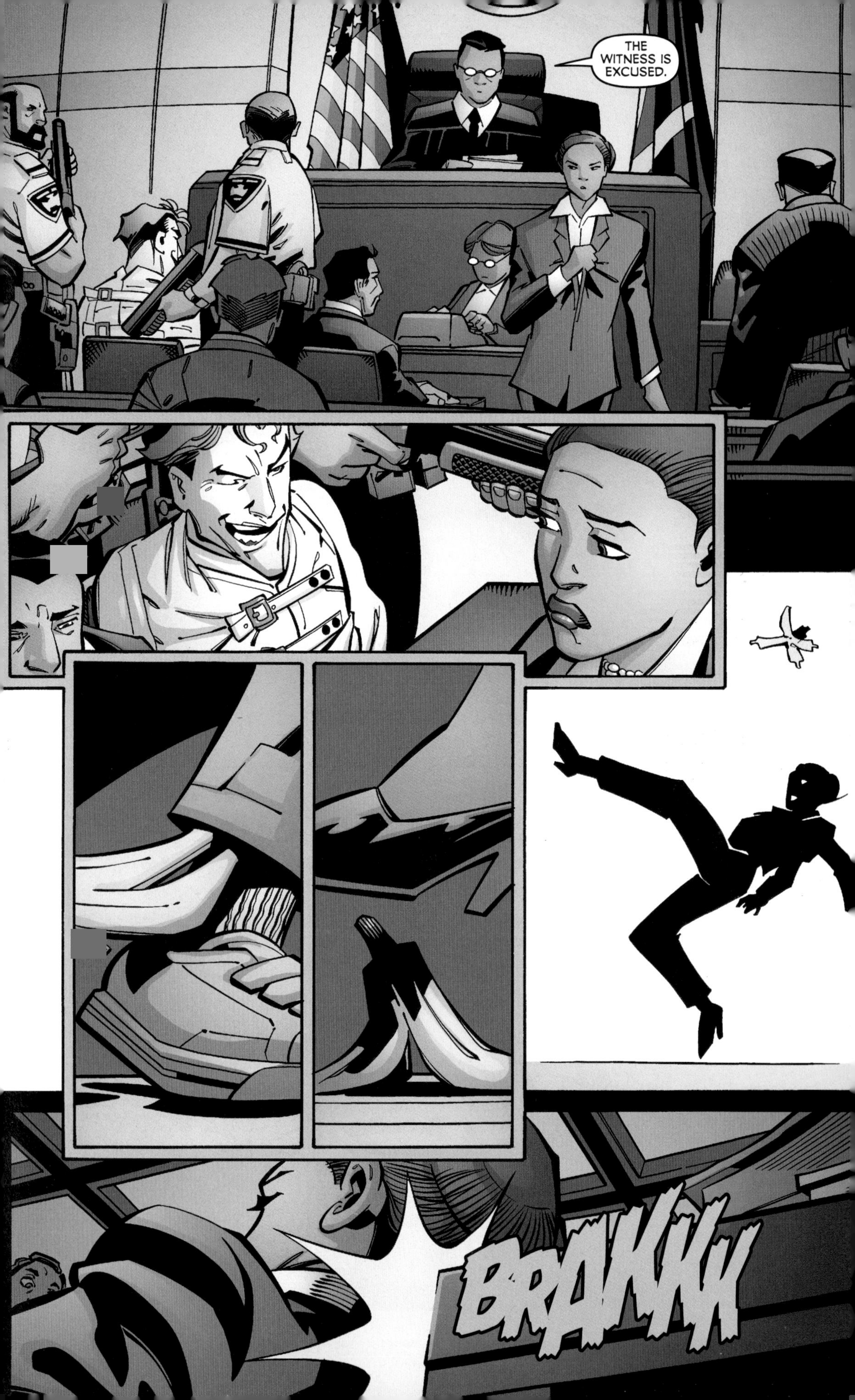
THE WITNESS IS EXCUSED.
BRAKKK

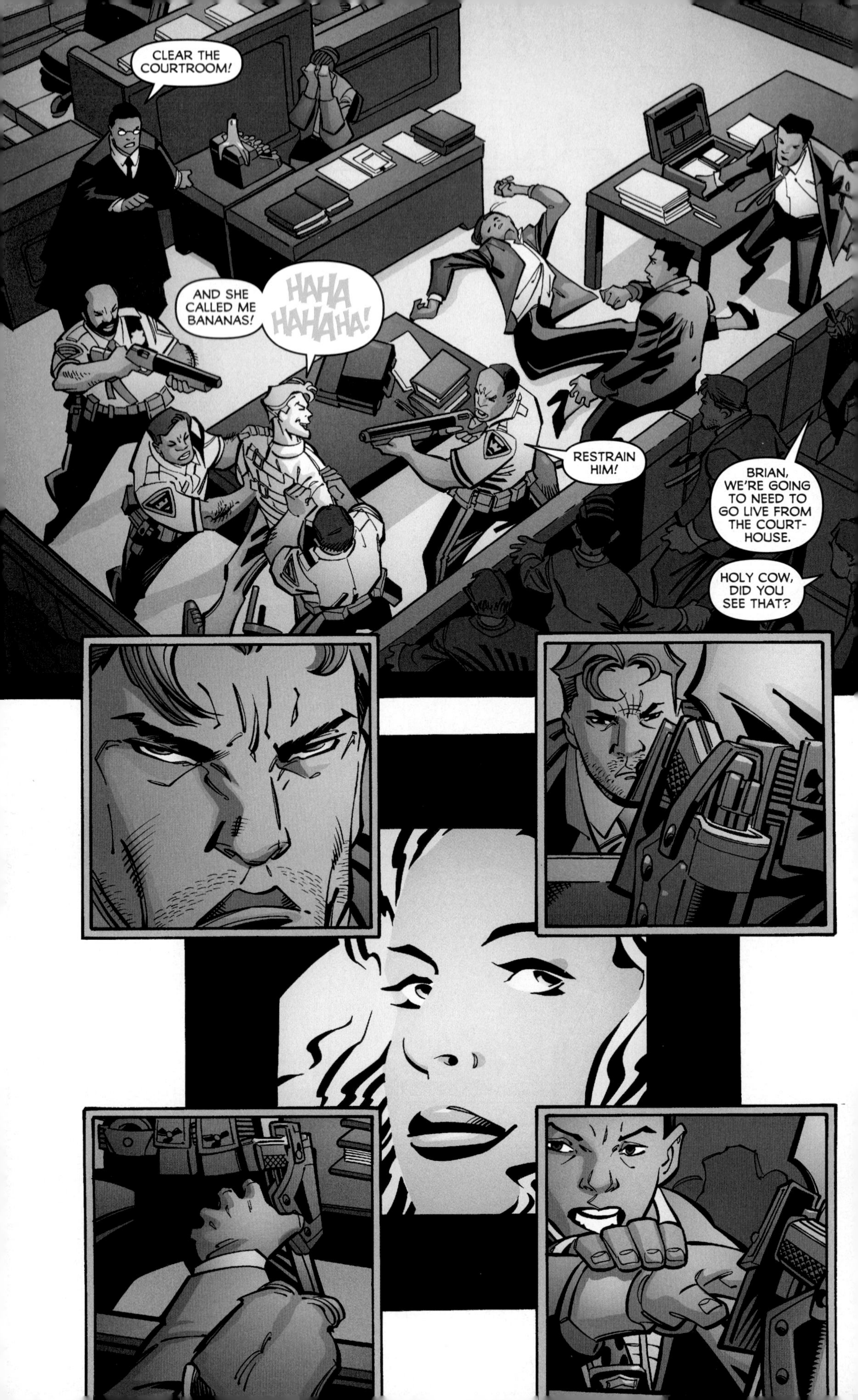
CLEAR THE COURTROOM!
AND SHE CALLED ME BANANAS!
HAHA HAHAHA!
RESTRAIN HIM!
BRIAN, WE'RE GOING TO NEED TO GO LIVE FROM THE COURT-HOUSE.
HOLY COW, DID YOU SEE THAT?

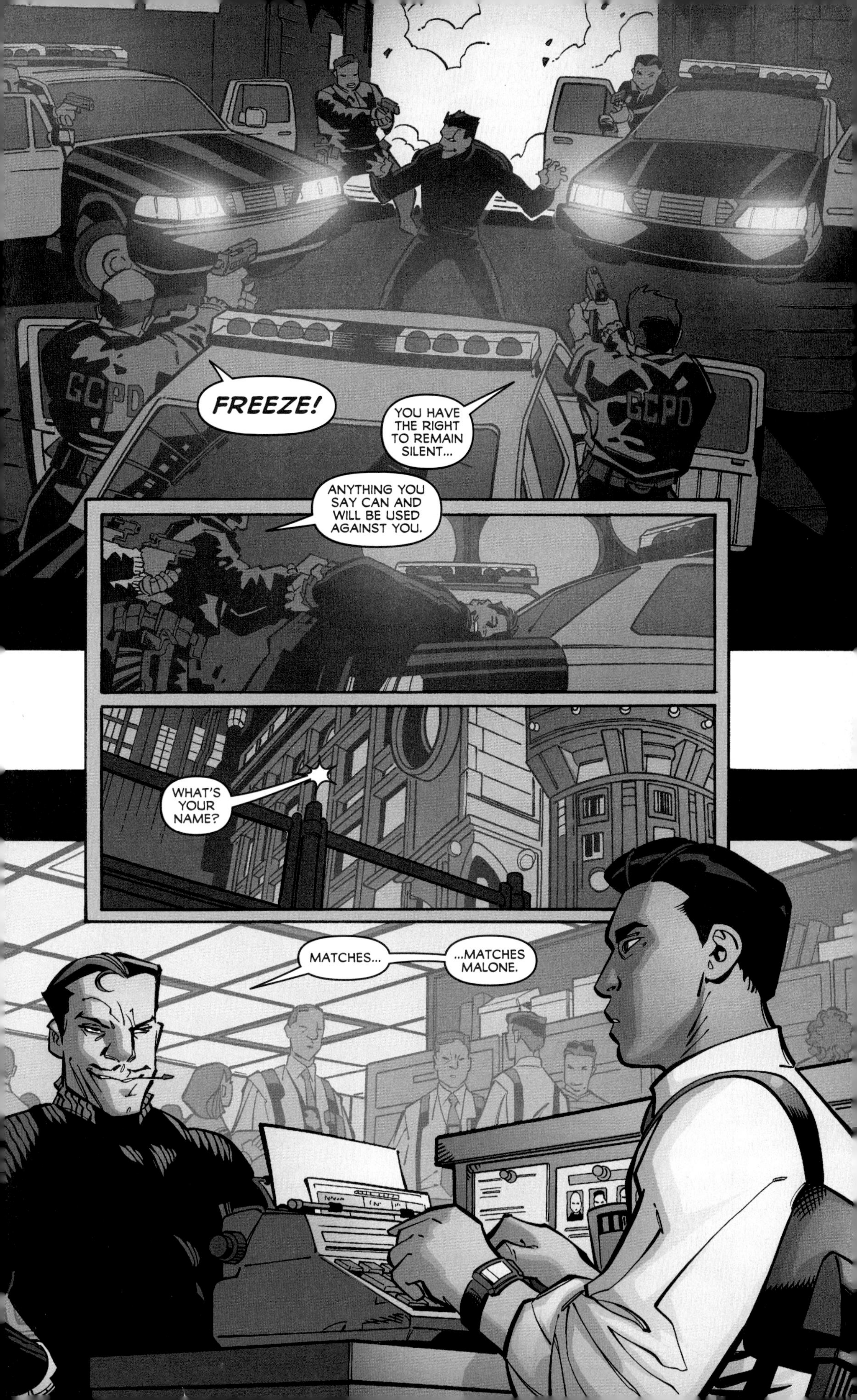
FREEZE!
YOU HAVE THE RIGHT TO REMAIN SILENT...
ANYTHING YOU SAY CAN AND WILL BE USED AGAINST YOU.
WHAT'S YOUR NAME?
MATCHES...
...MATCHES MALONE.

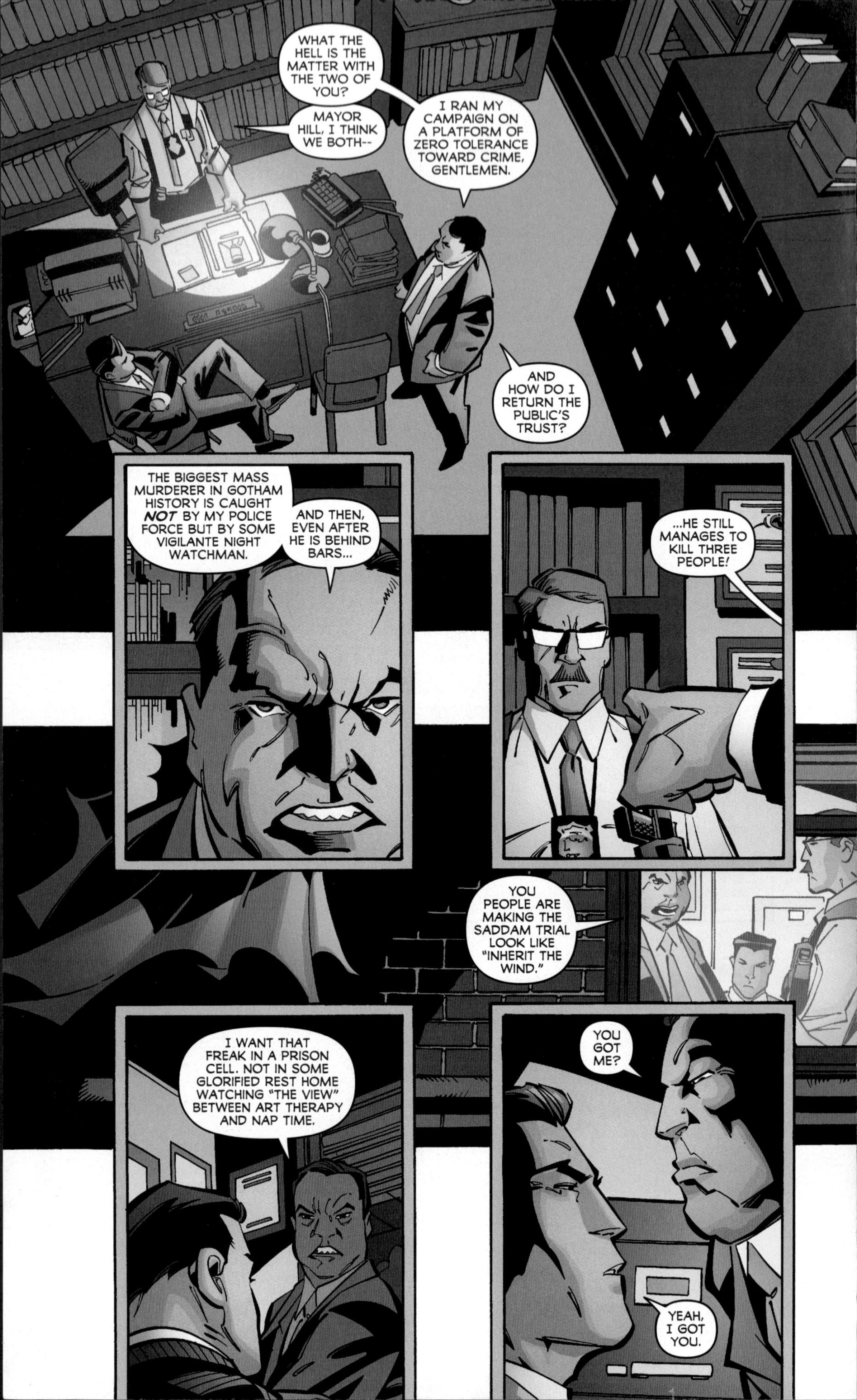
WHAT THE HELL IS THE MATTER WITH THE TWO OF YOU?
MAYOR HILL, I THINK WE BOTH--
I RAN MY CAMPAIGN ON A PLATFORM OF ZERO TOLERANCE TOWARD CRIME, GENTLEMEN.
AND HOW DO I RETURN THE PUBLIC'S TRUST?
THE BIGGEST MASS MURDERER IN GOTHAM HISTORY IS CAUGHT *NOT* BY MY POLICE FORCE BUT BY SOME VIGILANTE NIGHT WATCHMAN.
AND THEN, EVEN AFTER HE IS BEHIND BARS...
...HE STILL MANAGES TO KILL THREE PEOPLE!
YOU PEOPLE ARE MAKING THE SADDAM TRIAL LOOK LIKE "INHERIT THE WIND."
I WANT THAT FREAK IN A PRISON CELL. NOT IN SOME GLORIFIED REST HOME WATCHING "THE VIEW" BETWEEN ART THERAPY AND NAP TIME.
YOU GOT ME?
YEAH, I GOT YOU.

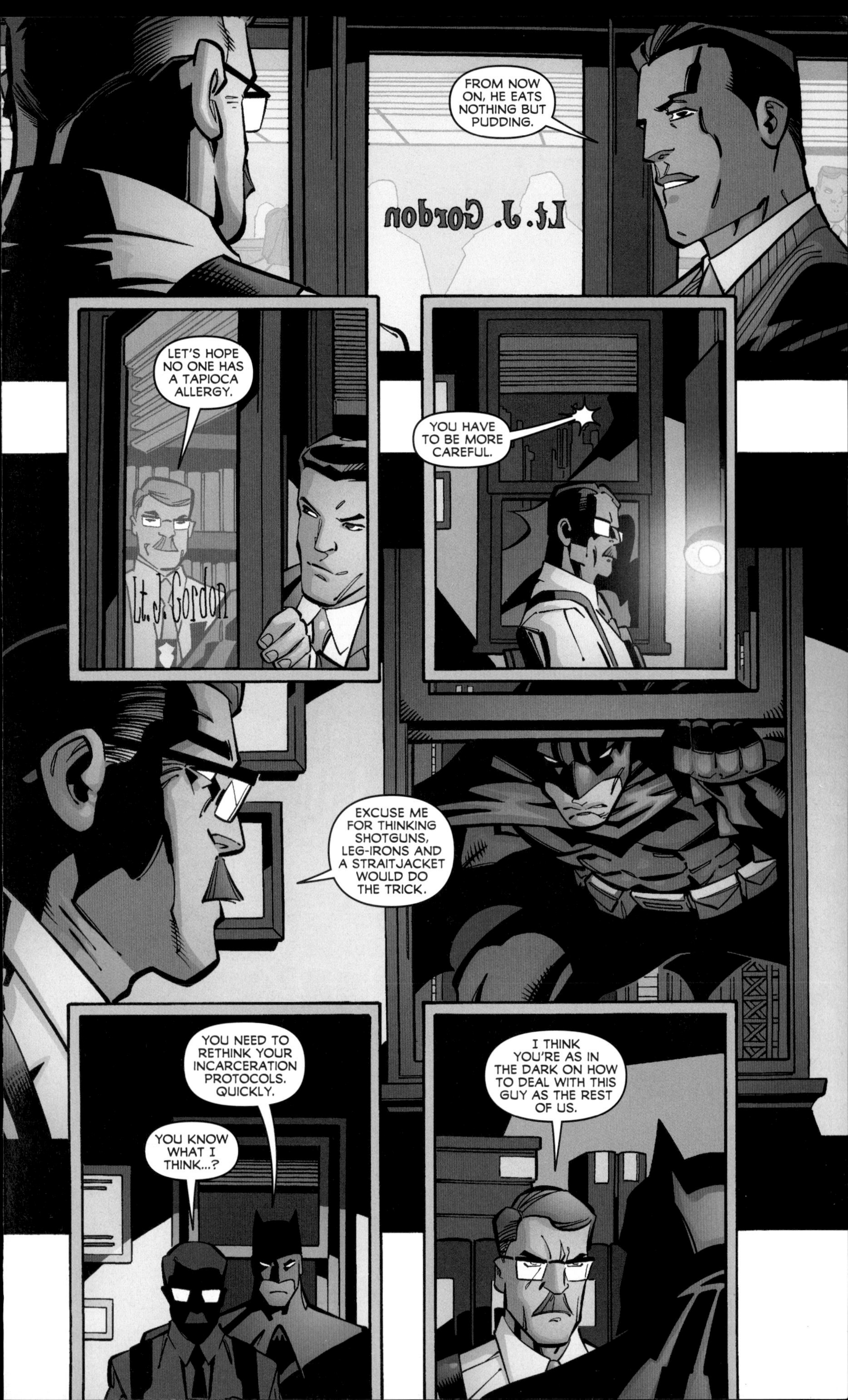
FROM NOW ON, HE EATS NOTHING BUT PUDDING.
Lt. J. Gordon
LET'S HOPE NO ONE HAS A TAPIOCA ALLERGY.
Lt. J. Gordon
YOU HAVE TO BE MORE CAREFUL.
EXCUSE ME FOR THINKING SHOTGUNS, LEG-IRONS AND A STRAITJACKET WOULD DO THE TRICK.
YOU NEED TO RETHINK YOUR INCARCERATION PROTOCOLS. QUICKLY.
YOU KNOW WHAT I THINK...?
I THINK YOU'RE AS IN THE DARK ON HOW TO DEAL WITH THIS GUY AS THE REST OF US.

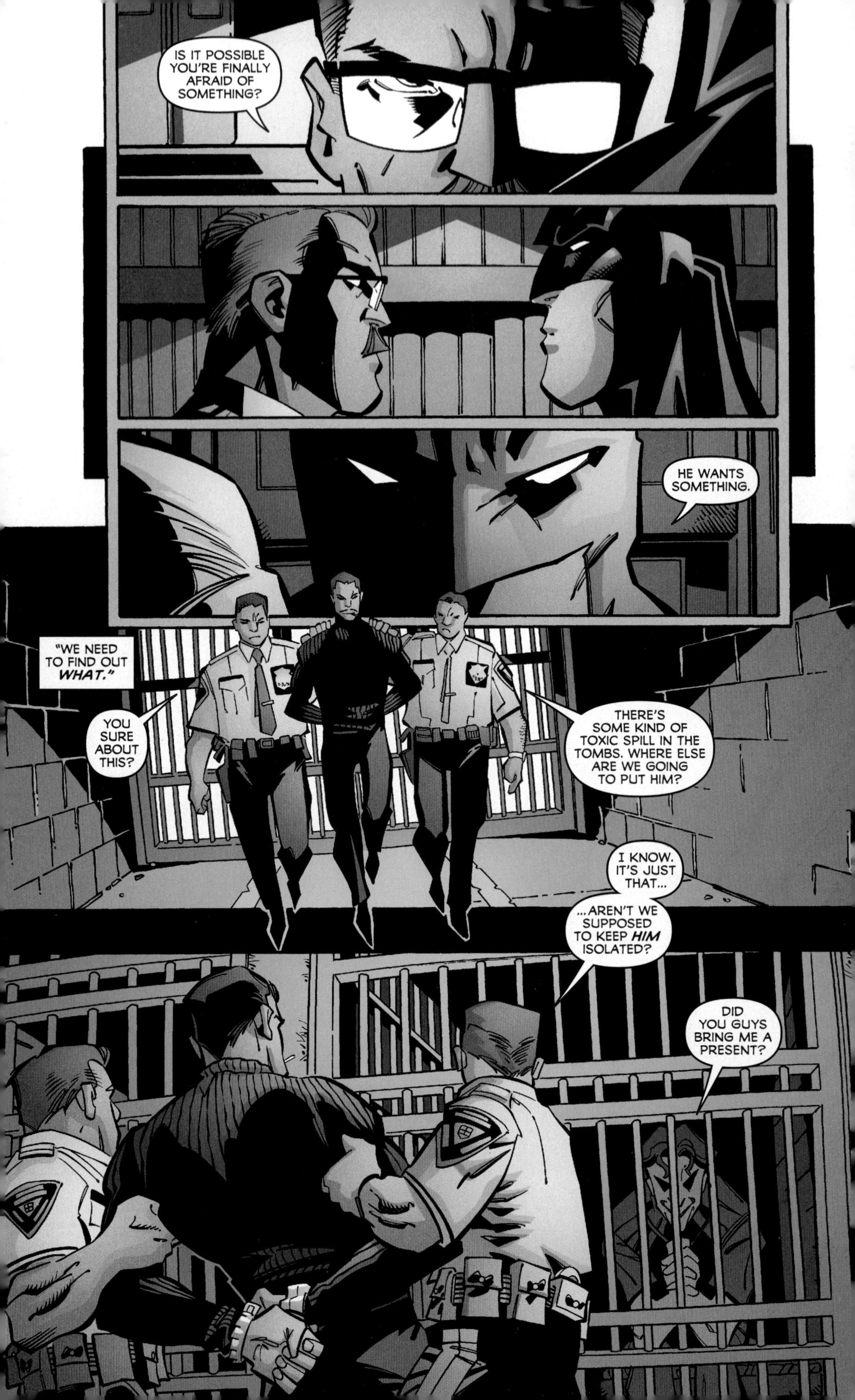

IS IT POSSIBLE YOU'RE FINALLY AFRAID OF SOMETHING?
HE WANTS SOMETHING.
"WE NEED TO FIND OUT *WHAT.*"
YOU SURE ABOUT THIS?
THERE'S SOME KIND OF TOXIC SPILL IN THE TOMBS. WHERE ELSE ARE WE GOING TO PUT HIM?
I KNOW. IT'S JUST THAT...
...AREN'T WE SUPPOSED TO KEEP *HIM* ISOLATED?
DID YOU GUYS BRING ME A PRESENT?

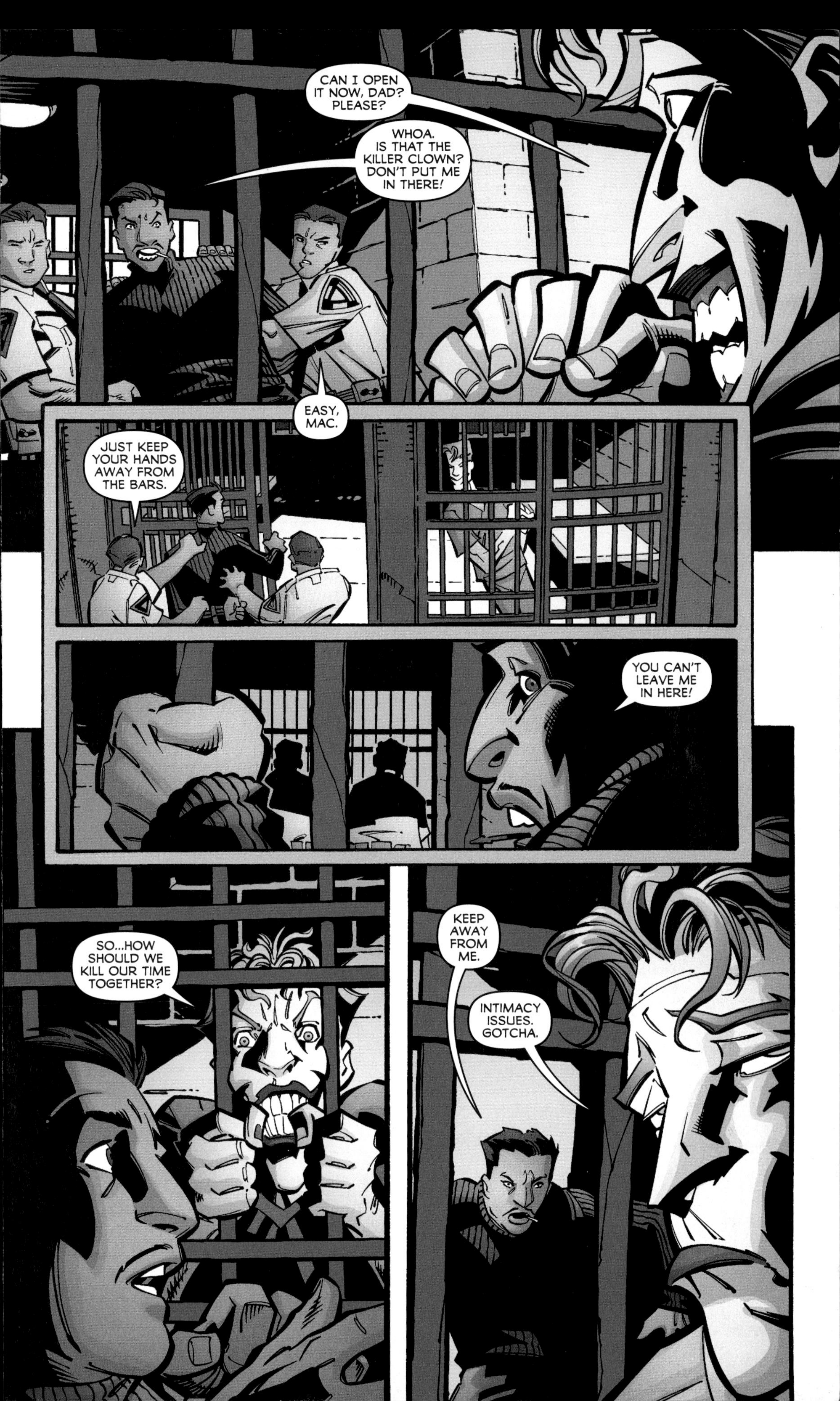
CAN I OPEN IT NOW, DAD? PLEASE?
WHOA. IS THAT THE KILLER CLOWN? DON'T PUT ME IN THERE!
EASY, MAC.
JUST KEEP YOUR HANDS AWAY FROM THE BARS.
YOU CAN'T LEAVE ME IN HERE!
SO...HOW SHOULD WE KILL OUR TIME TOGETHER?
KEEP AWAY FROM ME.
INTIMACY ISSUES. GOTCHA.

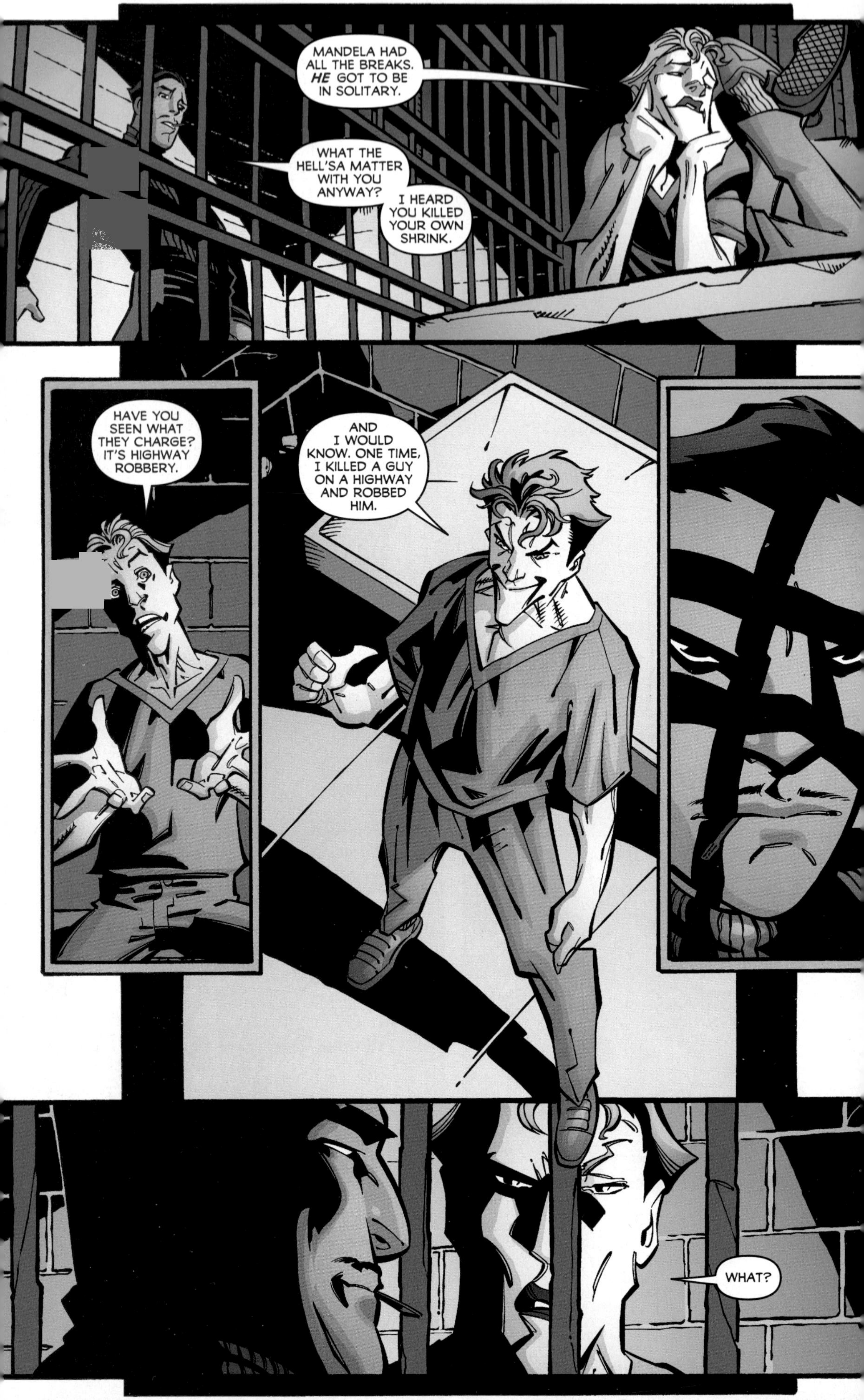
MANDELA HAD ALL THE BREAKS. HE GOT TO BE IN SOLITARY.
WHAT THE HELL'SA MATTER WITH YOU ANYWAY?
I HEARD YOU KILLED YOUR OWN SHRINK.
HAVE YOU SEEN WHAT THEY CHARGE? IT'S HIGHWAY ROBBERY.
AND I WOULD KNOW. ONE TIME, I KILLED A GUY ON A HIGHWAY AND ROBBED HIM.
WHAT?

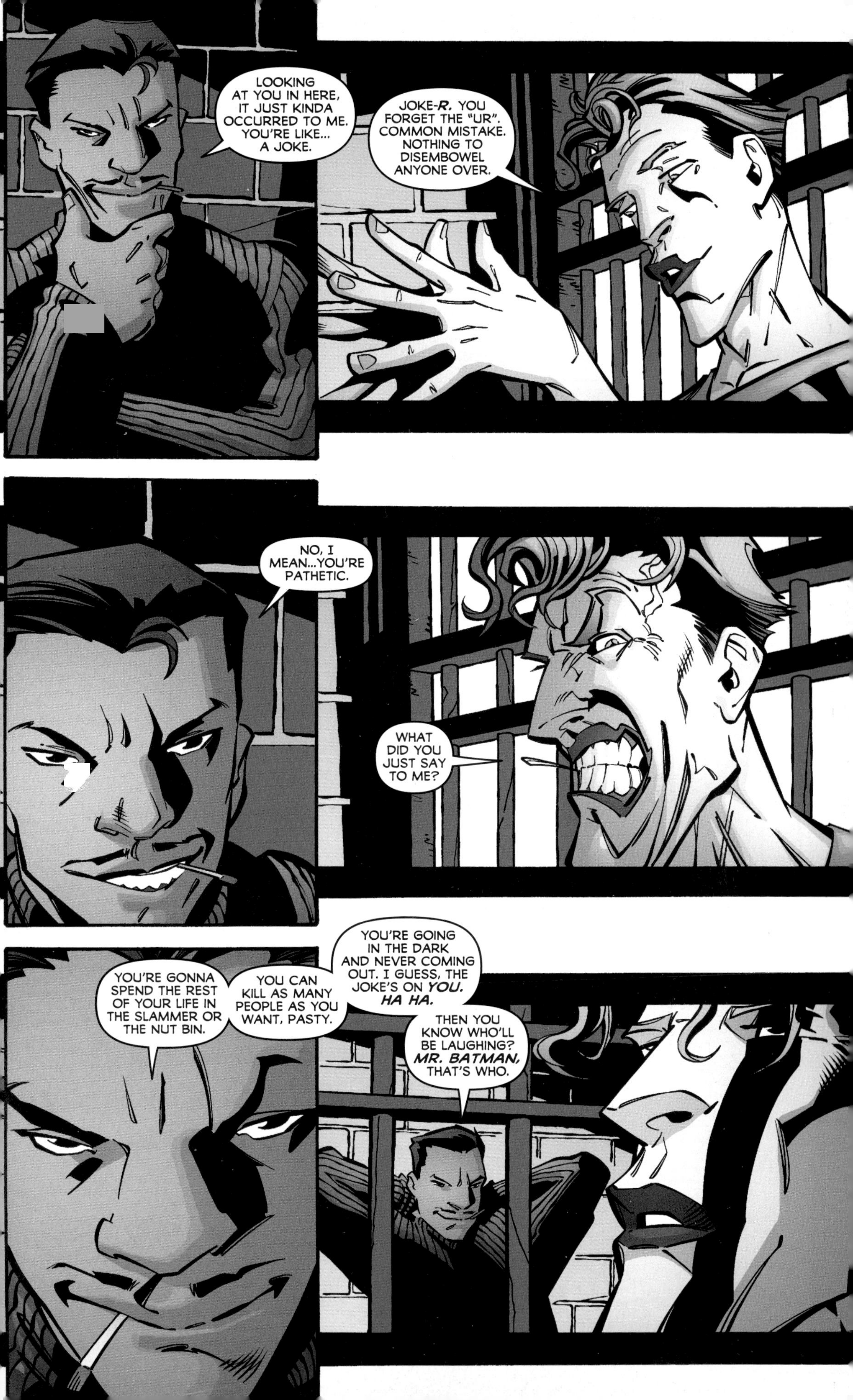
LOOKING AT YOU IN HERE, IT JUST KINDA OCCURRED TO ME. YOU'RE LIKE... A JOKE.
JOKE-R. YOU FORGET THE "UR". COMMON MISTAKE. NOTHING TO DISEMBOWEL ANYONE OVER.
NO, I MEAN...YOU'RE PATHETIC.
WHAT DID YOU JUST SAY TO ME?
YOU'RE GONNA SPEND THE REST OF YOUR LIFE IN THE SLAMMER OR THE NUT BIN.
YOU CAN KILL AS MANY PEOPLE AS YOU WANT, PASTY.
YOU'RE GOING IN THE DARK AND NEVER COMING OUT. I GUESS, THE JOKE'S ON YOU. HA HA.
THEN YOU KNOW WHO'LL BE LAUGHING? MR. BATMAN, THAT'S WHO.

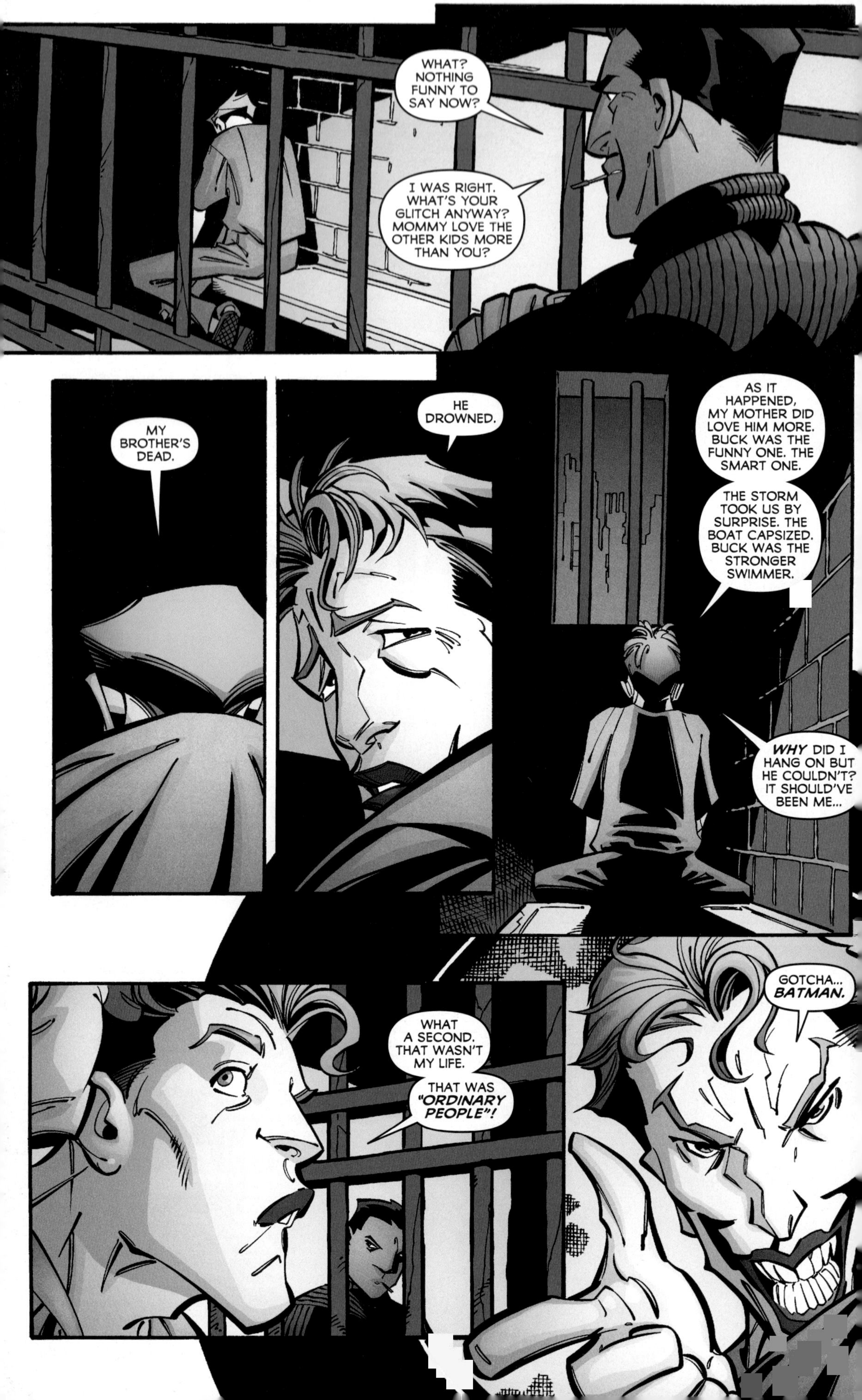

WHAT? NOTHING FUNNY TO SAY NOW?
I WAS RIGHT. WHAT'S YOUR GLITCH ANYWAY? MOMMY LOVE THE OTHER KIDS MORE THAN YOU?
MY BROTHER'S DEAD.
HE DROWNED.
AS IT HAPPENED, MY MOTHER DID LOVE HIM MORE. BUCK WAS THE FUNNY ONE. THE SMART ONE.
THE STORM TOOK US BY SURPRISE. THE BOAT CAPSIZED. BUCK WAS THE STRONGER SWIMMER.
WHY DID I HANG ON BUT HE COULDN'T? IT SHOULD'VE BEEN ME...
WHAT A SECOND. THAT WASN'T MY LIFE.
THAT WAS "ORDINARY PEOPLE"!
GOTCHA... BATMAN.

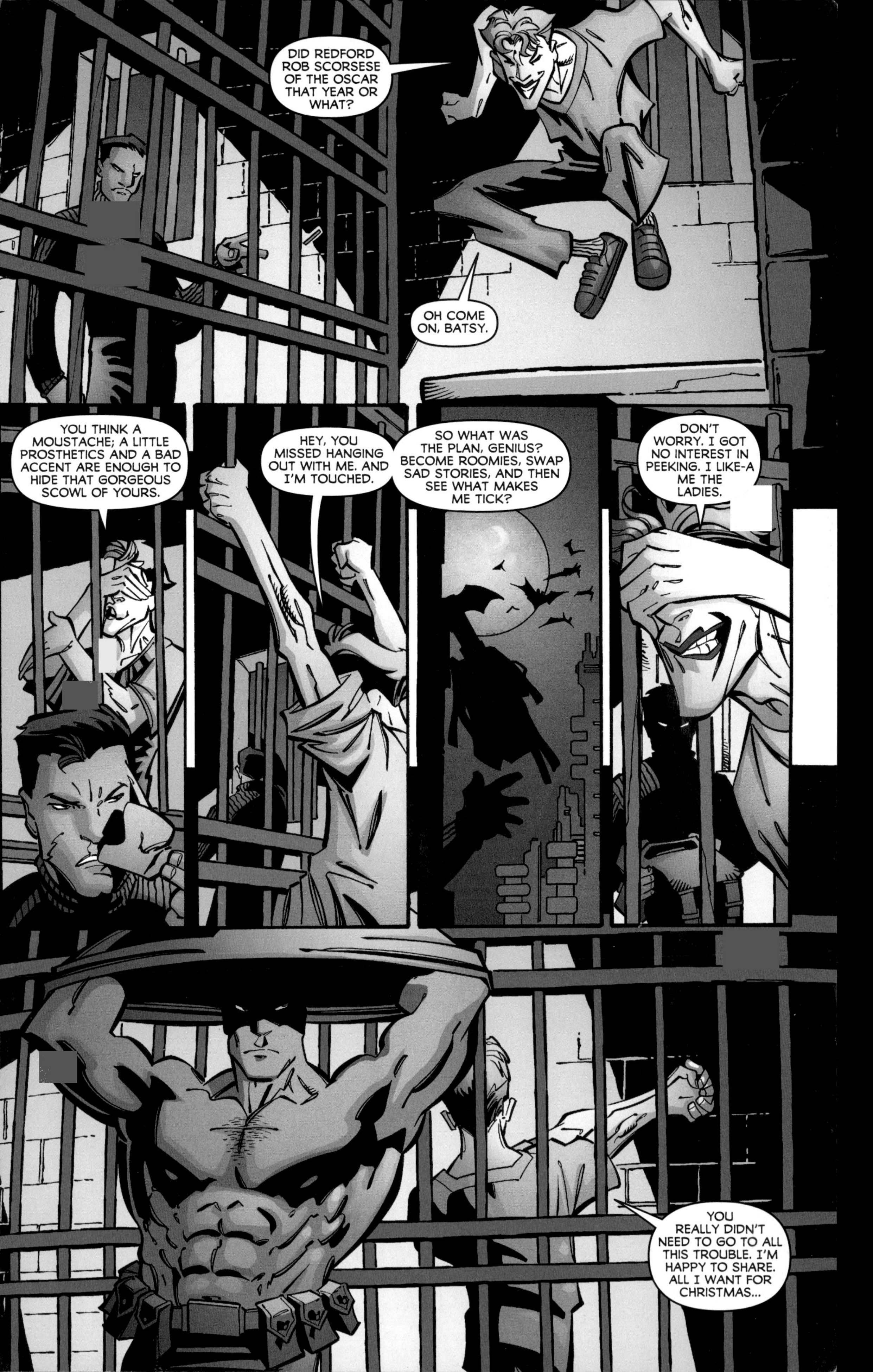
DID REDFORD ROB SCORSESE OF THE OSCAR THAT YEAR OR WHAT?
OH COME ON, BATSY.
YOU THINK A MOUSTACHE; A LITTLE PROSTHETICS AND A BAD ACCENT ARE ENOUGH TO HIDE THAT GORGEOUS SCOWL OF YOURS.
HEY, YOU MISSED HANGING OUT WITH ME. AND I'M TOUCHED.
SO WHAT WAS THE PLAN, GENIUS? BECOME ROOMIES, SWAP SAD STORIES, AND THEN SEE WHAT MAKES ME TICK?
DON'T WORRY. I GOT NO INTEREST IN PEEKING. I LIKE-A ME THE LADIES.
YOU REALLY DIDN'T NEED TO GO TO ALL THIS TROUBLE. I'M HAPPY TO SHARE. ALL I WANT FOR CHRISTMAS...

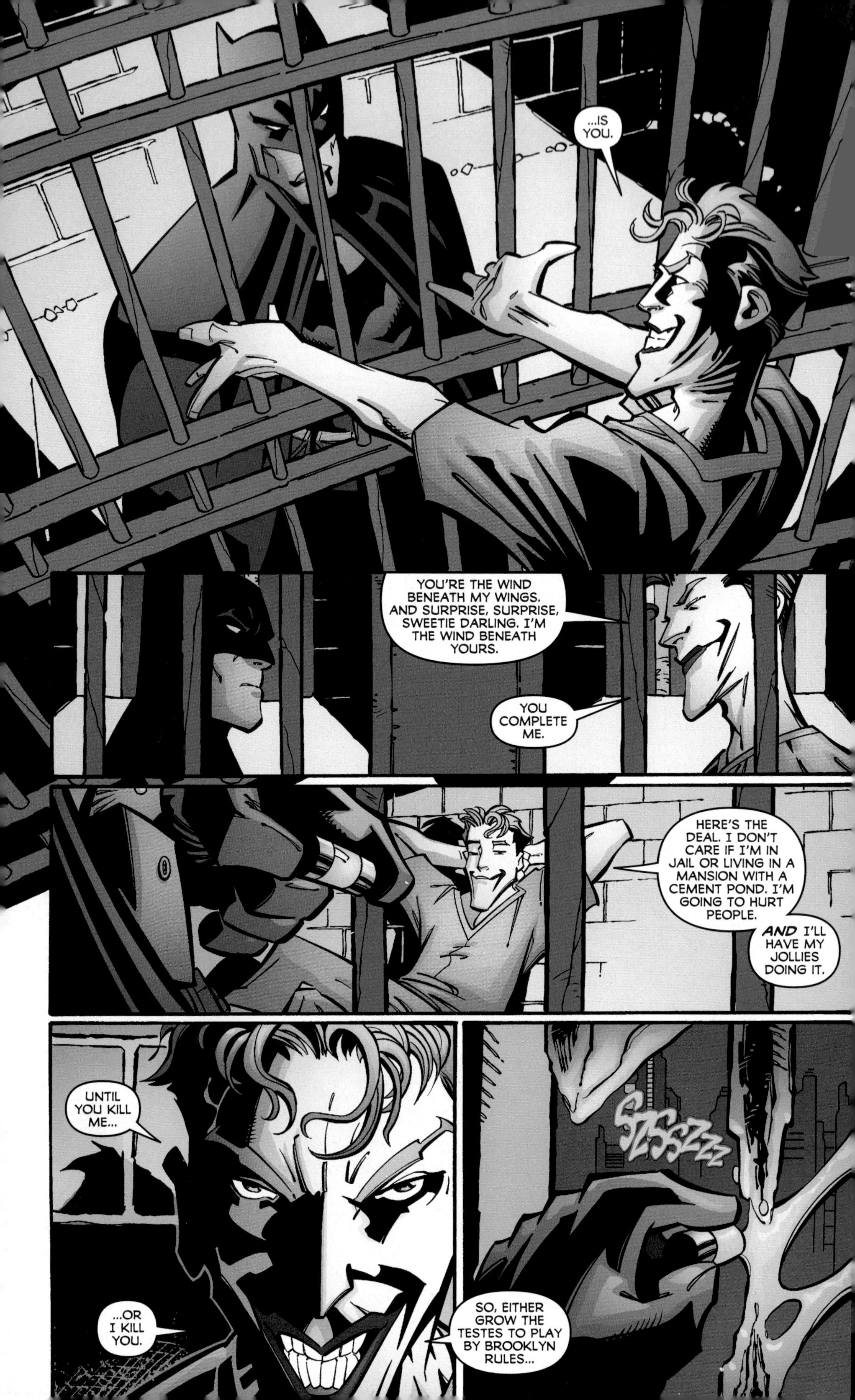
...IS YOU.
YOU'RE THE WIND BENEATH MY WINGS. AND SURPRISE, SURPRISE, SWEETIE DARLING. I'M THE WIND BENEATH YOURS.
YOU COMPLETE ME.
HERE'S THE DEAL. I DON'T CARE IF I'M IN JAIL OR LIVING IN A MANSION WITH A CEMENT POND. I'M GOING TO HURT PEOPLE.
AND I'LL HAVE MY JOLLIES DOING IT.
UNTIL YOU KILL ME...
...OR I KILL YOU.
SO, EITHER GROW THE TESTES TO PLAY BY BROOKLYN RULES...
SZSSZZZ

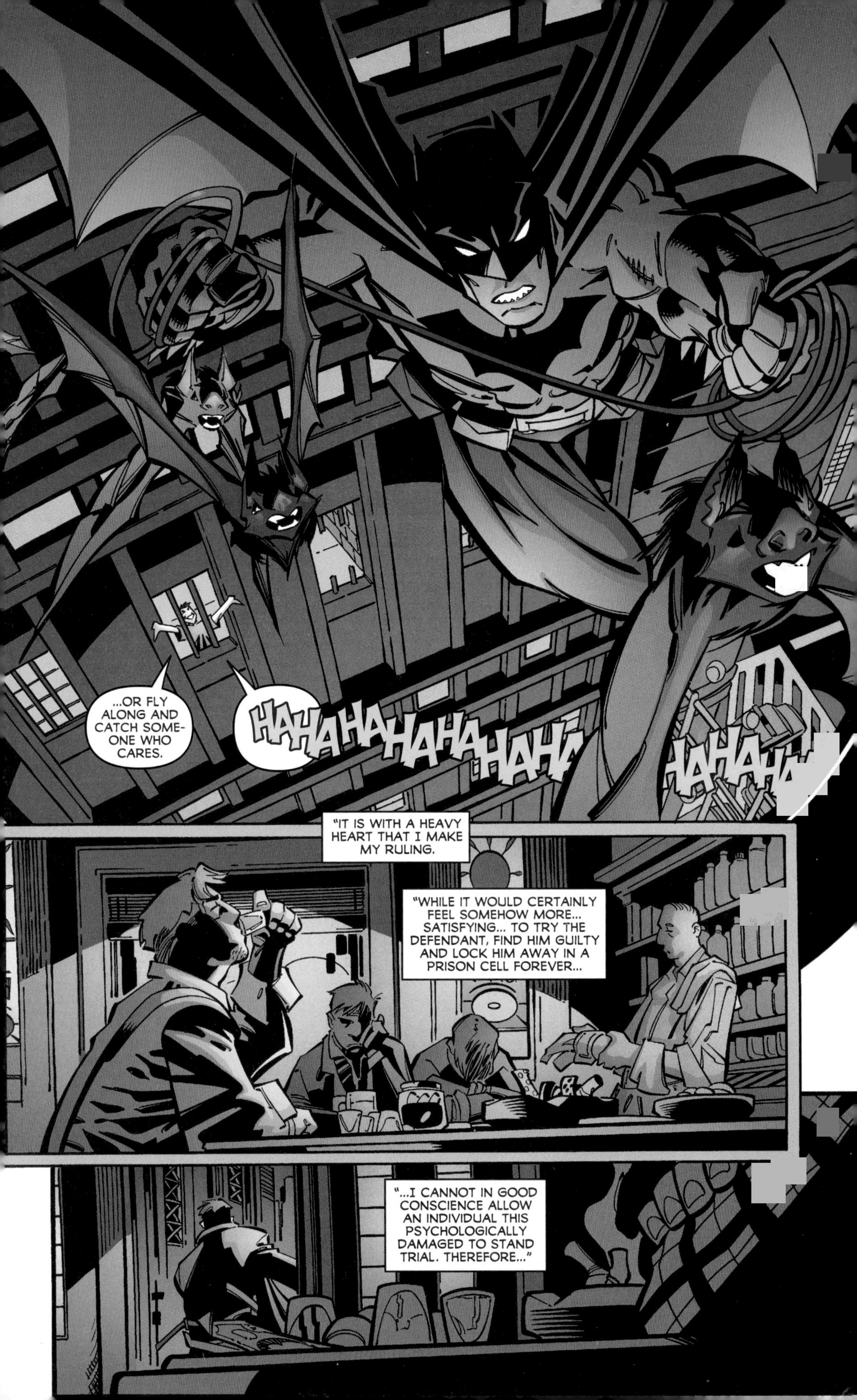
...OR FLY ALONG AND CATCH SOME-ONE WHO CARES.
HAHAHAHAHAHAHAHAHAHAHA
"IT IS WITH A HEAVY HEART THAT I MAKE MY RULING.
"WHILE IT WOULD CERTAINLY FEEL SOMEHOW MORE... SATISFYING... TO TRY THE DEFENDANT, FIND HIM GUILTY AND LOCK HIM AWAY IN A PRISON CELL FOREVER...
"...I CANNOT IN GOOD CONSCIENCE ALLOW AN INDIVIDUAL THIS PSYCHOLOGICALLY DAMAGED TO STAND TRIAL. THEREFORE..."

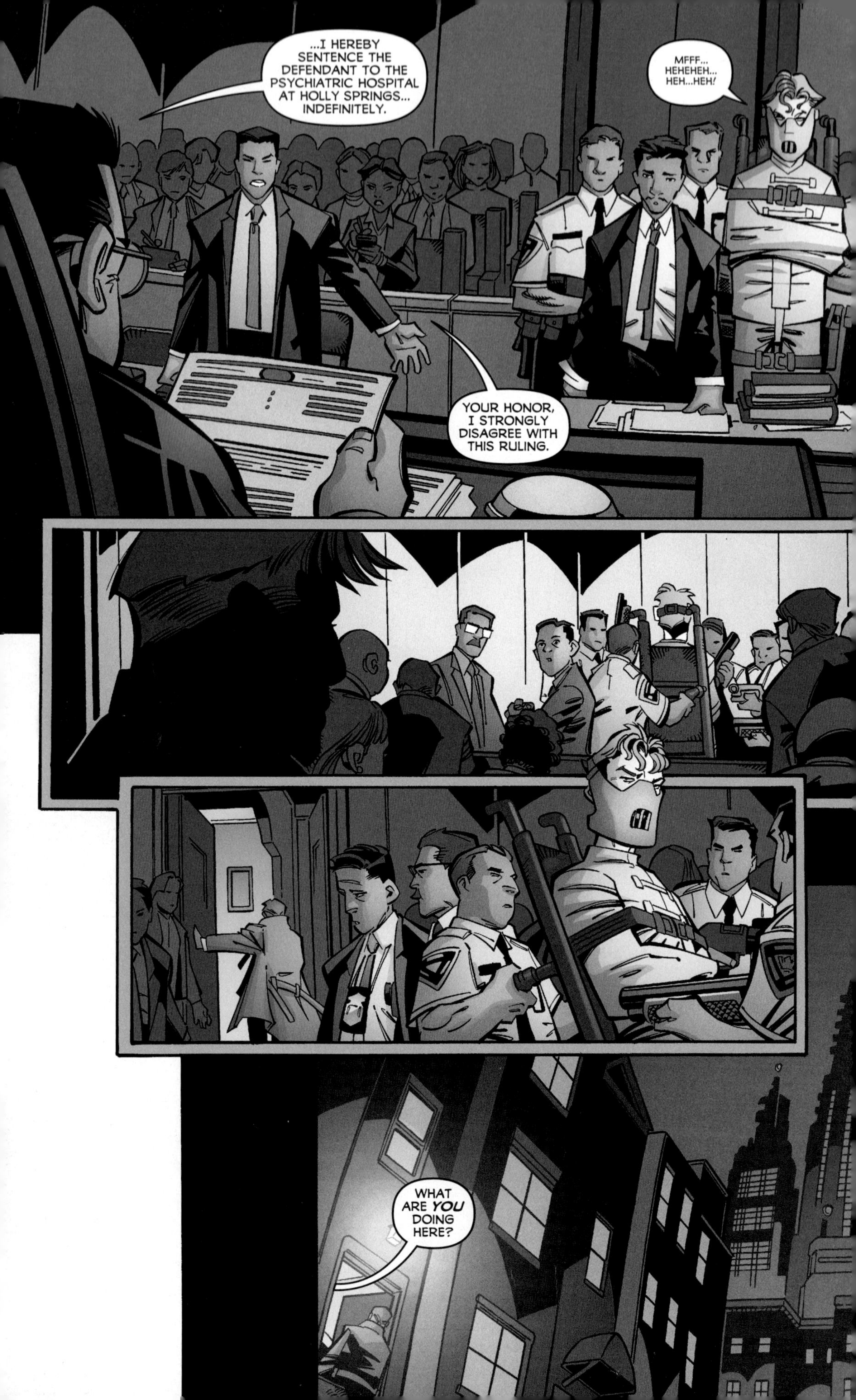
...I HEREBY SENTENCE THE DEFENDANT TO THE PSYCHIATRIC HOSPITAL AT HOLLY SPRINGS... INDEFINITELY.
MFFF... HEHEHEH... HEH...HEH!
YOUR HONOR, I STRONGLY DISAGREE WITH THIS RULING.
WHAT ARE *YOU* DOING HERE?

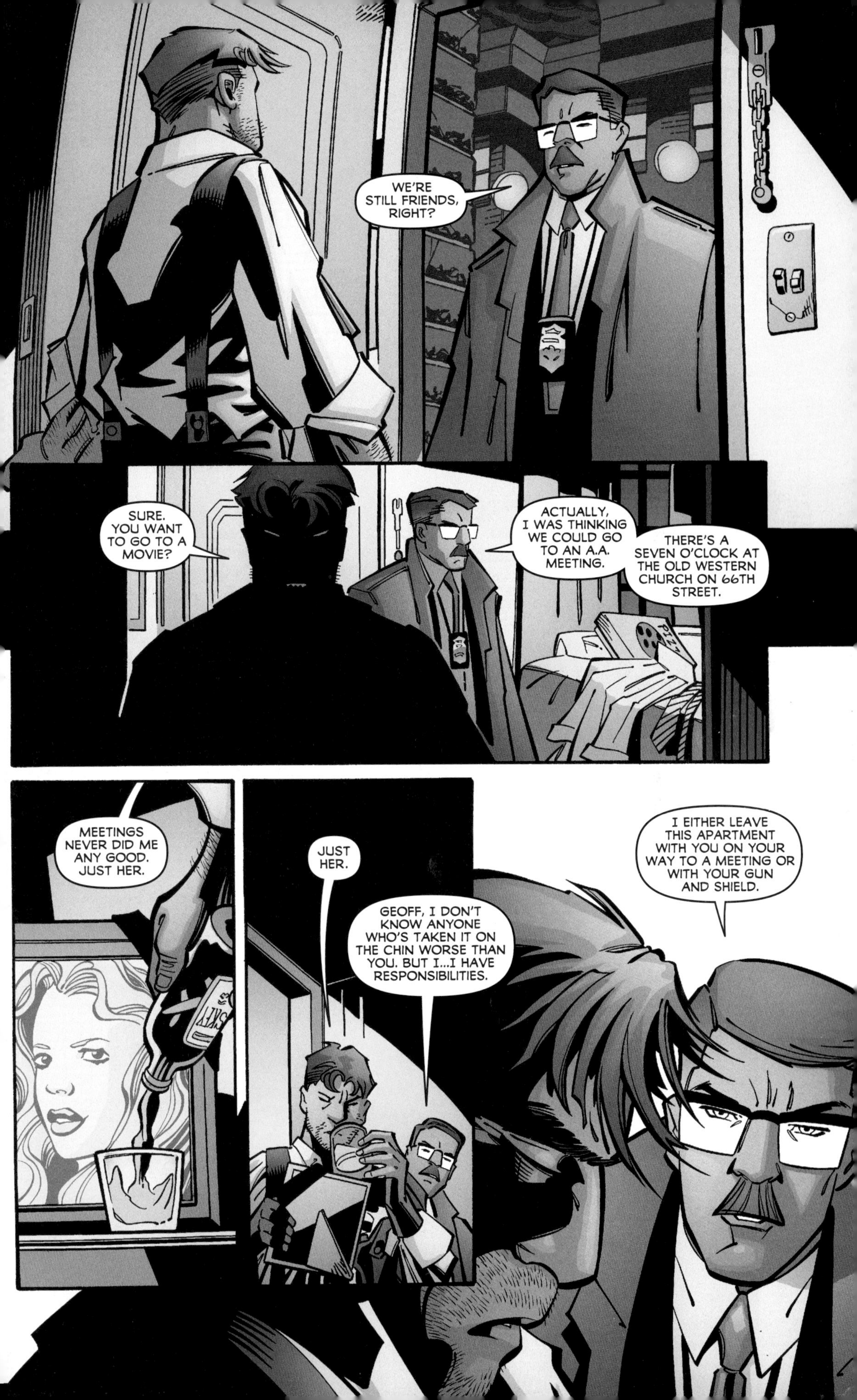
WE'RE STILL FRIENDS, RIGHT?
SURE. YOU WANT TO GO TO A MOVIE?
ACTUALLY, I WAS THINKING WE COULD GO TO AN A.A. MEETING.
THERE'S A SEVEN O'CLOCK AT THE OLD WESTERN CHURCH ON 66TH STREET.
MEETINGS NEVER DID ME ANY GOOD. JUST HER.
JUST HER.
GEOFF, I DON'T KNOW ANYONE WHO'S TAKEN IT ON THE CHIN WORSE THAN YOU. BUT I...I HAVE RESPONSIBILITIES.
I EITHER LEAVE THIS APARTMENT WITH YOU ON YOUR WAY TO A MEETING OR WITH YOUR GUN AND SHIELD.

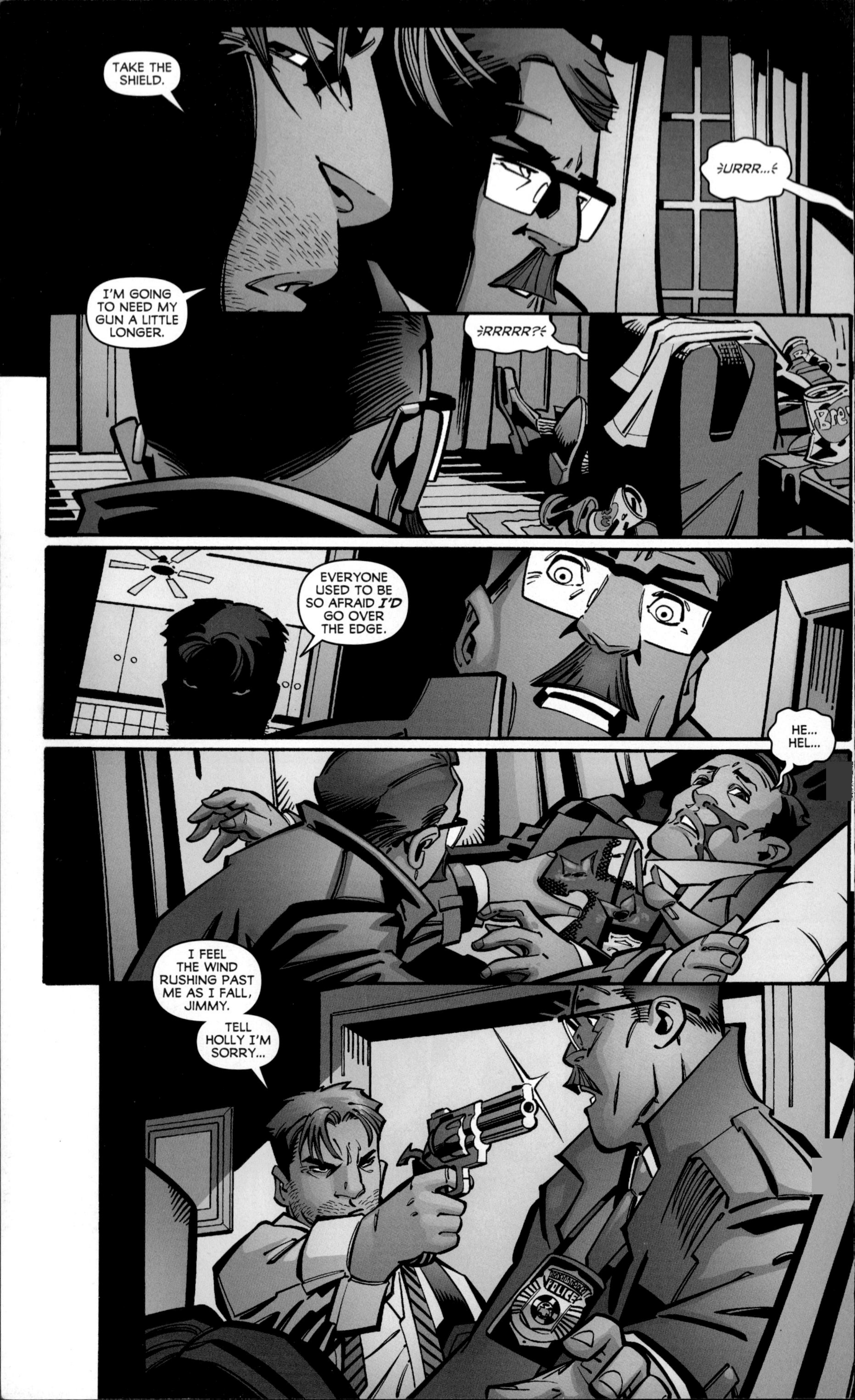
TAKE THE SHIELD.
URRR...
I'M GOING TO NEED MY GUN A LITTLE LONGER.
RRRRR?
EVERYONE USED TO BE SO AFRAID I'D GO OVER THE EDGE.
HE... HEL...
I FEEL THE WIND RUSHING PAST ME AS I FALL, JIMMY.
TELL HOLLY I'M SORRY...

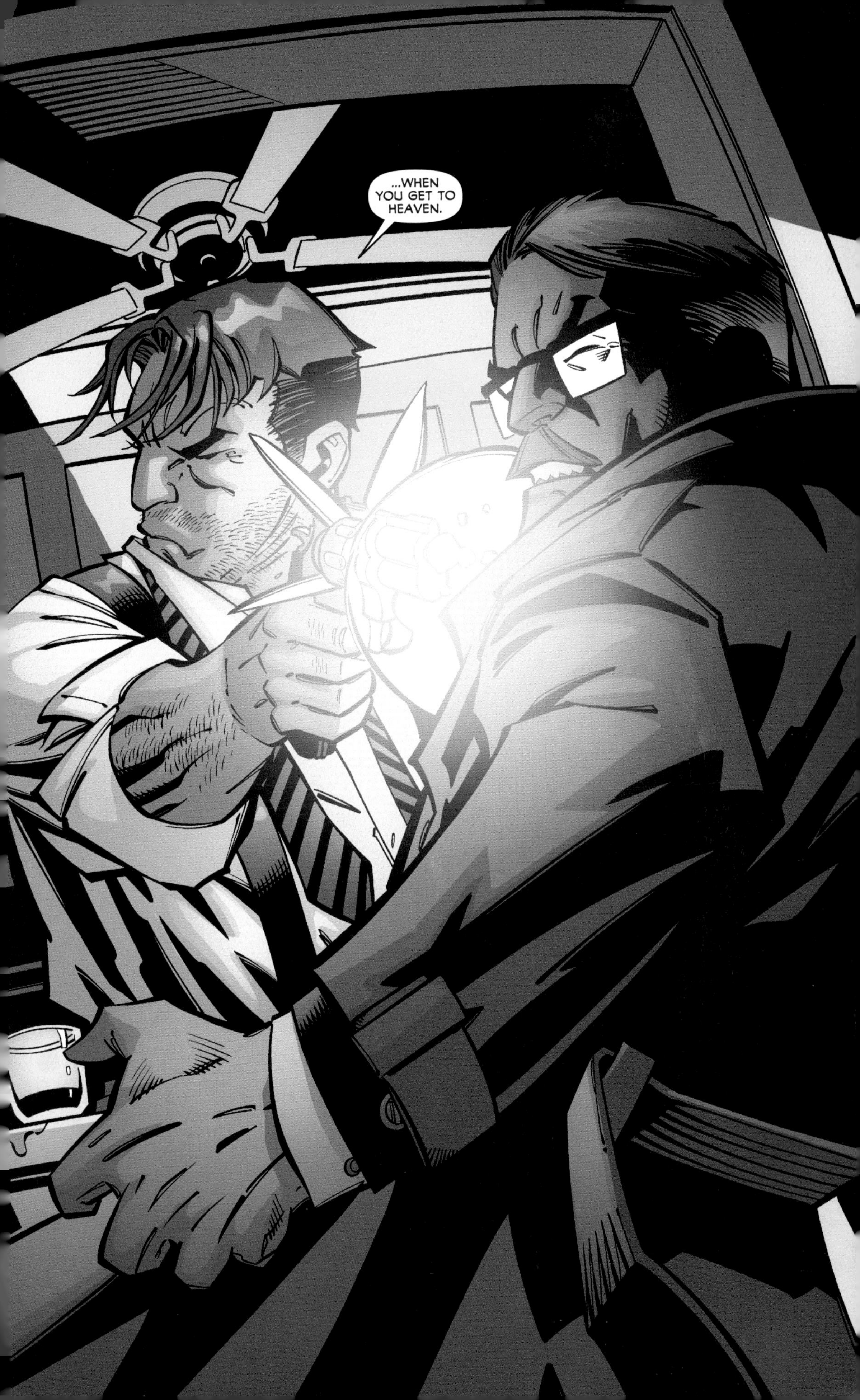
...WHEN YOU GET TO HEAVEN.

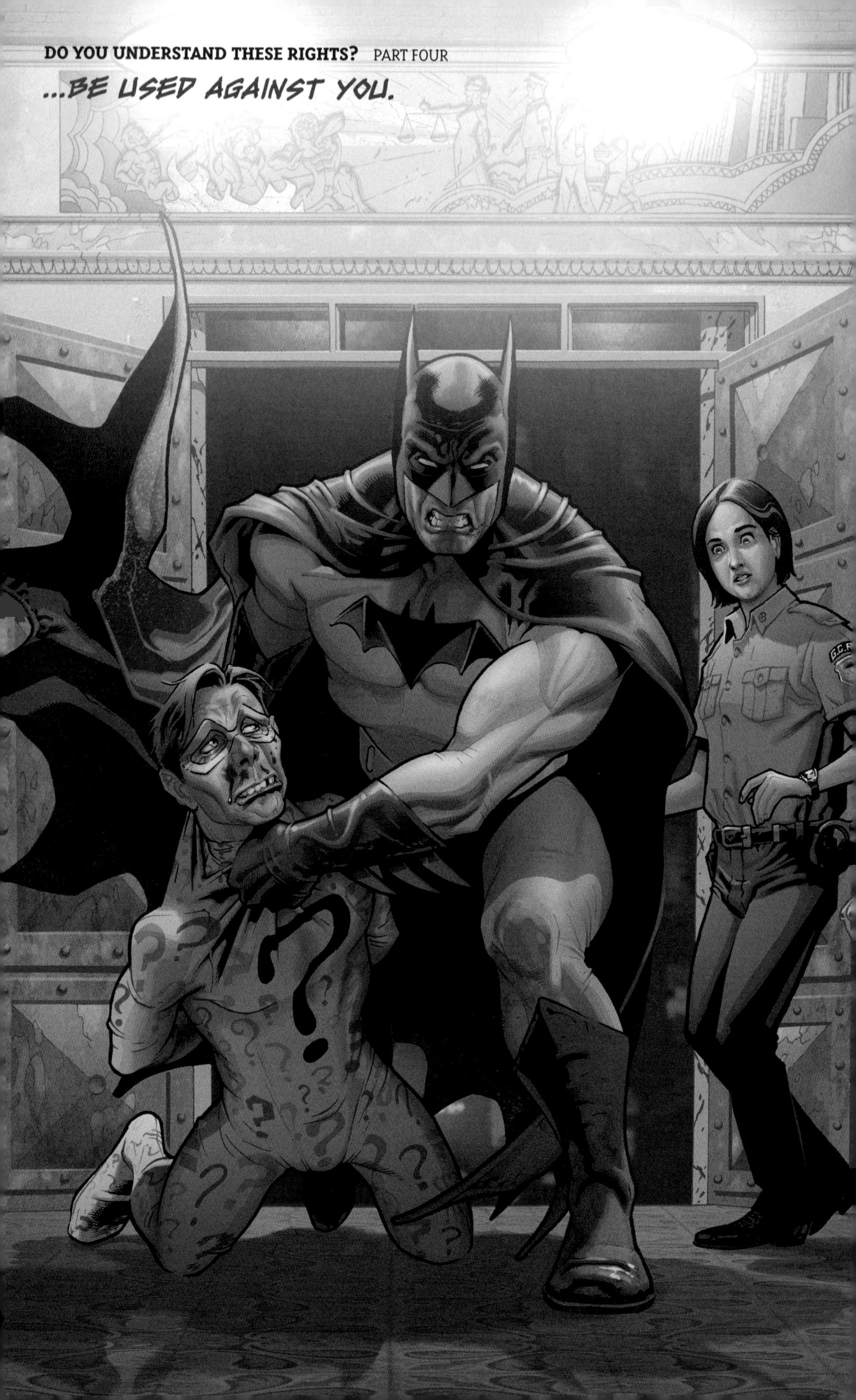
DO YOU UNDERSTAND THESE RIGHTS? PART FOUR
...BE USED AGAINST YOU.
G.C.P.D.

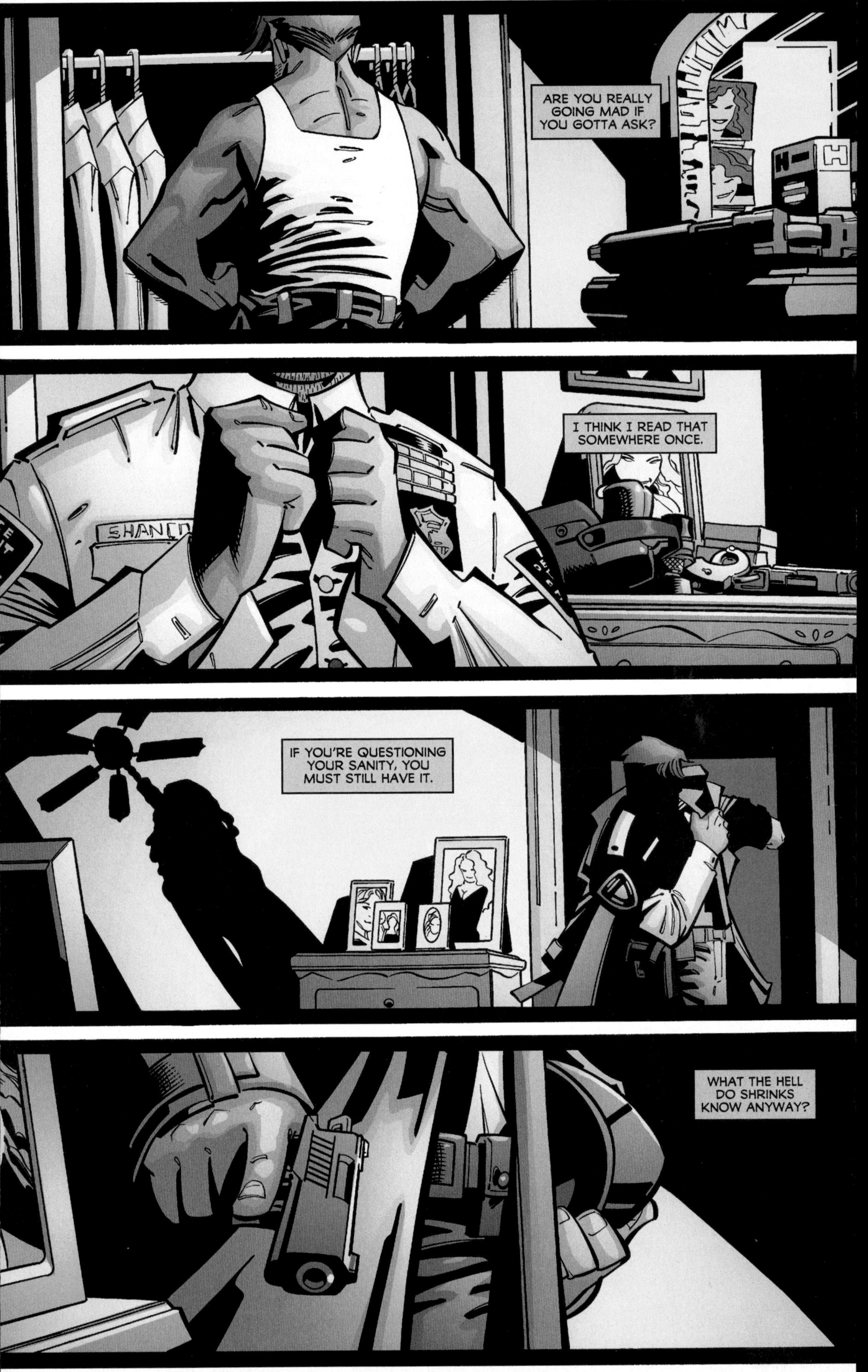
ARE YOU REALLY GOING MAD IF YOU GOTTA ASK?
I THINK I READ THAT SOMEWHERE ONCE.
IF YOU'RE QUESTIONING YOUR SANITY, YOU MUST STILL HAVE IT.
WHAT THE HELL DO SHRINKS KNOW ANYWAY?

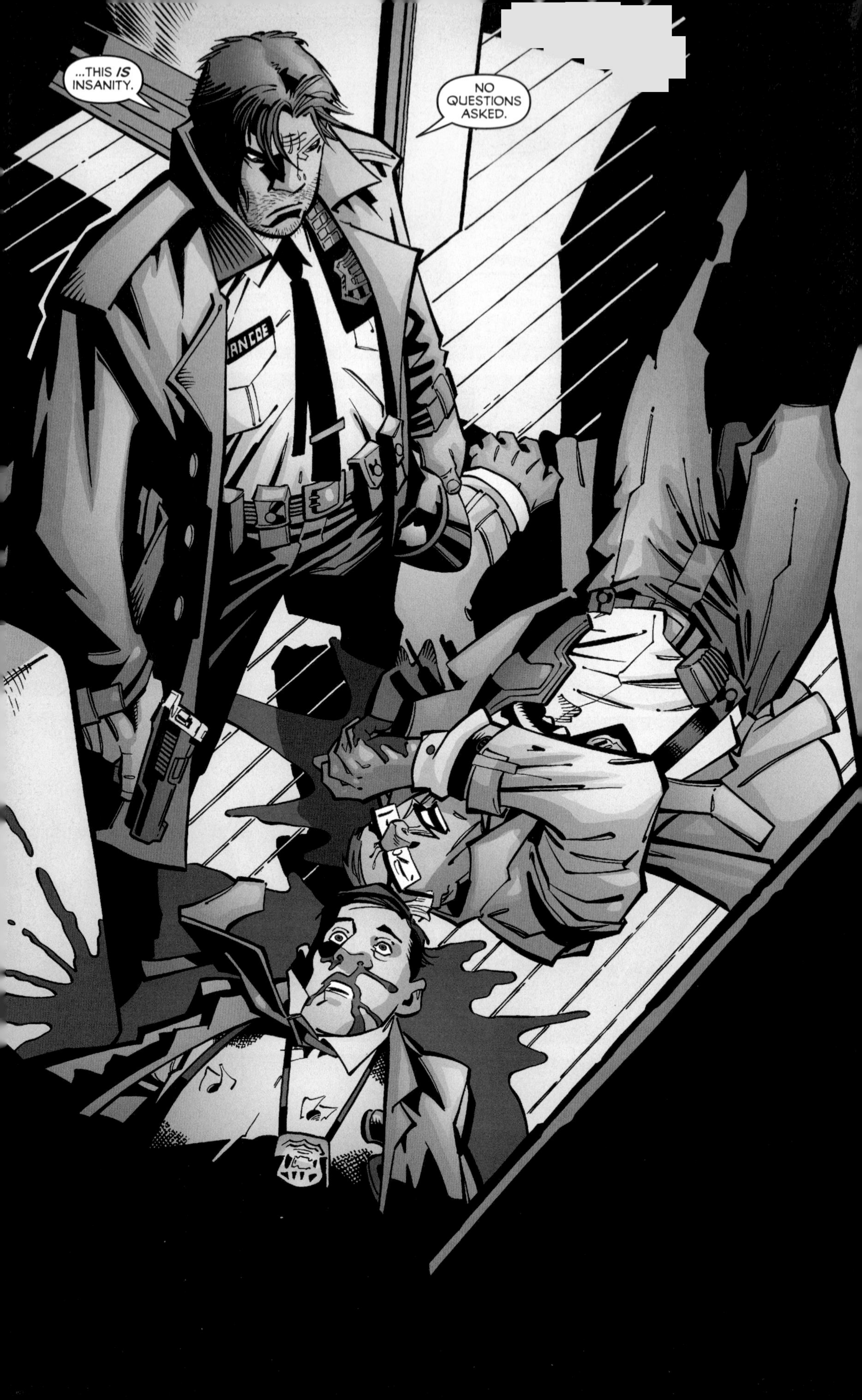
...THIS IS INSANITY.
NO QUESTIONS ASKED.

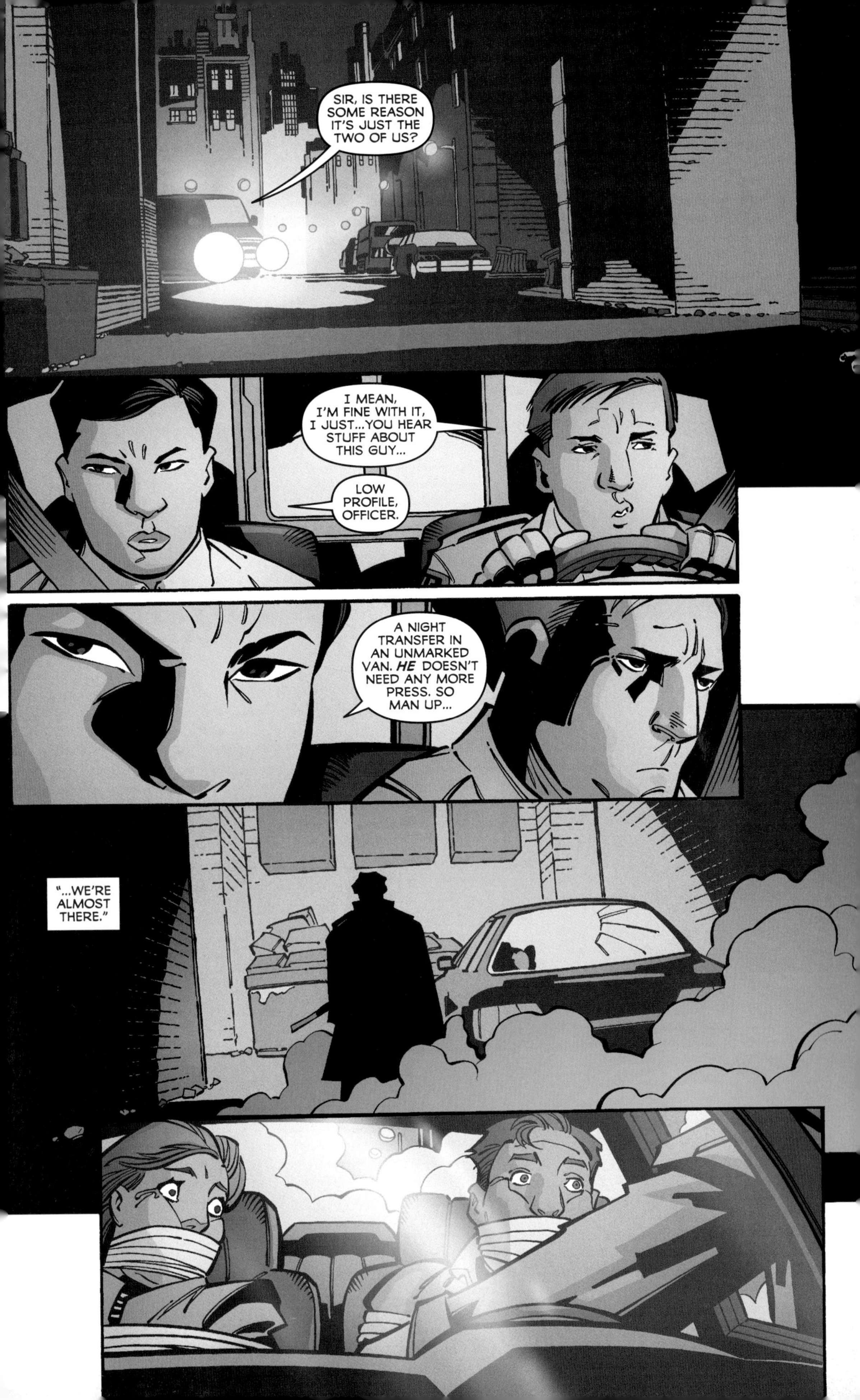
SIR, IS THERE SOME REASON IT'S JUST THE TWO OF US?
I MEAN, I'M FINE WITH IT, I JUST...YOU HEAR STUFF ABOUT THIS GUY...
LOW PROFILE, OFFICER.
A NIGHT TRANSFER IN AN UNMARKED VAN. HE DOESN'T NEED ANY MORE PRESS. SO MAN UP...
"...WE'RE ALMOST THERE."

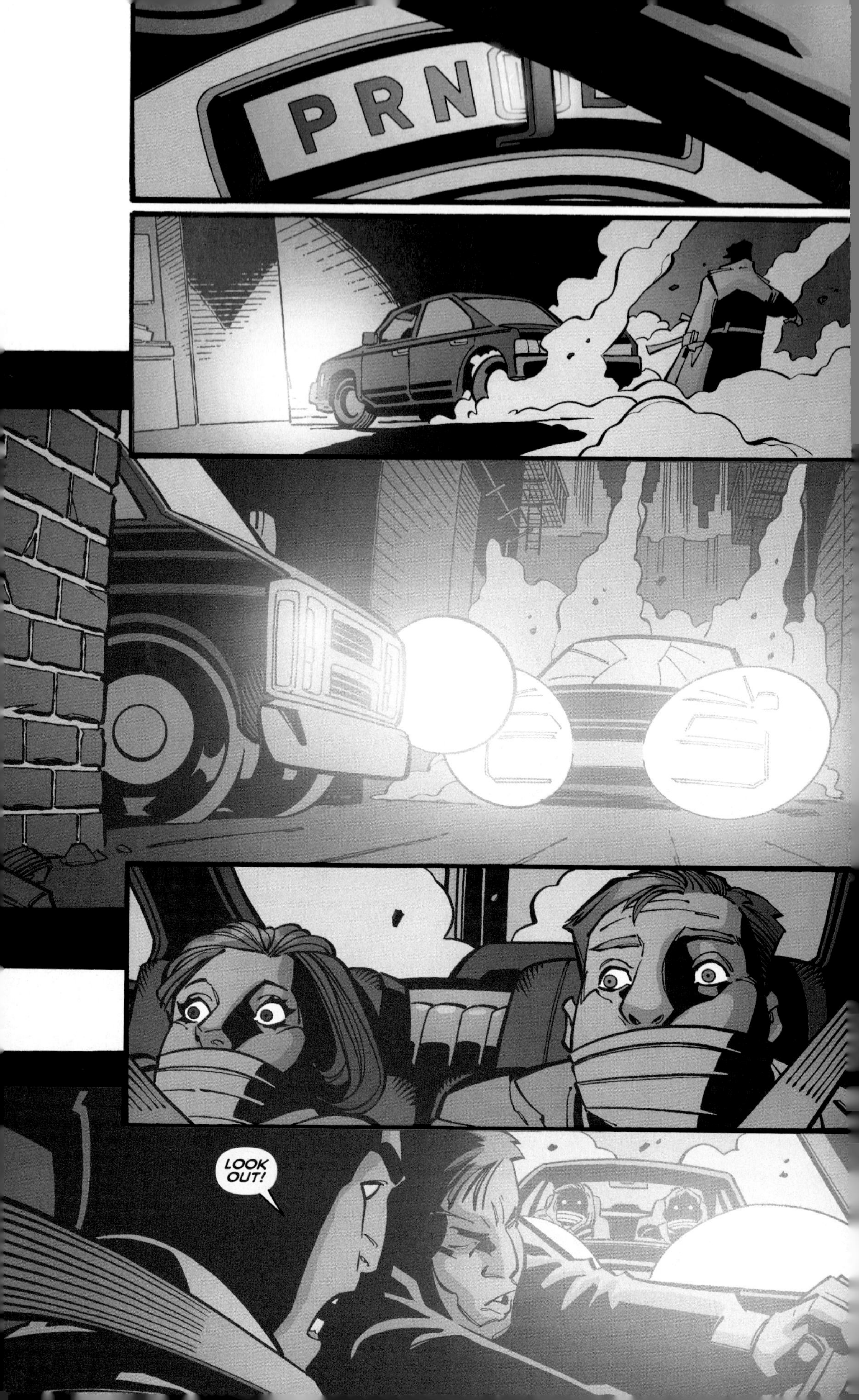

PRN
LOOK OUT!

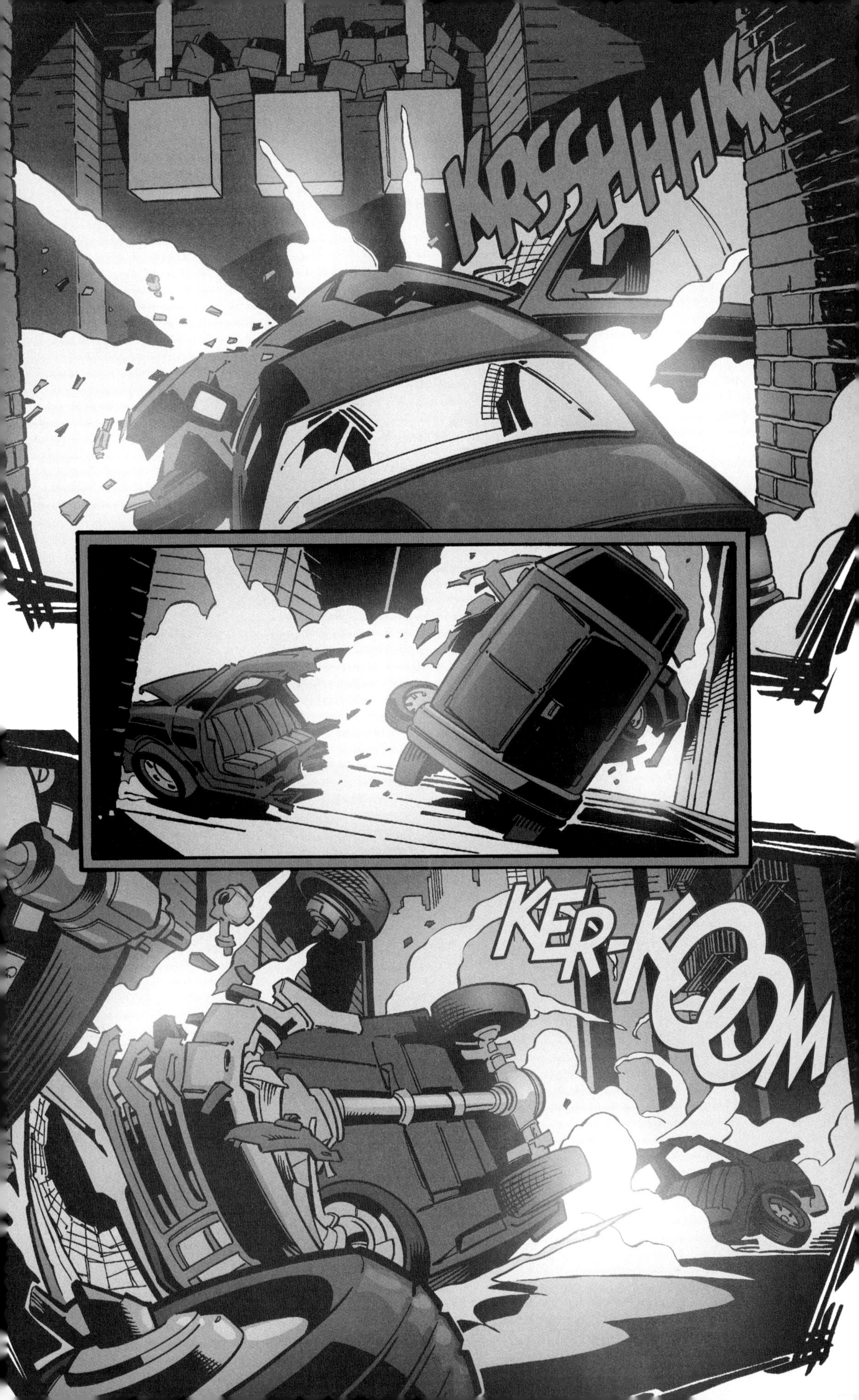
KRSSHHHKK
KER-KOOM

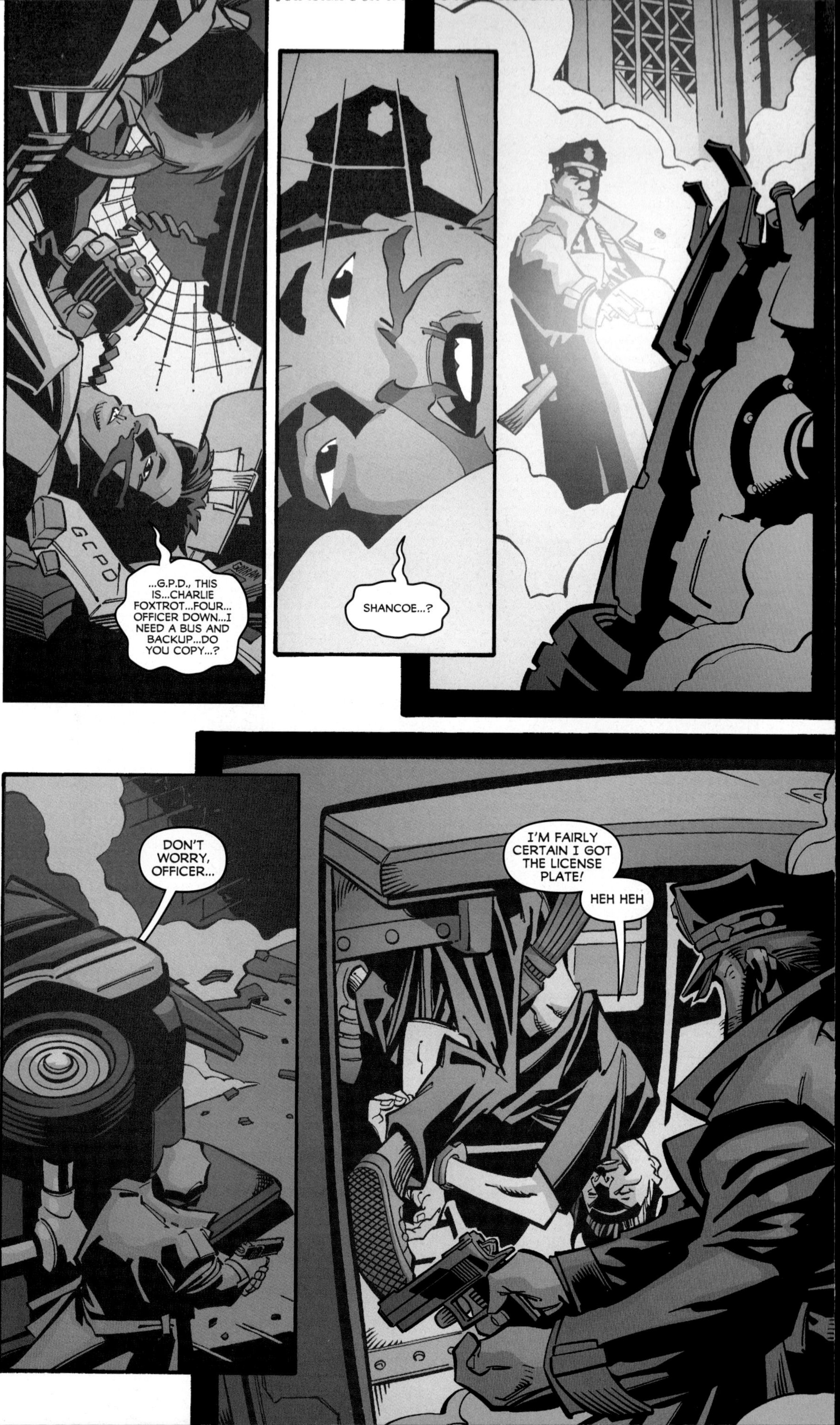
...G.P.D., THIS IS...CHARLIE FOXTROT...FOUR... OFFICER DOWN...I NEED A BUS AND BACKUP...DO YOU COPY...?
SHANCOE...?
DON'T WORRY, OFFICER...
I'M FAIRLY CERTAIN I GOT THE LICENSE PLATE!
HEH HEH

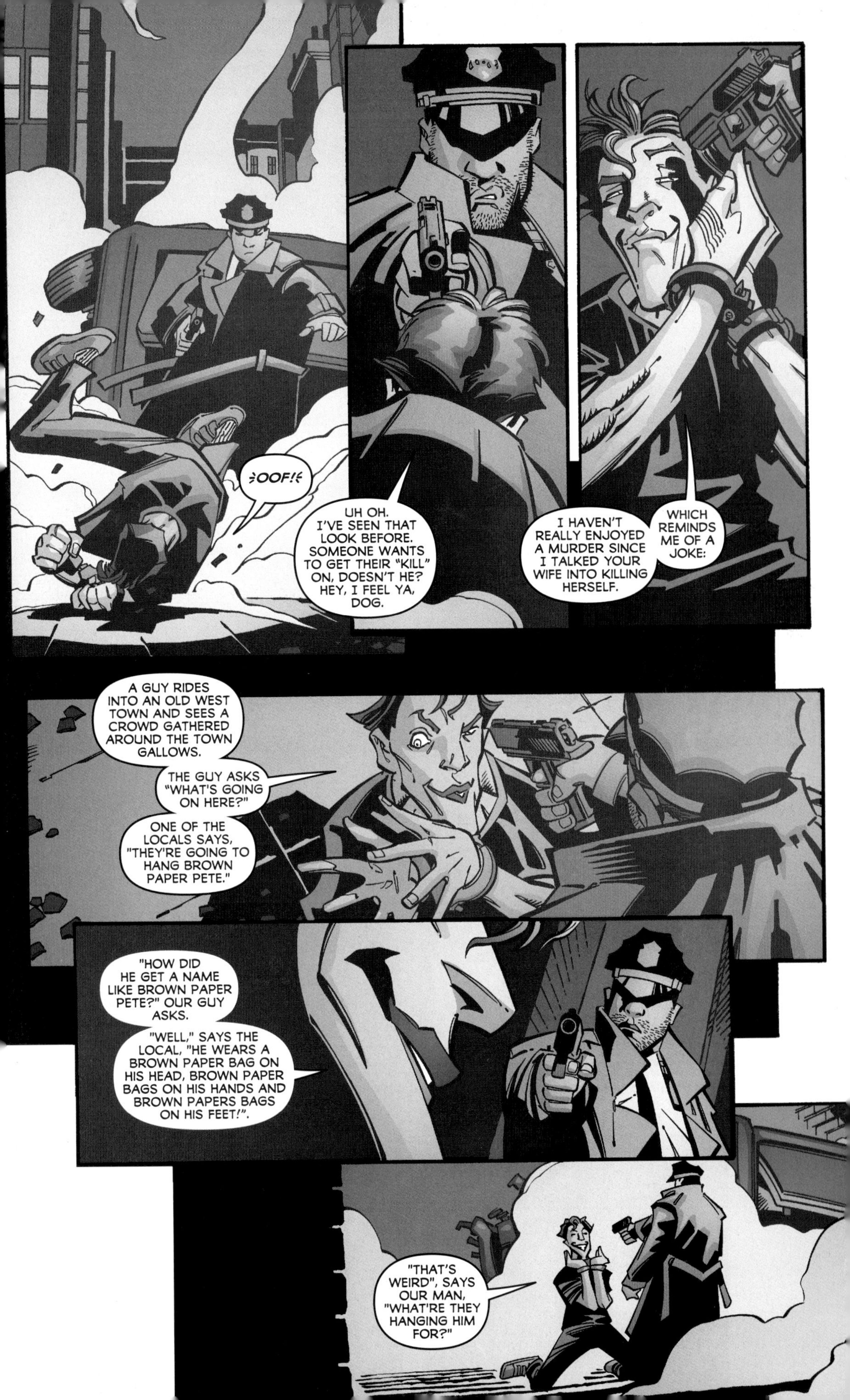
OOF!
UH OH. I'VE SEEN THAT LOOK BEFORE. SOMEONE WANTS TO GET THEIR "KILL" ON, DOESN'T HE? HEY, I FEEL YA, DOG.
I HAVEN'T REALLY ENJOYED A MURDER SINCE I TALKED YOUR WIFE INTO KILLING HERSELF.
WHICH REMINDS ME OF A JOKE:
A GUY RIDES INTO AN OLD WEST TOWN AND SEES A CROWD GATHERED AROUND THE TOWN GALLOWS.
THE GUY ASKS "WHAT'S GOING ON HERE?"
ONE OF THE LOCALS SAYS, "THEY'RE GOING TO HANG BROWN PAPER PETE."
"HOW DID HE GET A NAME LIKE BROWN PAPER PETE?" OUR GUY ASKS.
"WELL," SAYS THE LOCAL, "HE WEARS A BROWN PAPER BAG ON HIS HEAD, BROWN PAPER BAGS ON HIS HANDS AND BROWN PAPERS BAGS ON HIS FEET!".
"THAT'S WEIRD", SAYS OUR MAN, "WHAT'RE THEY HANGING HIM FOR?"

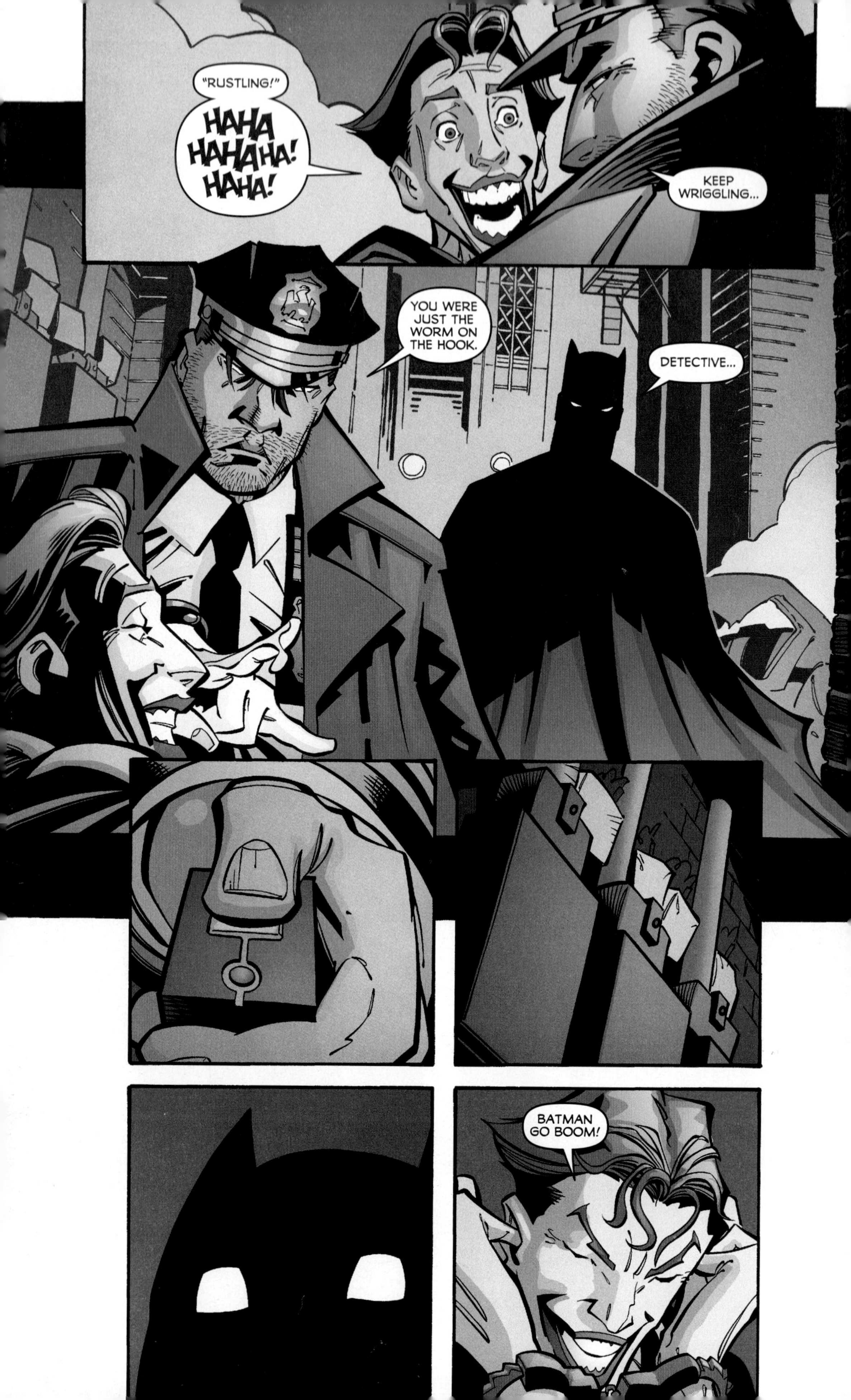
"RUSTLING!"
HAHA HAHAHA! HAHA!
KEEP WRIGGLING...
YOU WERE JUST THE WORM ON THE HOOK.
DETECTIVE...
BATMAN GO BOOM!

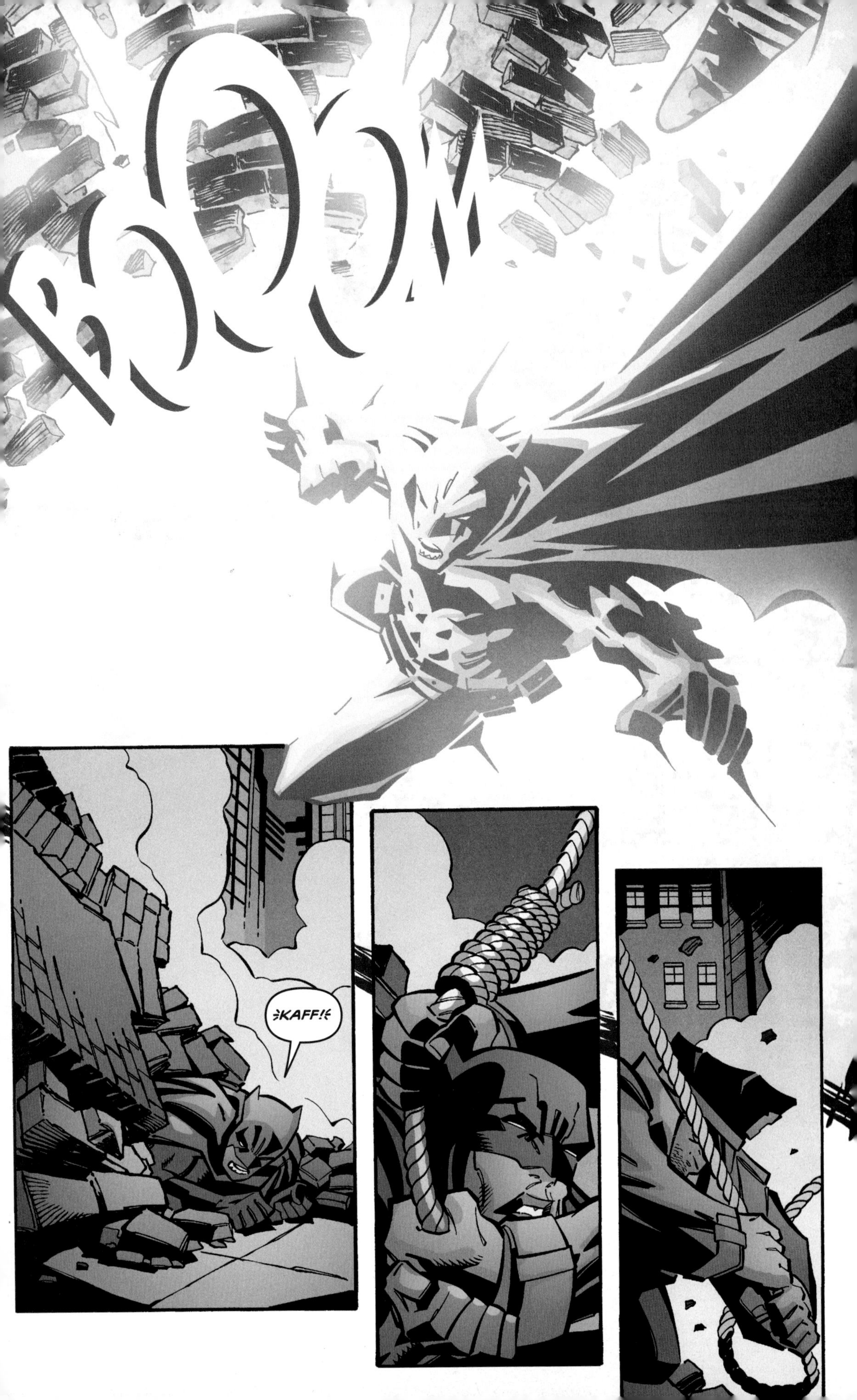
BOOOM
KAFF!

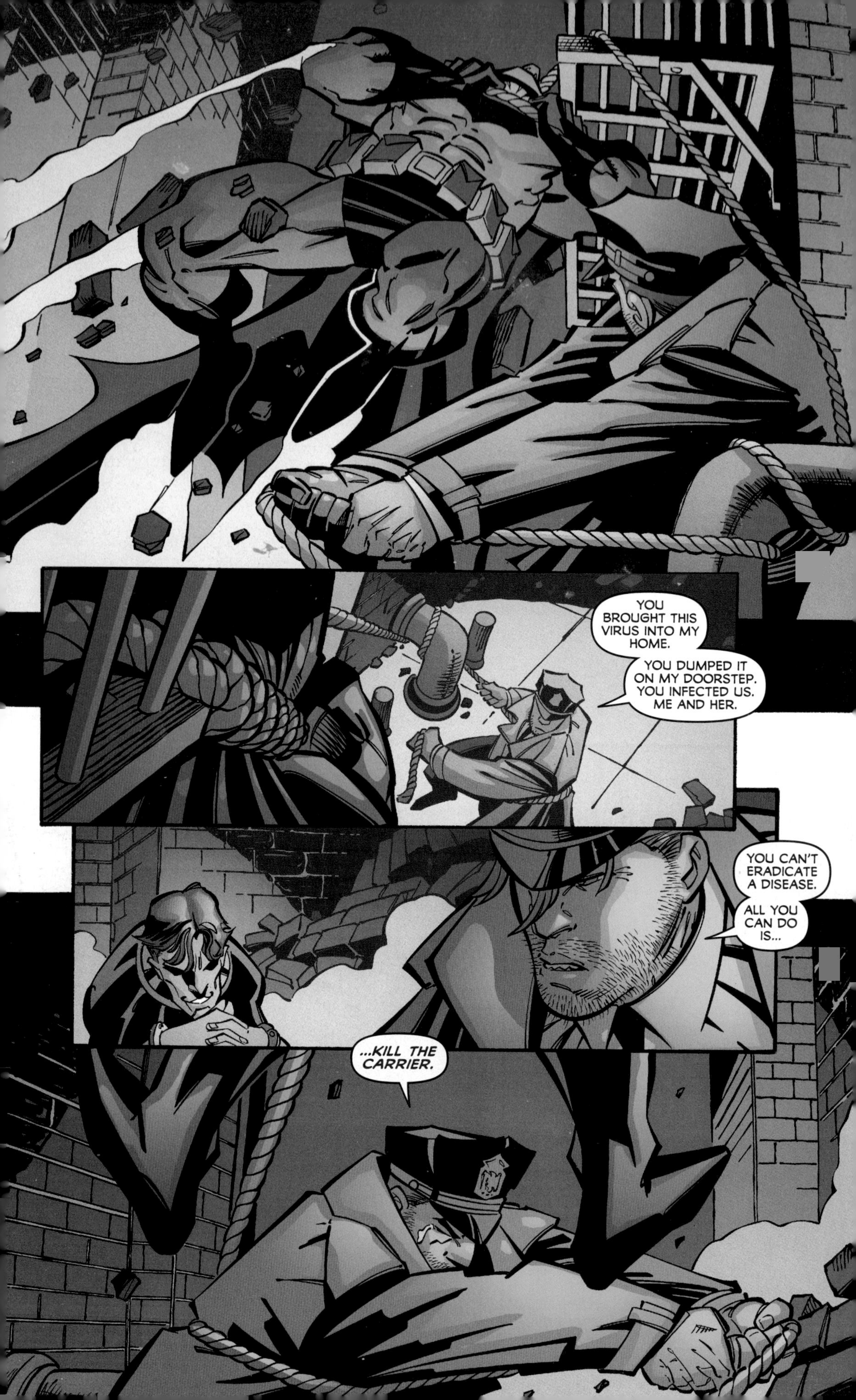
YOU BROUGHT THIS VIRUS INTO MY HOME.
YOU DUMPED IT ON MY DOORSTEP. YOU INFECTED US. ME AND HER.
YOU CAN'T ERADICATE A DISEASE.
ALL YOU CAN DO IS...
...KILL THE CARRIER.

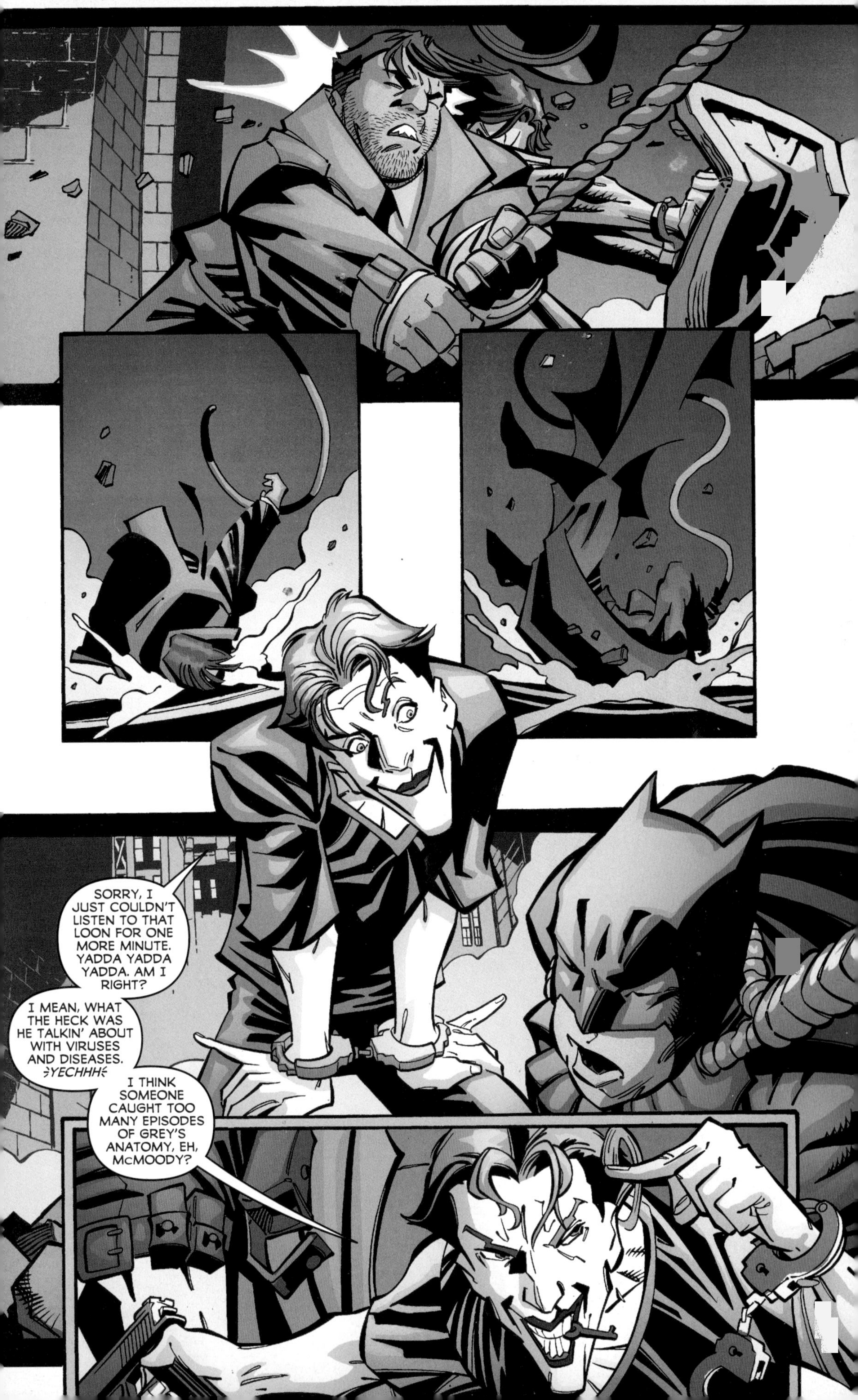
SORRY, I JUST COULDN'T LISTEN TO THAT LOON FOR ONE MORE MINUTE. YADDA YADDA YADDA. AM I RIGHT?
I MEAN, WHAT THE HECK WAS HE TALKIN' ABOUT WITH VIRUSES AND DISEASES. *YECHHH*
I THINK SOMEONE CAUGHT TOO MANY EPISODES OF GREY'S ANATOMY, EH, McMOODY?

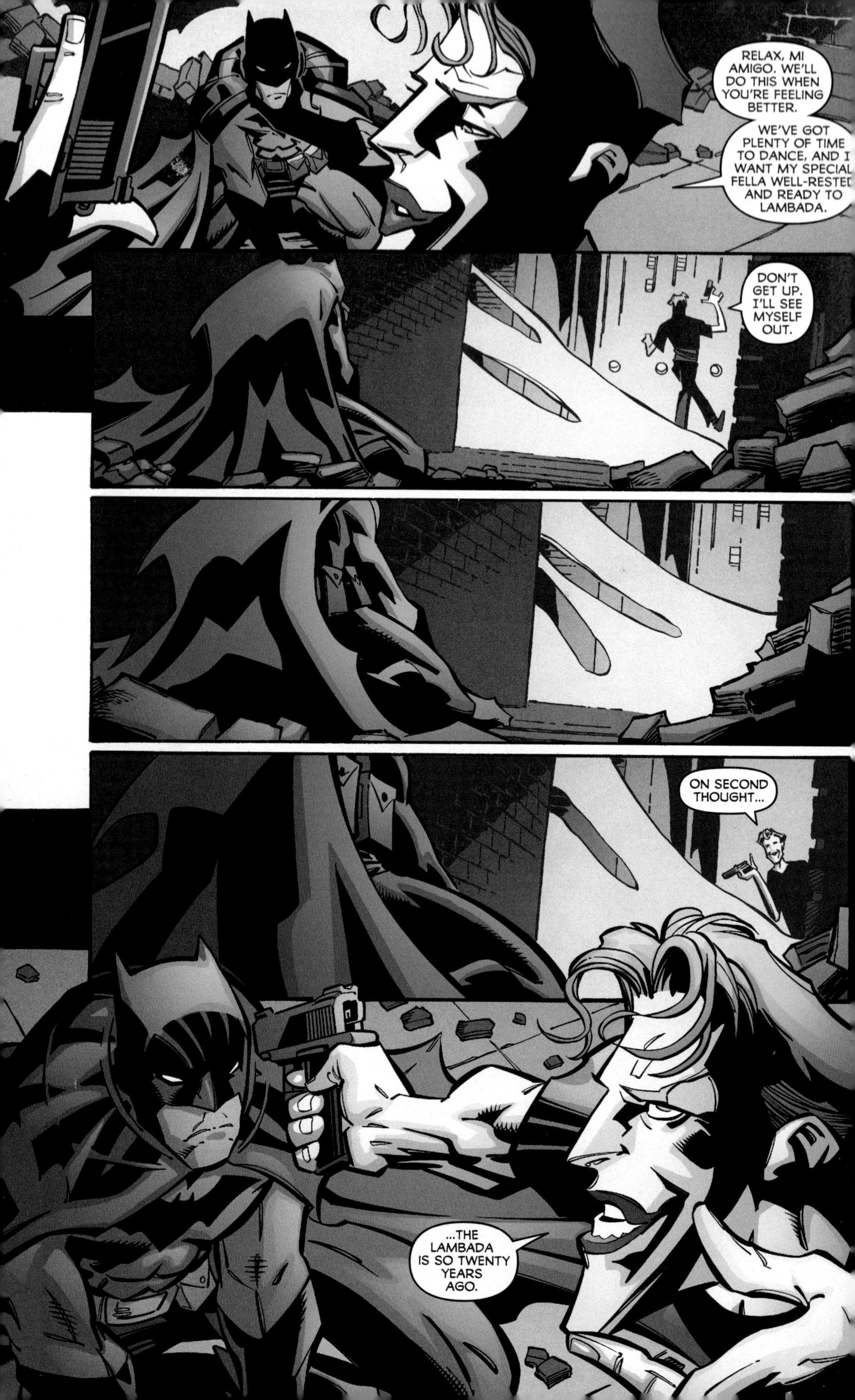
RELAX, MI AMIGO. WE'LL DO THIS WHEN YOU'RE FEELING BETTER.
WE'VE GOT PLENTY OF TIME TO DANCE, AND I WANT MY SPECIAL FELLA WELL-RESTED AND READY TO LAMBADA.
DON'T GET UP. I'LL SEE MYSELF OUT.
ON SECOND THOUGHT...
...THE LAMBADA IS SO TWENTY YEARS AGO.

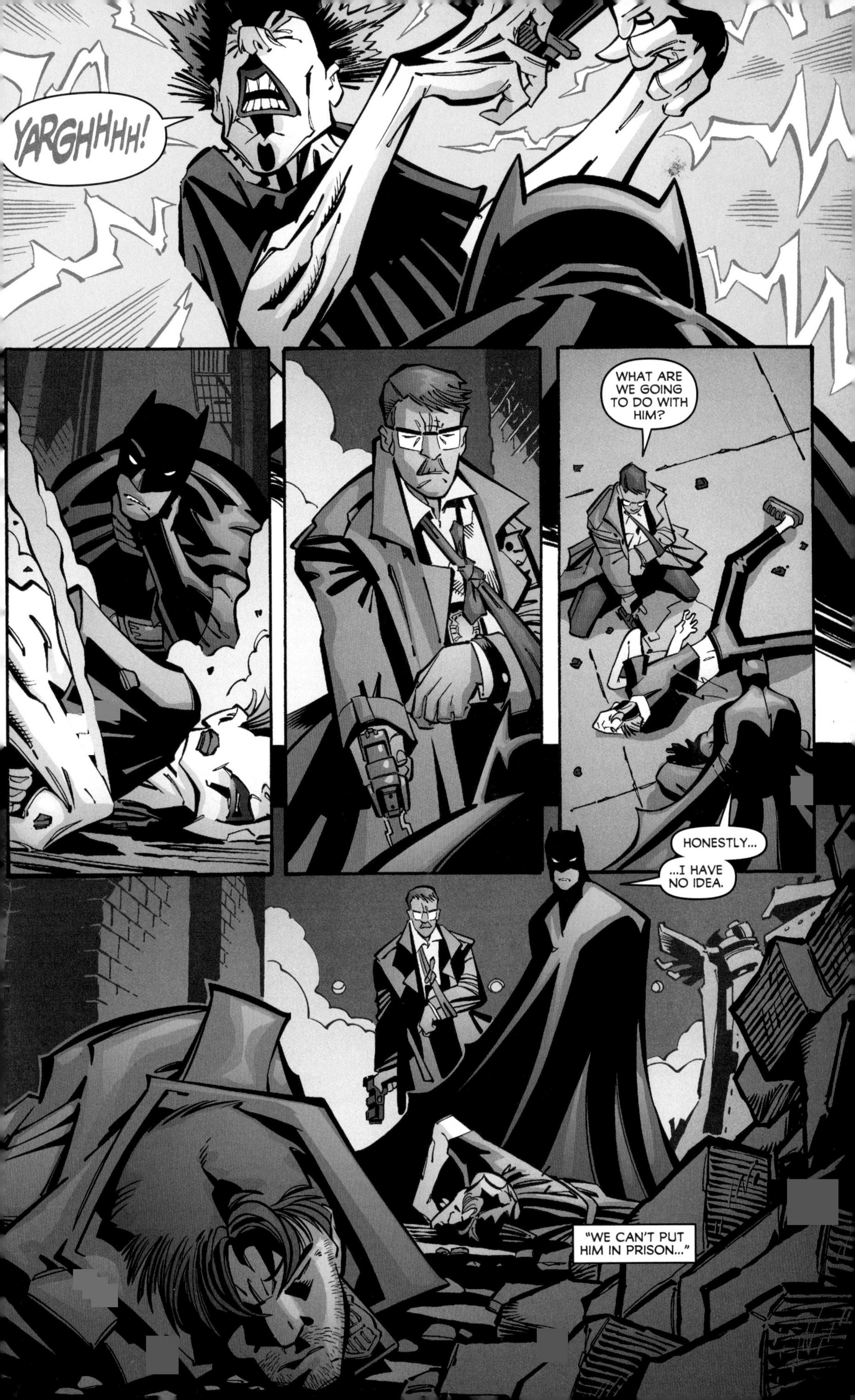
YARGHHHH!
WHAT ARE WE GOING TO DO WITH HIM?
HONESTLY...
...I HAVE NO IDEA.
"WE CAN'T PUT HIM IN PRISON..."

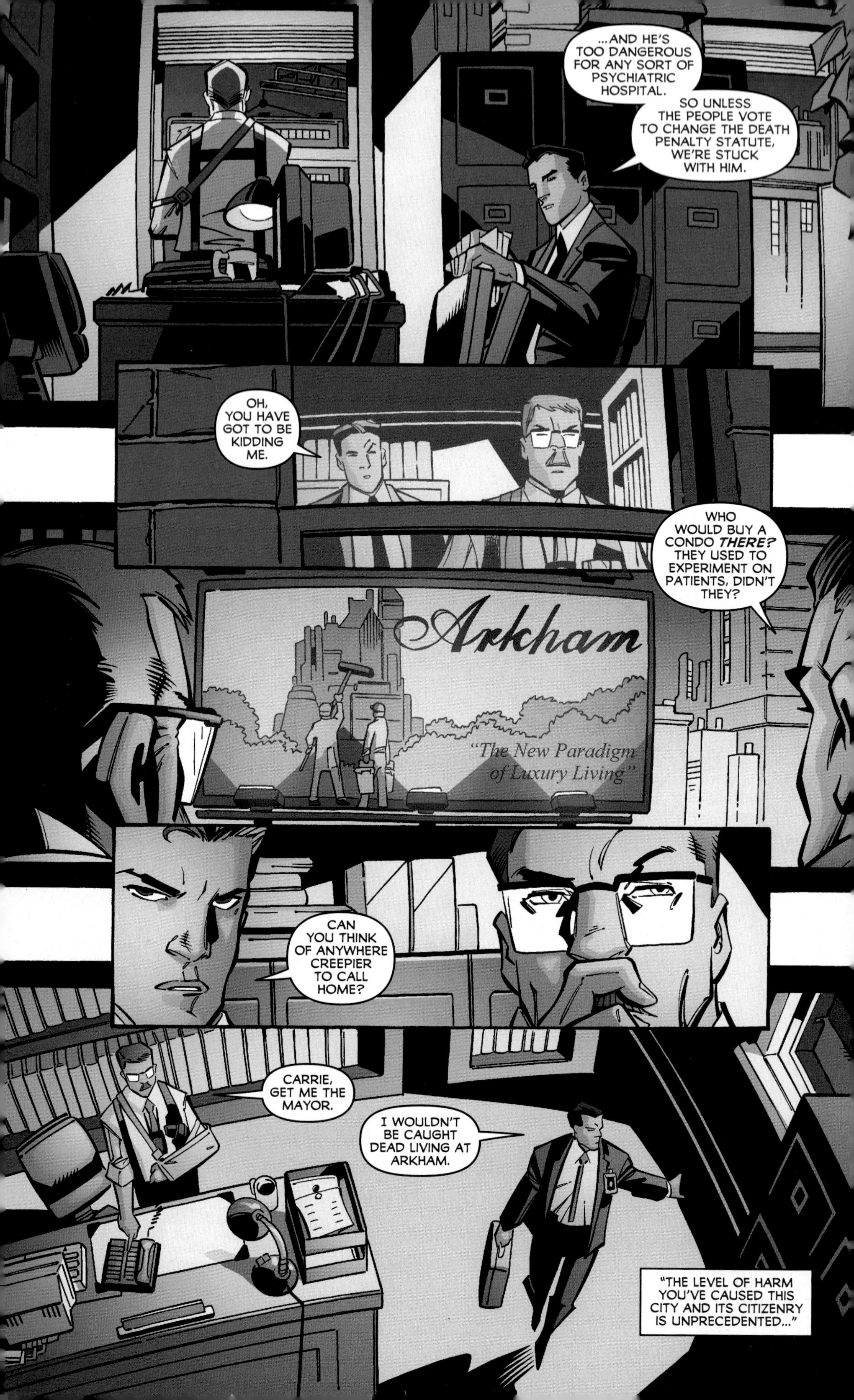
...AND HE'S TOO DANGEROUS FOR ANY SORT OF PSYCHIATRIC HOSPITAL.
SO UNLESS THE PEOPLE VOTE TO CHANGE THE DEATH PENALTY STATUTE, WE'RE STUCK WITH HIM.
OH, YOU HAVE GOT TO BE KIDDING ME.
WHO WOULD BUY A CONDO THERE? THEY USED TO EXPERIMENT ON PATIENTS, DIDN'T THEY?
Arkham
"The New Paradigm of Luxury Living"
CAN YOU THINK OF ANYWHERE CREEPIER TO CALL HOME?
CARRIE, GET ME THE MAYOR.
I WOULDN'T BE CAUGHT DEAD LIVING AT ARKHAM.
"THE LEVEL OF HARM YOU'VE CAUSED THIS CITY AND ITS CITIZENRY IS UNPRECEDENTED..."

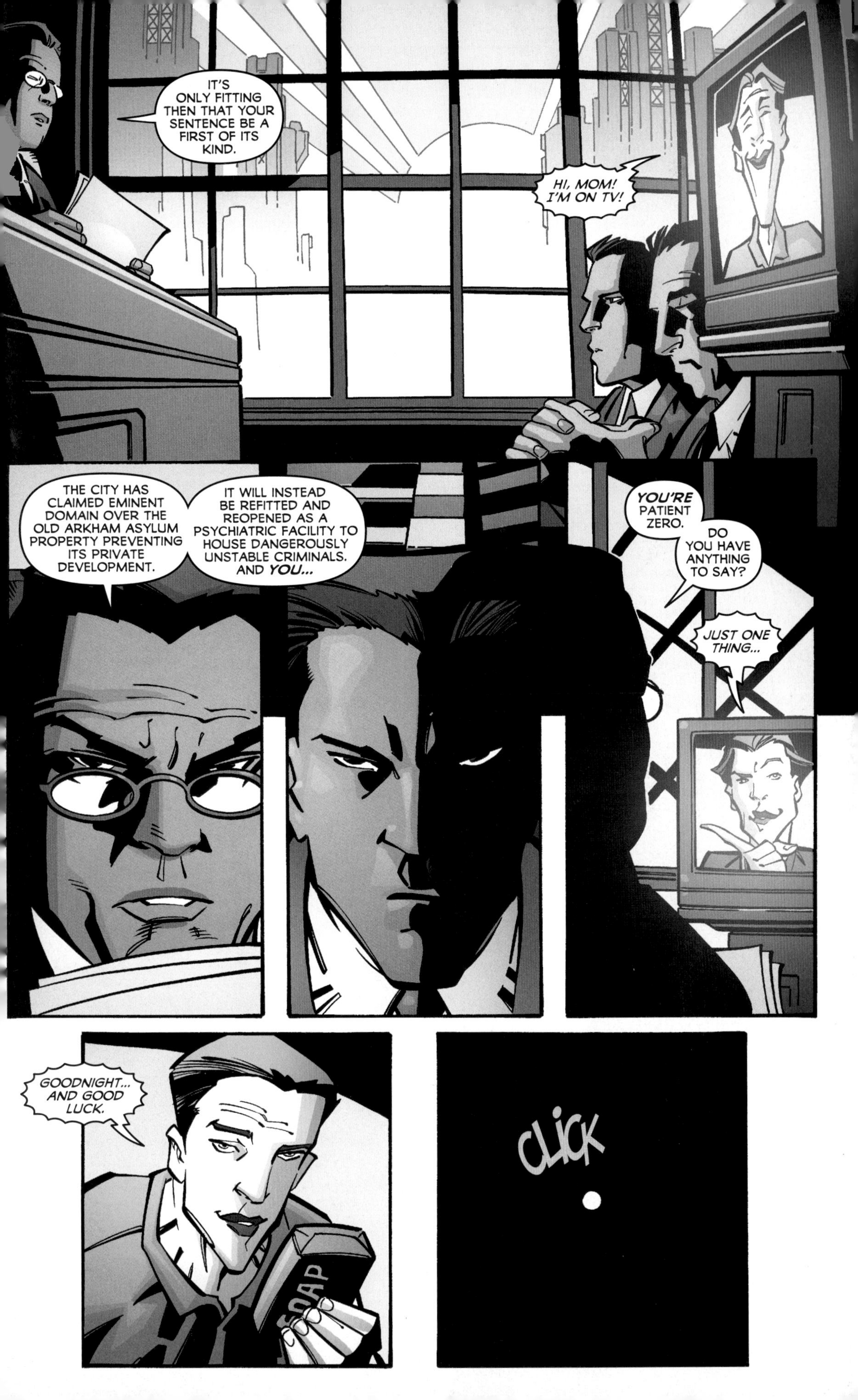
IT'S ONLY FITTING THEN THAT YOUR SENTENCE BE A FIRST OF ITS KIND.
HI, MOM! I'M ON TV!
THE CITY HAS CLAIMED EMINENT DOMAIN OVER THE OLD ARKHAM ASYLUM PROPERTY PREVENTING ITS PRIVATE DEVELOPMENT.
IT WILL INSTEAD BE REFITTED AND REOPENED AS A PSYCHIATRIC FACILITY TO HOUSE DANGEROUSLY UNSTABLE CRIMINALS. AND *YOU...*
YOU'RE PATIENT ZERO.
DO YOU HAVE ANYTHING TO SAY?
JUST ONE THING...
GOODNIGHT... AND GOOD LUCK.
SOAP
CLICK

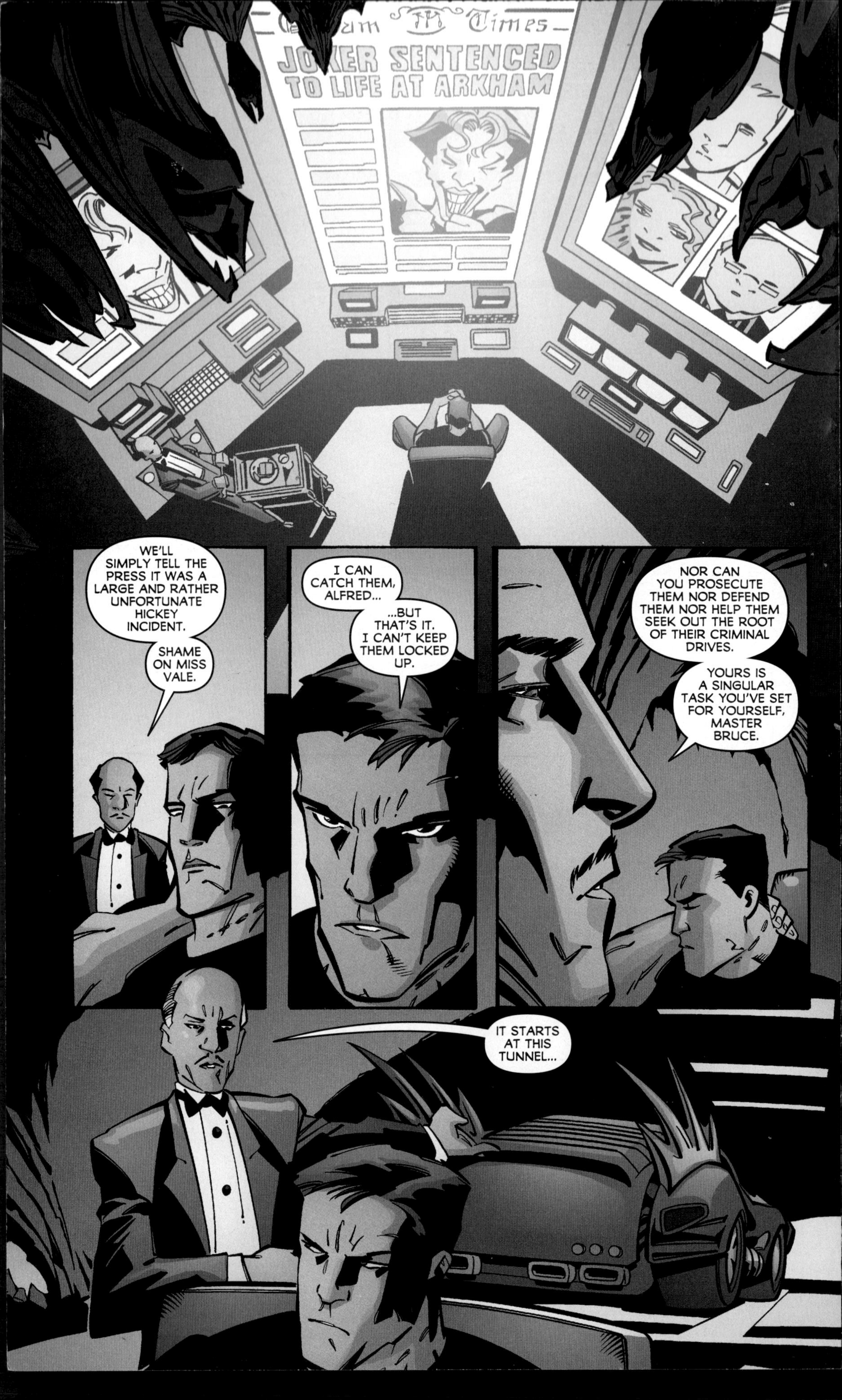
Gotham Times
JOKER SENTENCED TO LIFE AT ARKHAM
WE'LL SIMPLY TELL THE PRESS IT WAS A LARGE AND RATHER UNFORTUNATE HICKEY INCIDENT.
SHAME ON MISS VALE.
I CAN CATCH THEM, ALFRED...
...BUT THAT'S IT. I CAN'T KEEP THEM LOCKED UP.
NOR CAN YOU PROSECUTE THEM NOR DEFEND THEM NOR HELP THEM SEEK OUT THE ROOT OF THEIR CRIMINAL DRIVES.
YOURS IS A SINGULAR TASK YOU'VE SET FOR YOURSELF, MASTER BRUCE.
IT STARTS AT THIS TUNNEL...

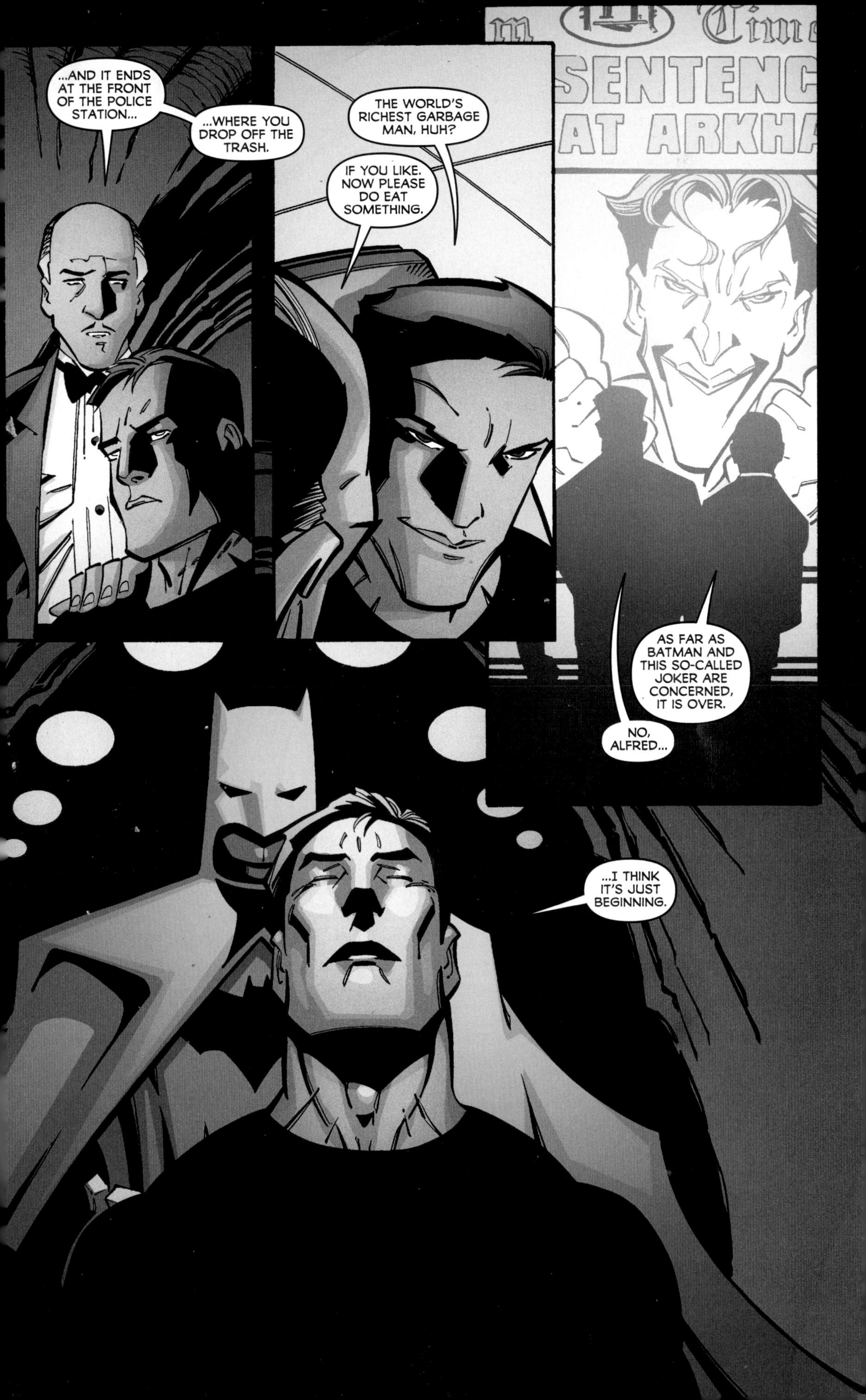
...AND IT ENDS AT THE FRONT OF THE POLICE STATION...
...WHERE YOU DROP OFF THE TRASH.
THE WORLD'S RICHEST GARBAGE MAN, HUH?
IF YOU LIKE. NOW PLEASE DO EAT SOMETHING.
SENTENC
AT ARKHA
AS FAR AS BATMAN AND THIS SO-CALLED JOKER ARE CONCERNED, IT IS OVER.
NO, ALFRED...
...I THINK IT'S JUST BEGINNING.

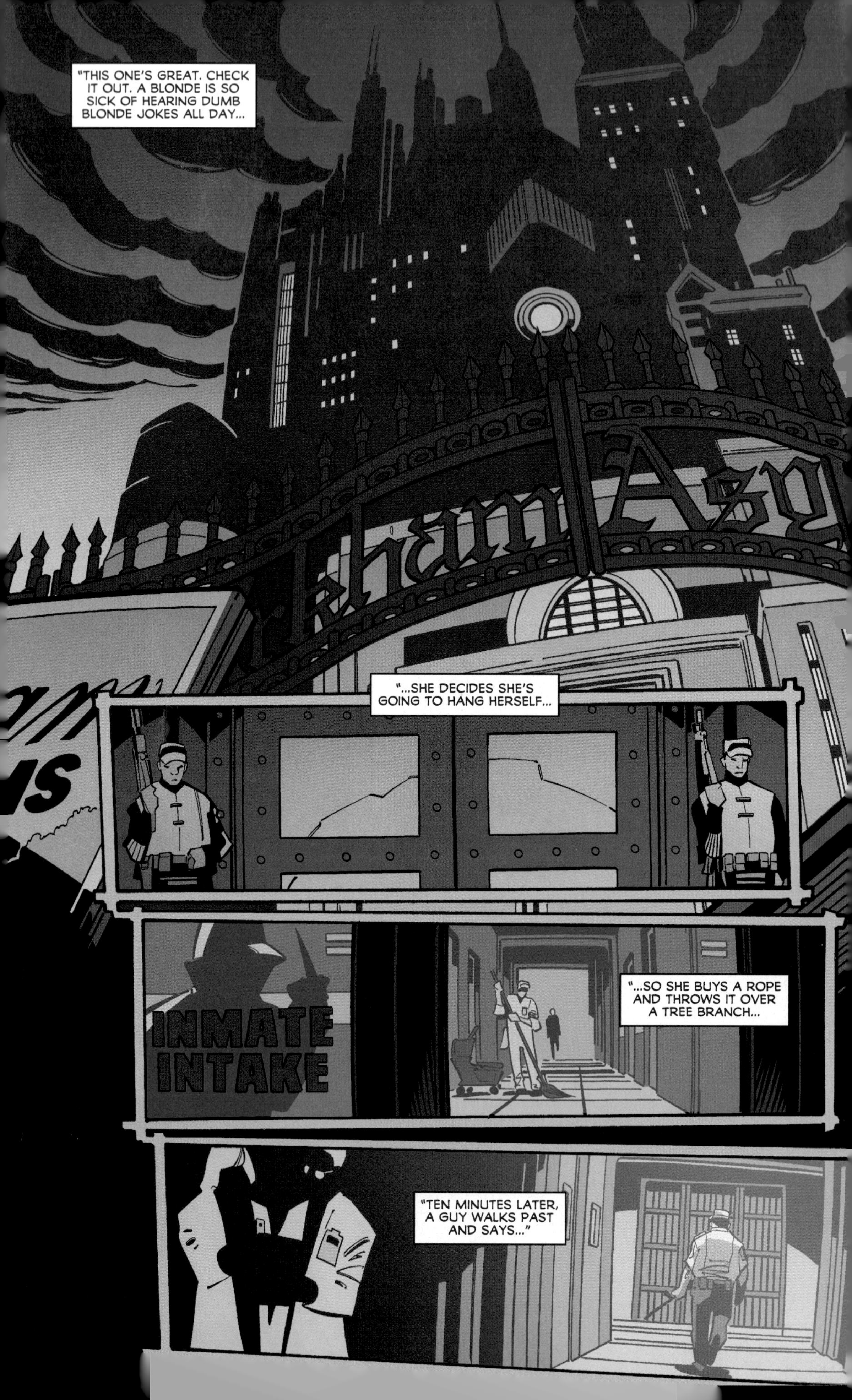
"THIS ONE'S GREAT. CHECK IT OUT. A BLONDE IS SO SICK OF HEARING DUMB BLONDE JOKES ALL DAY...
"...SHE DECIDES SHE'S GOING TO HANG HERSELF...
INMATE INTAKE
"...SO SHE BUYS A ROPE AND THROWS IT OVER A TREE BRANCH...
"TEN MINUTES LATER, A GUY WALKS PAST AND SAYS..."

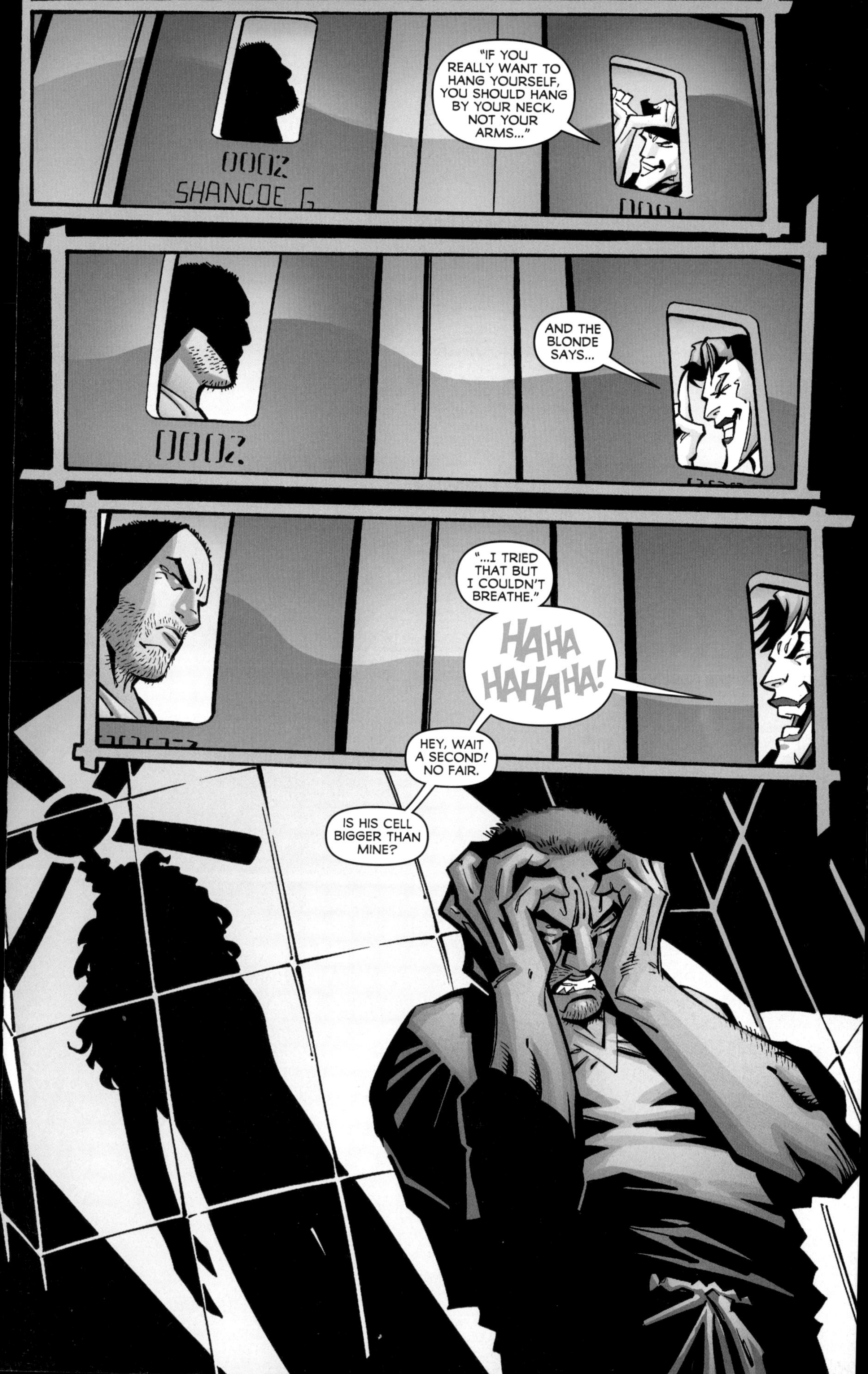
"IF YOU REALLY WANT TO HANG YOURSELF, YOU SHOULD HANG BY YOUR NECK, NOT YOUR ARMS..."
0002
SHANCOE G
AND THE BLONDE SAYS...
0002
"...I TRIED THAT BUT I COULDN'T BREATHE."
HAHA HAHAHA!
HEY, WAIT A SECOND! NO FAIR.
IS HIS CELL BIGGER THAN MINE?

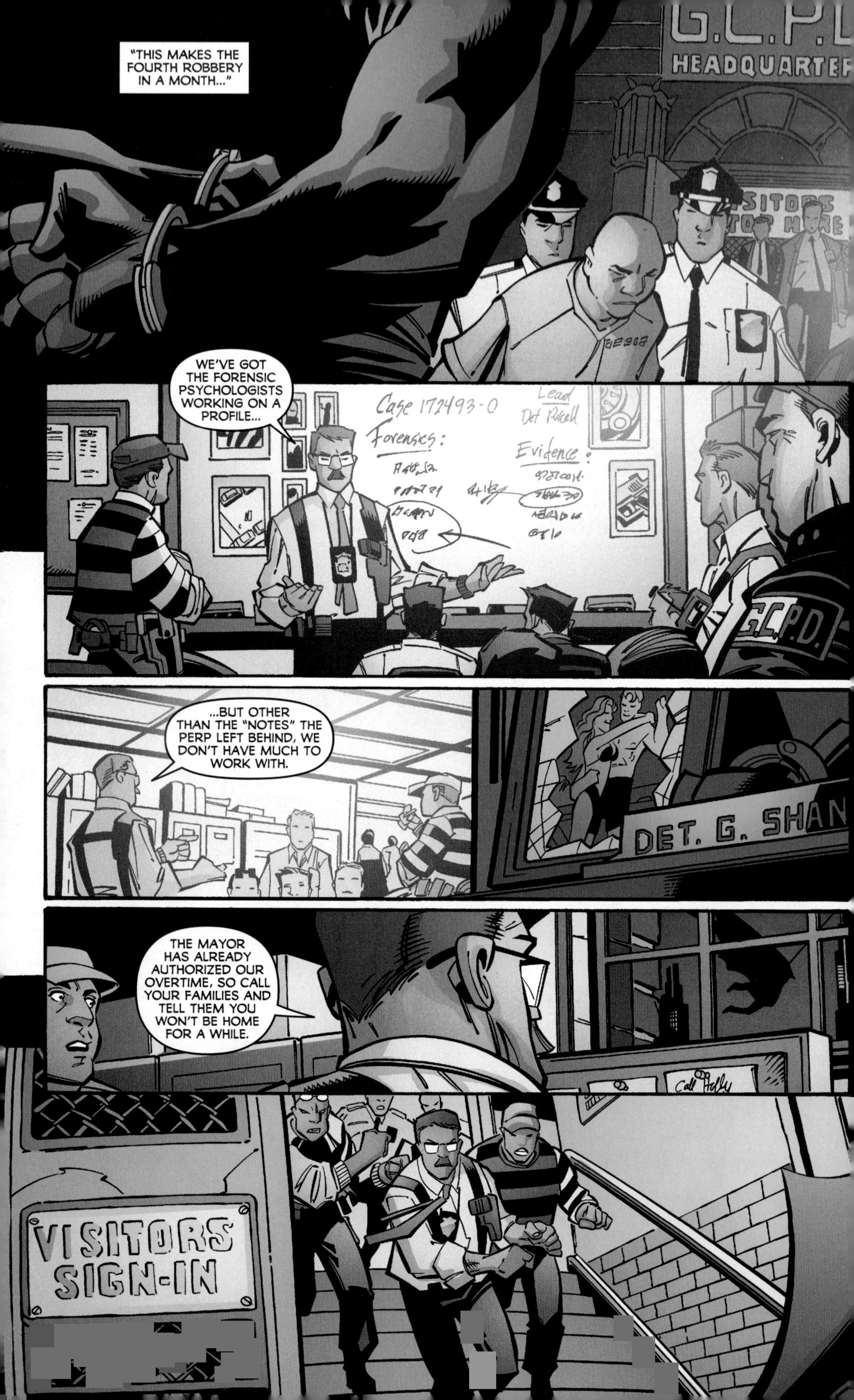
"THIS MAKES THE FOURTH ROBBERY IN A MONTH..."
WE'VE GOT THE FORENSIC PSYCHOLOGISTS WORKING ON A PROFILE...
Case 172493-0
Lead
Forensics:
Evidence:
G.C.P.D.
...BUT OTHER THAN THE "NOTES" THE PERP LEFT BEHIND, WE DON'T HAVE MUCH TO WORK WITH.
THE MAYOR HAS ALREADY AUTHORIZED OUR OVERTIME, SO CALL YOUR FAMILIES AND TELL THEM YOU WON'T BE HOME FOR A WHILE.
VISITORS SIGN-IN

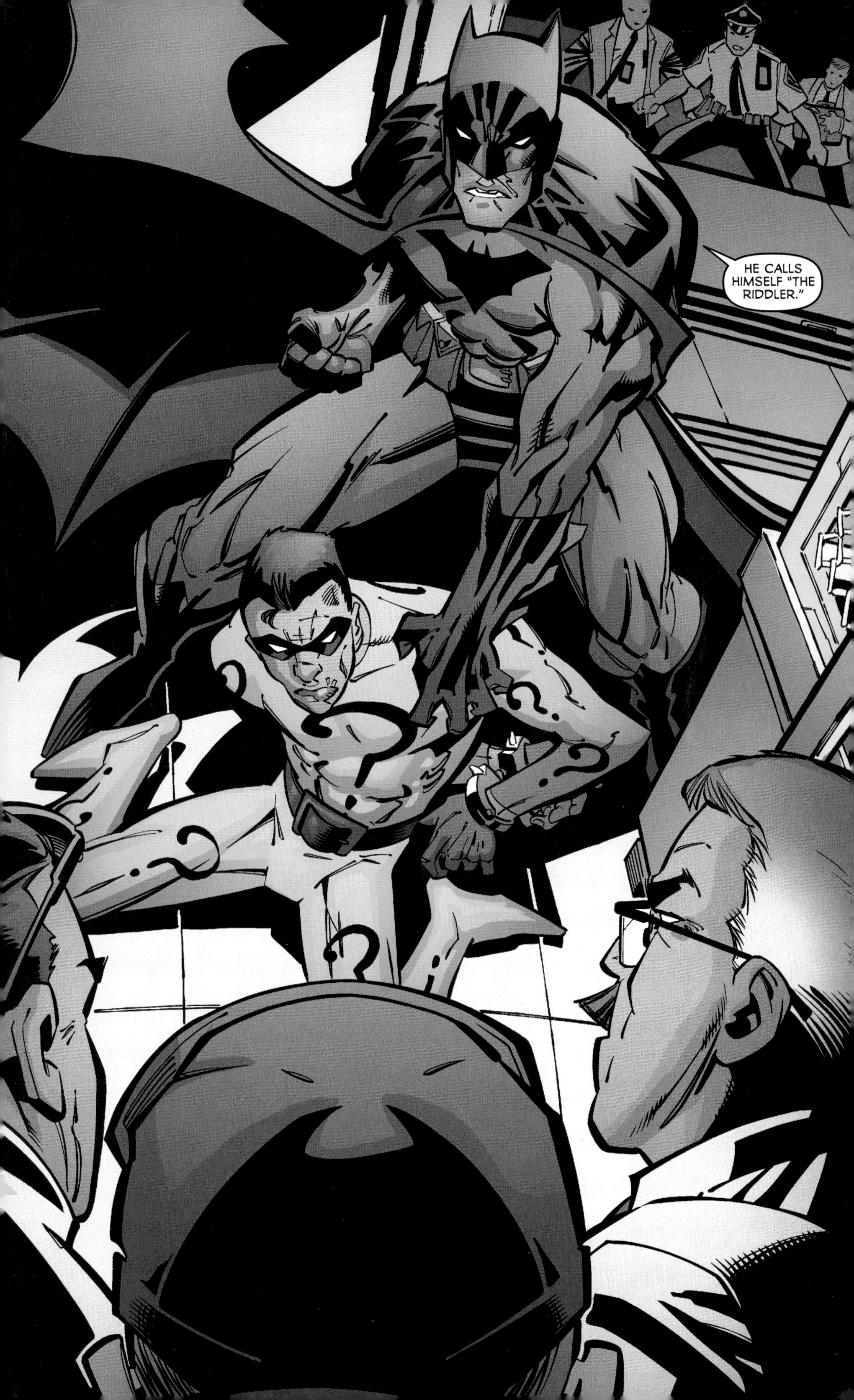
HE CALLS HIMSELF "THE RIDDLER."

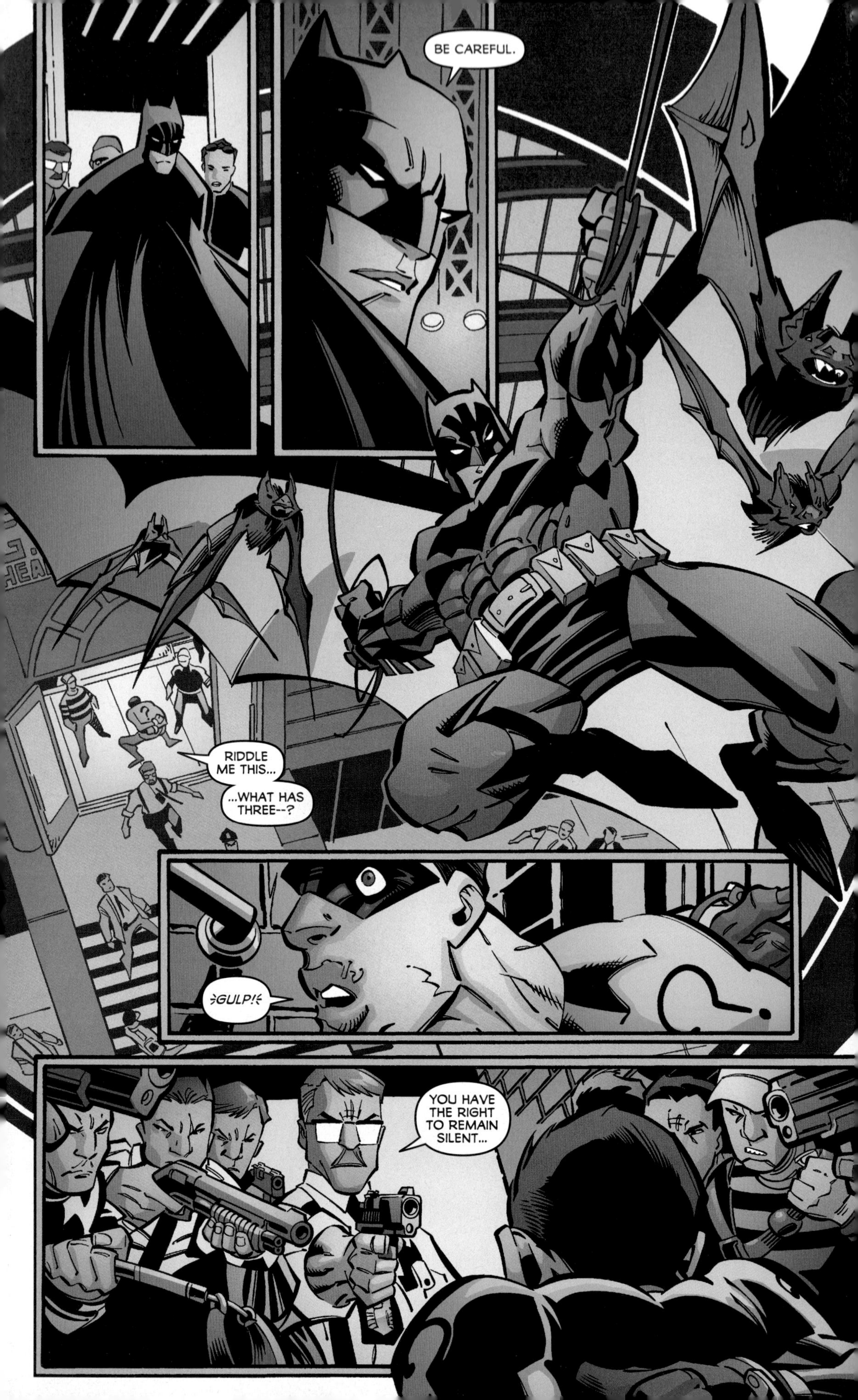
BE CAREFUL.
RIDDLE ME THIS...
...WHAT HAS THREE--?
GULP!
YOU HAVE THE RIGHT TO REMAIN SILENT...

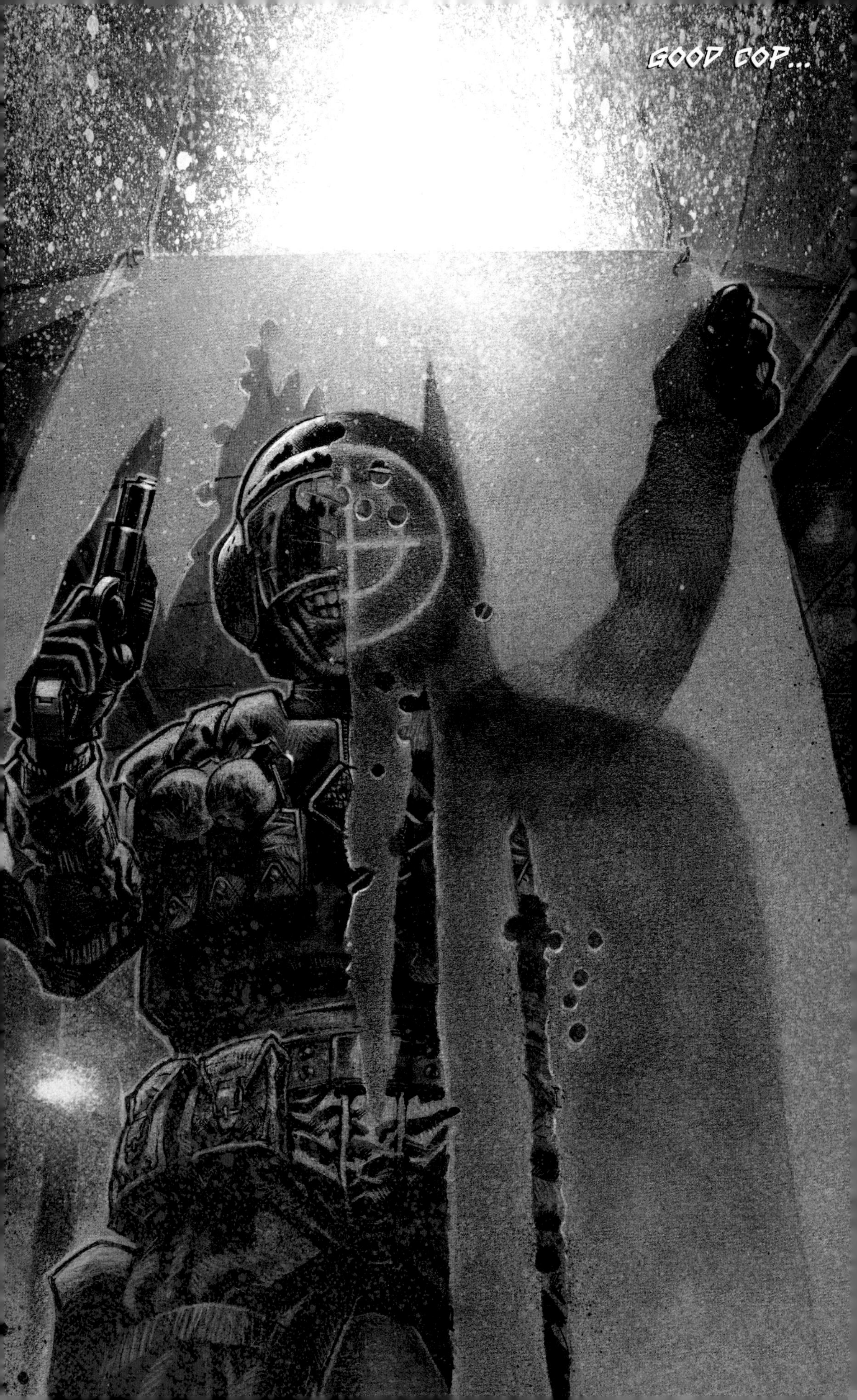
GOOD COP...

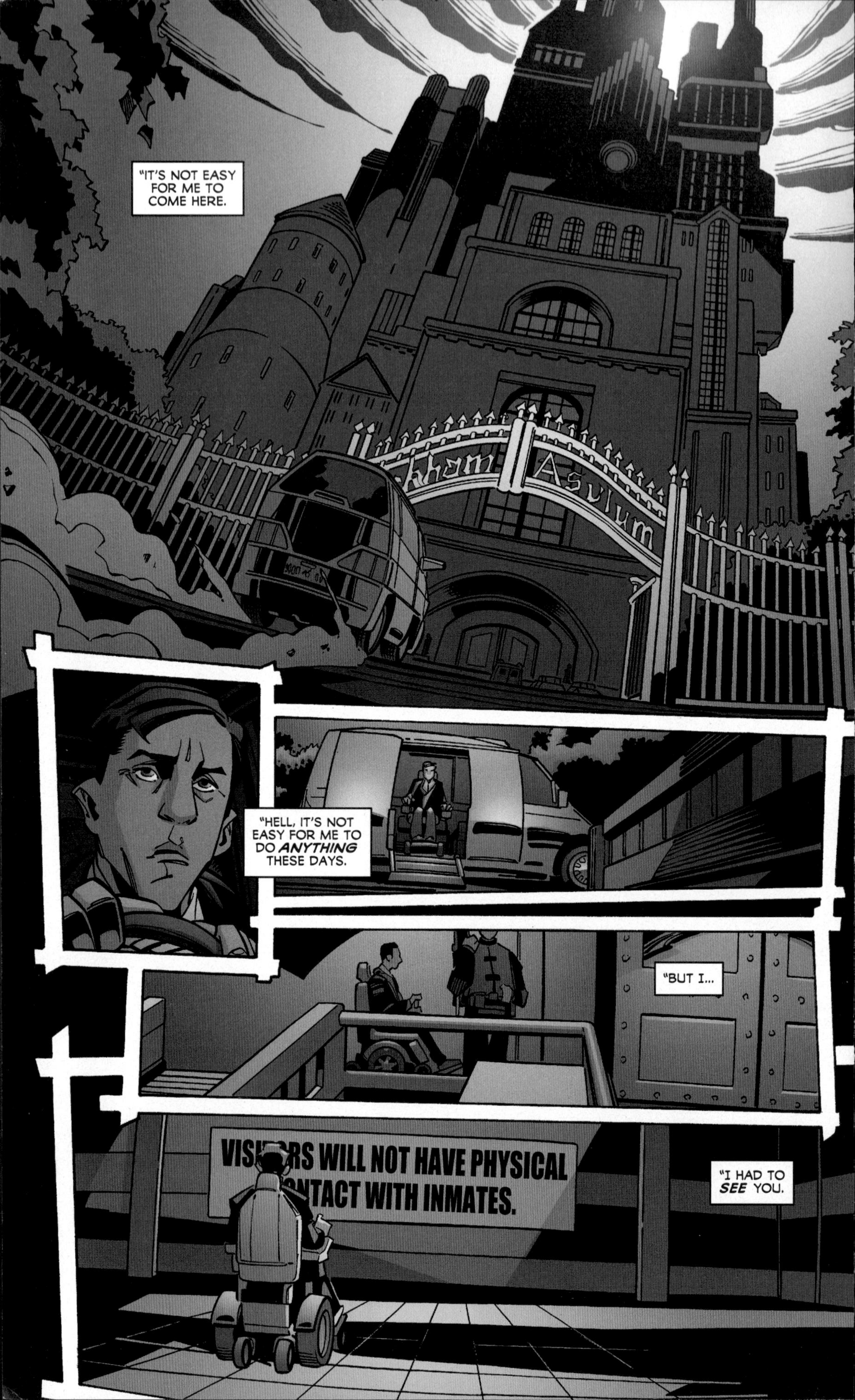
"IT'S NOT EASY FOR ME TO COME HERE.
Arkham Asylum
"HELL, IT'S NOT EASY FOR ME TO DO ANYTHING THESE DAYS.
"BUT I...
VISITORS WILL NOT HAVE PHYSICAL CONTACT WITH INMATES.
"I HAD TO SEE YOU.

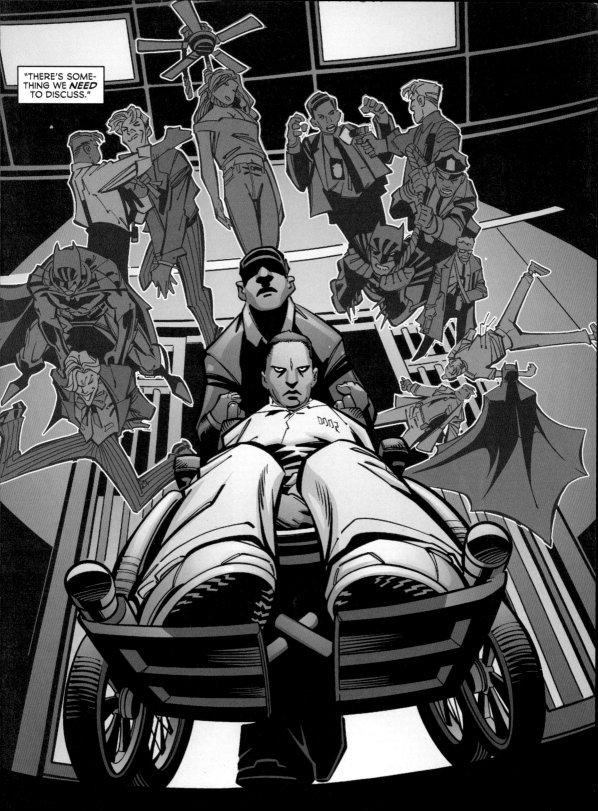

"THERE'S SOME-
THING WE *NEED*
TO DISCUSS."

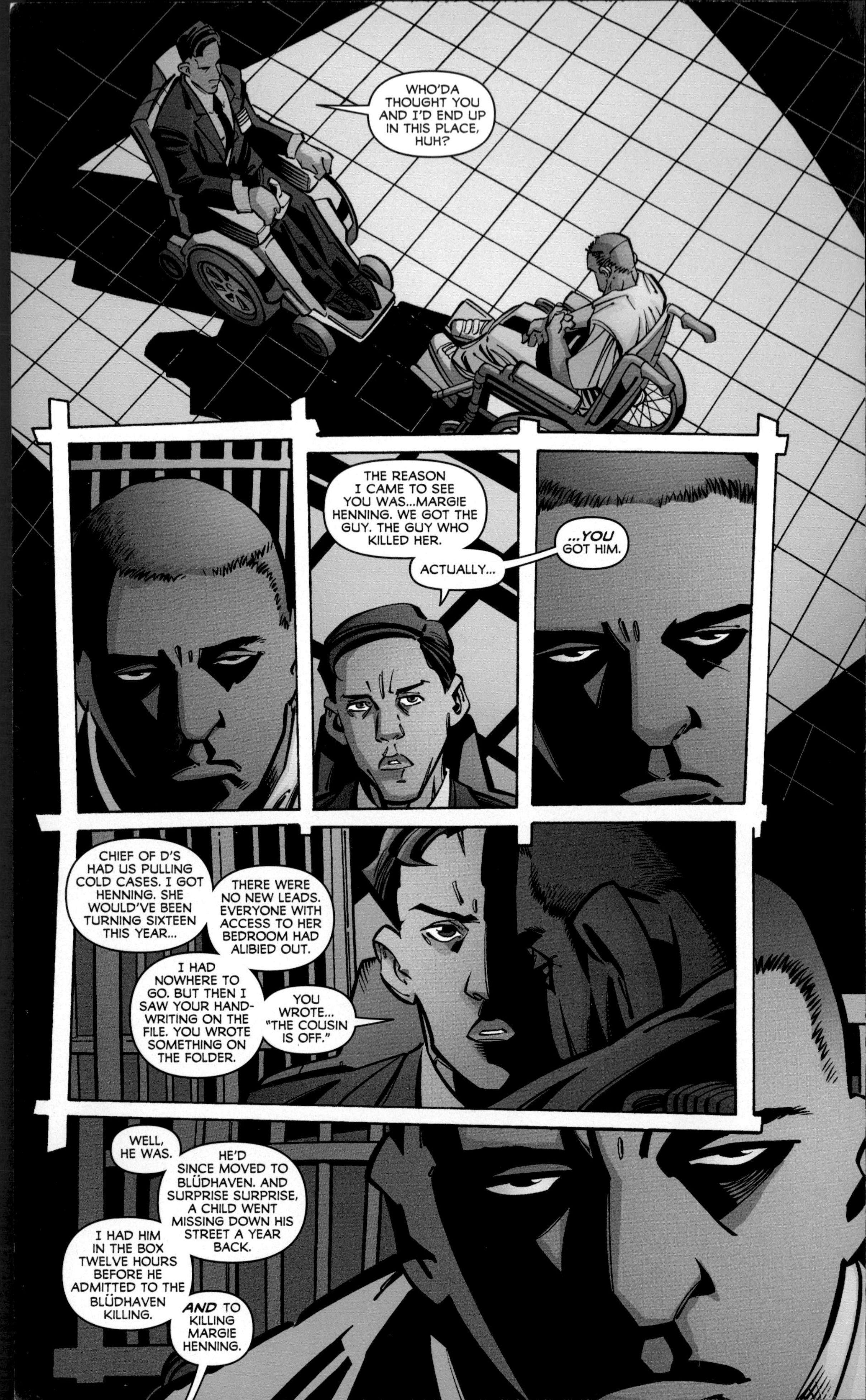

WHO'DA THOUGHT YOU AND I'D END UP IN THIS PLACE, HUH?
THE REASON I CAME TO SEE YOU WAS...MARGIE HENNING. WE GOT THE GUY. THE GUY WHO KILLED HER.
ACTUALLY...
...YOU GOT HIM.
CHIEF OF D'S HAD US PULLING COLD CASES. I GOT HENNING. SHE WOULD'VE BEEN TURNING SIXTEEN THIS YEAR...
THERE WERE NO NEW LEADS. EVERYONE WITH ACCESS TO HER BEDROOM HAD ALIBIED OUT.
I HAD NOWHERE TO GO. BUT THEN I SAW YOUR HAND-WRITING ON THE FILE. YOU WROTE SOMETHING ON THE FOLDER.
YOU WROTE... "THE COUSIN IS OFF."
WELL, HE WAS.
HE'D SINCE MOVED TO BLÜDHAVEN. AND SURPRISE SURPRISE, A CHILD WENT MISSING DOWN HIS STREET A YEAR BACK.
I HAD HIM IN THE BOX TWELVE HOURS BEFORE HE ADMITTED TO THE BLÜDHAVEN KILLING.
AND TO KILLING MARGIE HENNING.

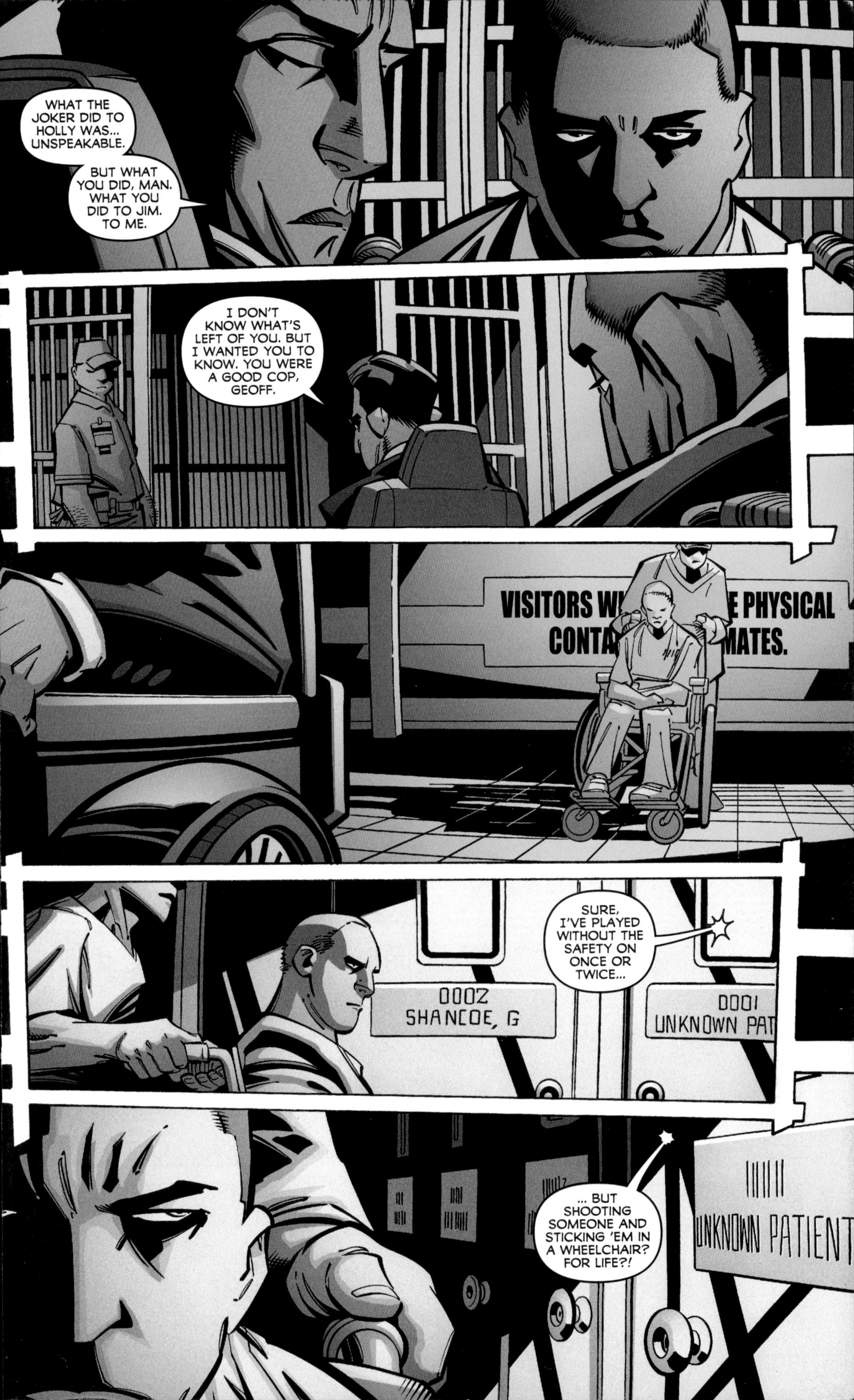
WHAT THE JOKER DID TO HOLLY WAS... UNSPEAKABLE.
BUT WHAT YOU DID, MAN. WHAT YOU DID TO JIM. TO ME.
I DON'T KNOW WHAT'S LEFT OF YOU. BUT I WANTED YOU TO KNOW. YOU WERE A GOOD COP, GEOFF.
VISITORS W
E PHYSICAL
CONTA
MATES.
SURE, I'VE PLAYED WITHOUT THE SAFETY ON ONCE OR TWICE...
0002
SHANCOE, G
0001
UNKNOWN PAT
... BUT SHOOTING SOMEONE AND STICKING 'EM IN A WHEELCHAIR? FOR LIFE?!
UNKNOWN PATIENT

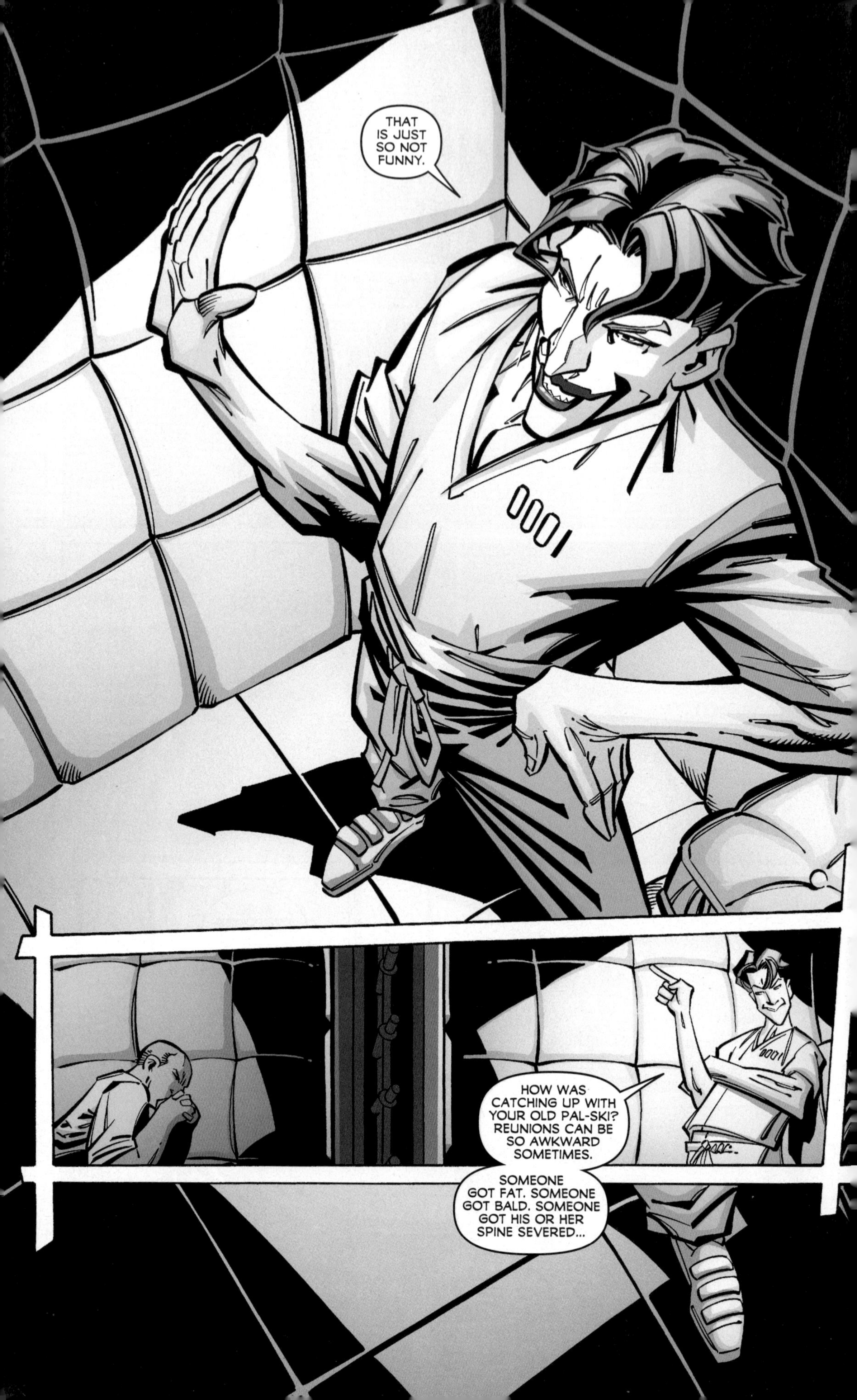
THAT IS JUST SO NOT FUNNY.
0001
0001
HOW WAS CATCHING UP WITH YOUR OLD PAL-SKI? REUNIONS CAN BE SO AWKWARD SOMETIMES.
SOMEONE GOT FAT. SOMEONE GOT BALD. SOMEONE GOT HIS OR HER SPINE SEVERED...

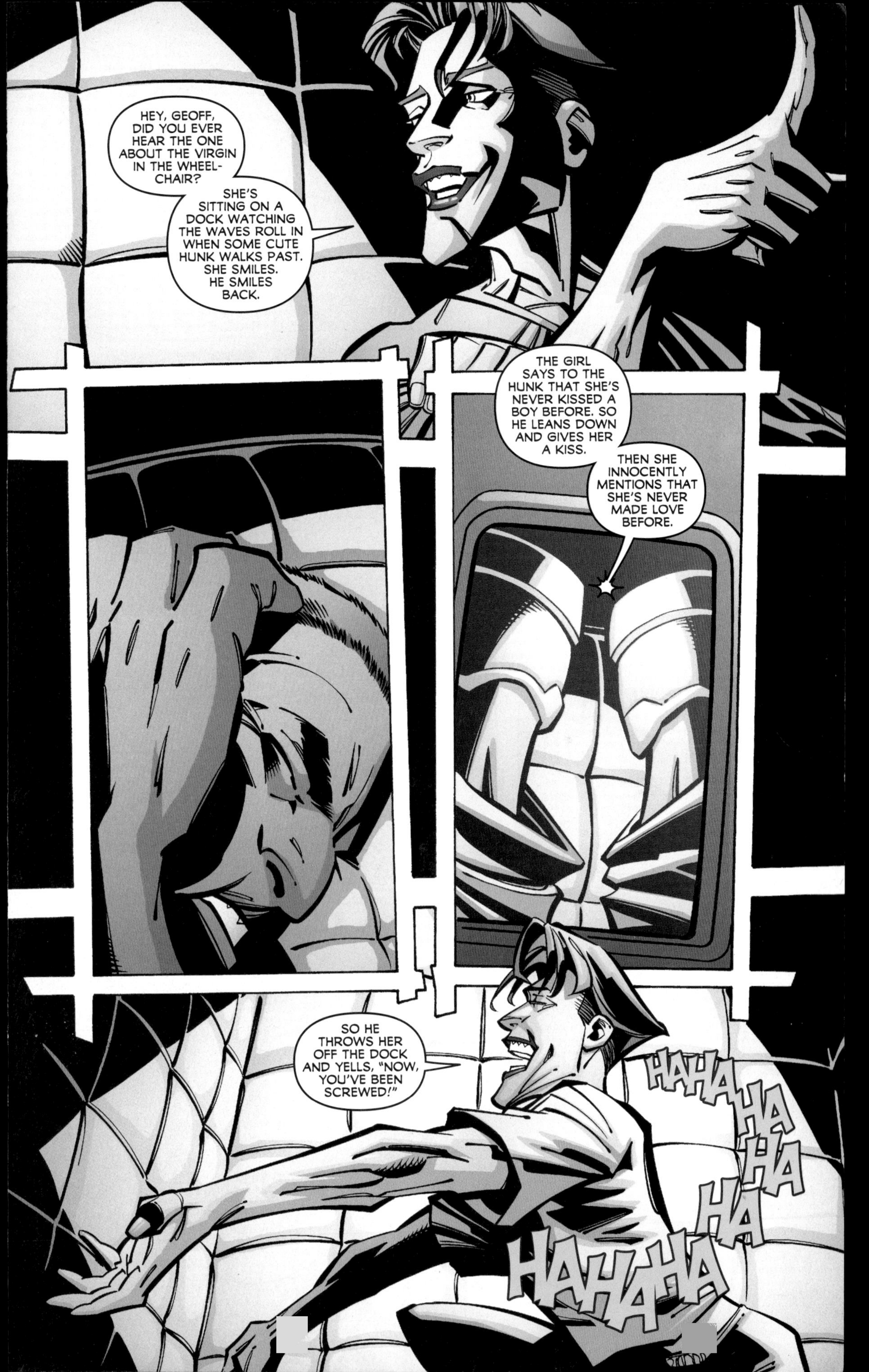
HEY, GEOFF, DID YOU EVER HEAR THE ONE ABOUT THE VIRGIN IN THE WHEEL-CHAIR?
SHE'S SITTING ON A DOCK WATCHING THE WAVES ROLL IN WHEN SOME CUTE HUNK WALKS PAST. SHE SMILES. HE SMILES BACK.
THE GIRL SAYS TO THE HUNK THAT SHE'S NEVER KISSED A BOY BEFORE. SO HE LEANS DOWN AND GIVES HER A KISS.
THEN SHE INNOCENTLY MENTIONS THAT SHE'S NEVER MADE LOVE BEFORE.
SO HE THROWS HER OFF THE DOCK AND YELLS, "NOW, YOU'VE BEEN SCREWED!"
HAHAHA HA HA HA
HAHAHA

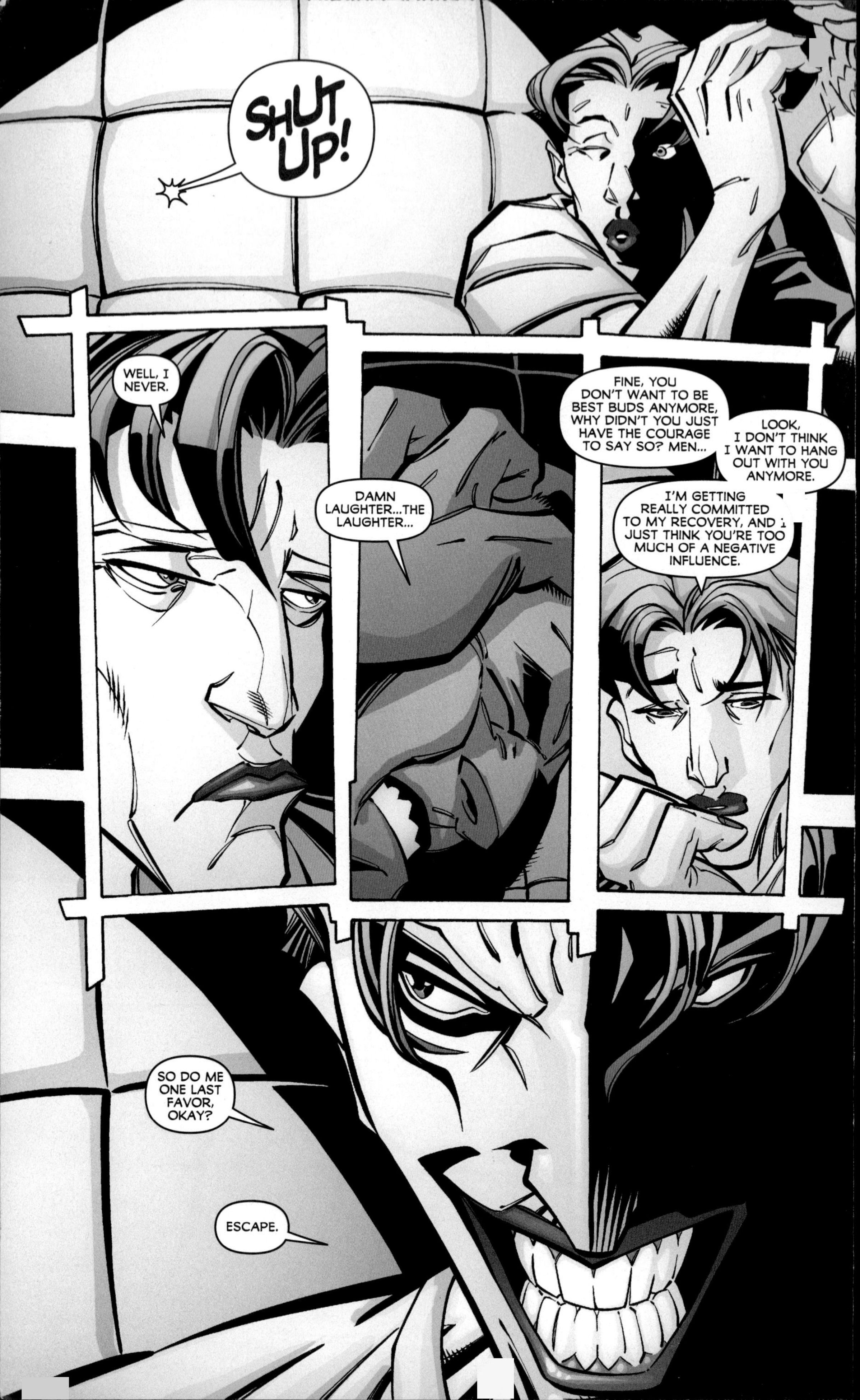
SHUT UP!
WELL, I NEVER.
DAMN LAUGHTER...THE LAUGHTER...
FINE, YOU DON'T WANT TO BE BEST BUDS ANYMORE, WHY DIDN'T YOU JUST HAVE THE COURAGE TO SAY SO? MEN...
LOOK, I DON'T THINK I WANT TO HANG OUT WITH YOU ANYMORE.
I'M GETTING REALLY COMMITTED TO MY RECOVERY, AND I JUST THINK YOU'RE TOO MUCH OF A NEGATIVE INFLUENCE.
SO DO ME ONE LAST FAVOR, OKAY?
ESCAPE.

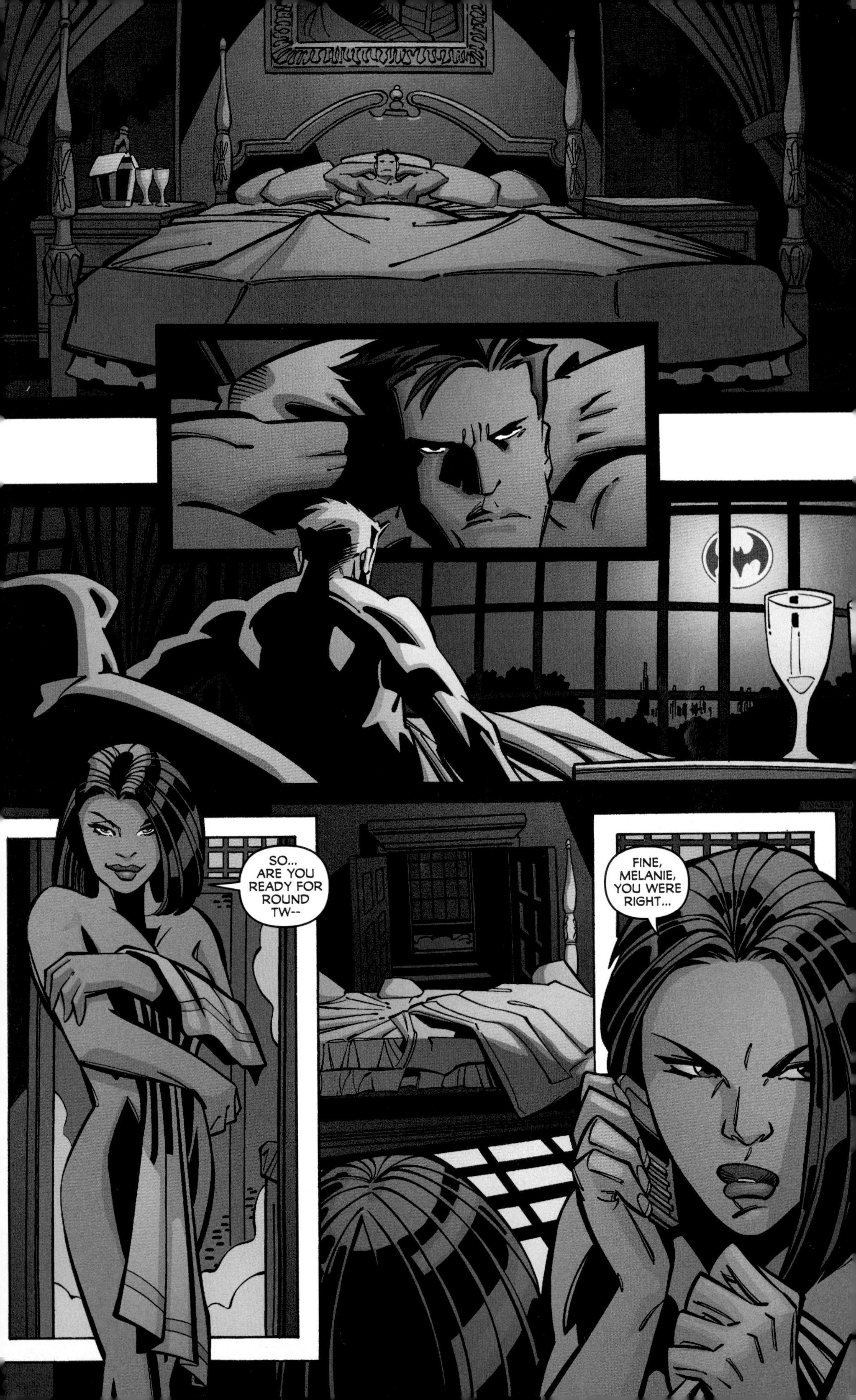
SO... ARE YOU READY FOR ROUND TW--
FINE, MELANIE, YOU WERE RIGHT...

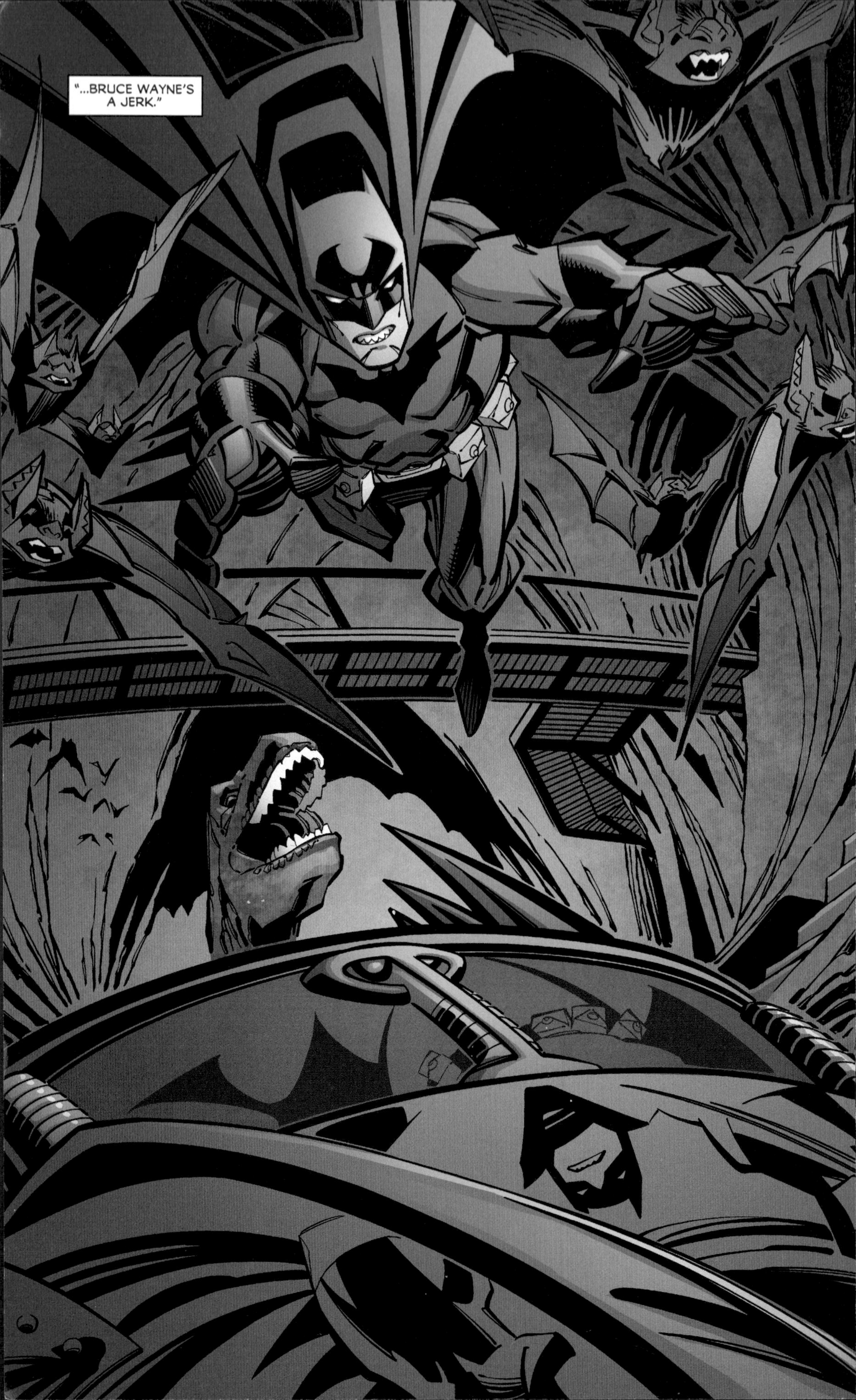
"...BRUCE WAYNE'S A JERK."

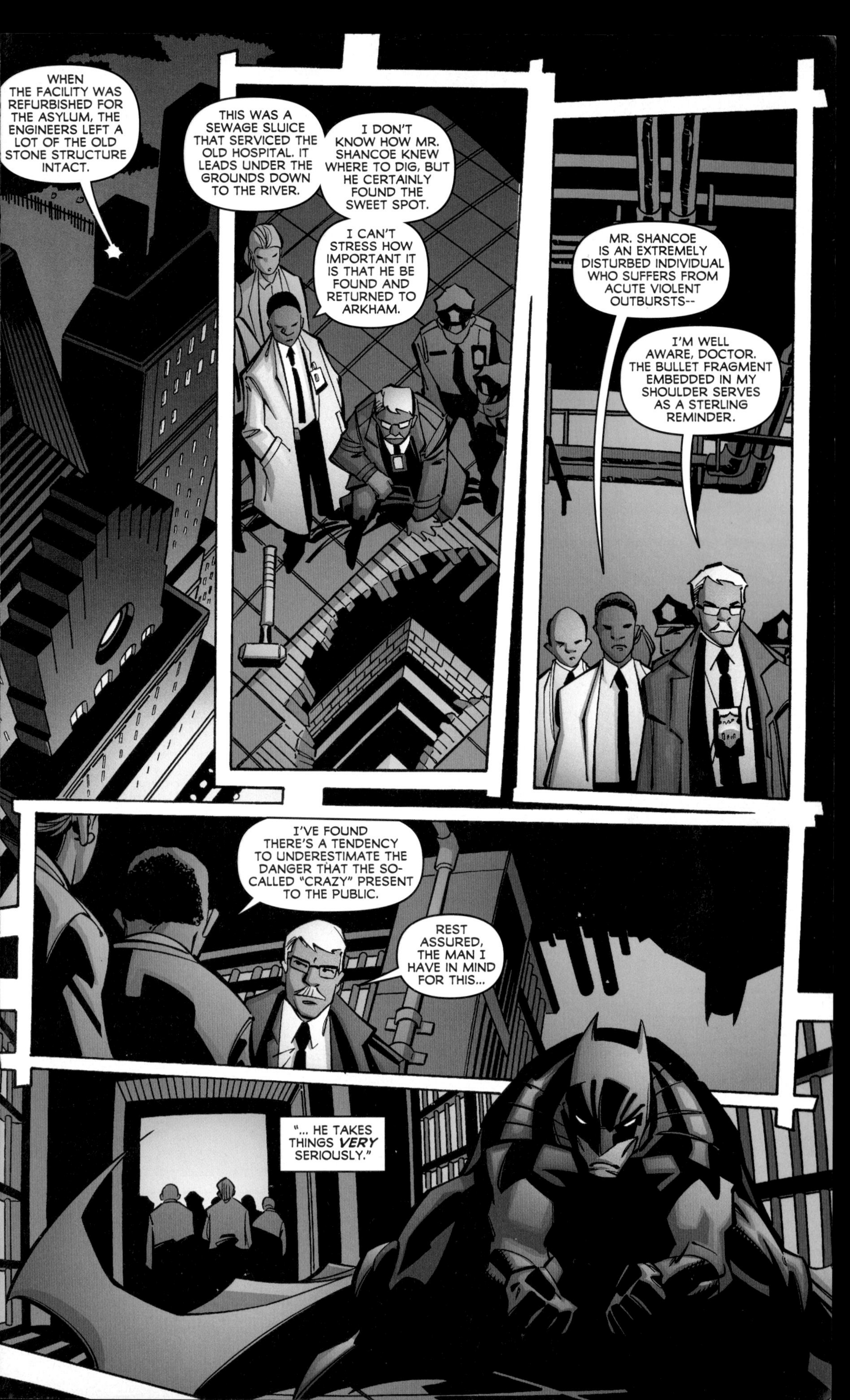
WHEN THE FACILITY WAS REFURBISHED FOR THE ASYLUM, THE ENGINEERS LEFT A LOT OF THE OLD STONE STRUCTURE INTACT.
THIS WAS A SEWAGE SLUICE THAT SERVICED THE OLD HOSPITAL. IT LEADS UNDER THE GROUNDS DOWN TO THE RIVER.
I DON'T KNOW HOW MR. SHANCOE KNEW WHERE TO DIG, BUT HE CERTAINLY FOUND THE SWEET SPOT.
I CAN'T STRESS HOW IMPORTANT IT IS THAT HE BE FOUND AND RETURNED TO ARKHAM.
MR. SHANCOE IS AN EXTREMELY DISTURBED INDIVIDUAL WHO SUFFERS FROM ACUTE VIOLENT OUTBURSTS--
I'M WELL AWARE, DOCTOR. THE BULLET FRAGMENT EMBEDDED IN MY SHOULDER SERVES AS A STERLING REMINDER.
I'VE FOUND THERE'S A TENDENCY TO UNDERESTIMATE THE DANGER THAT THE SO-CALLED "CRAZY" PRESENT TO THE PUBLIC.
REST ASSURED, THE MAN I HAVE IN MIND FOR THIS...
"... HE TAKES THINGS *VERY* SERIOUSLY."

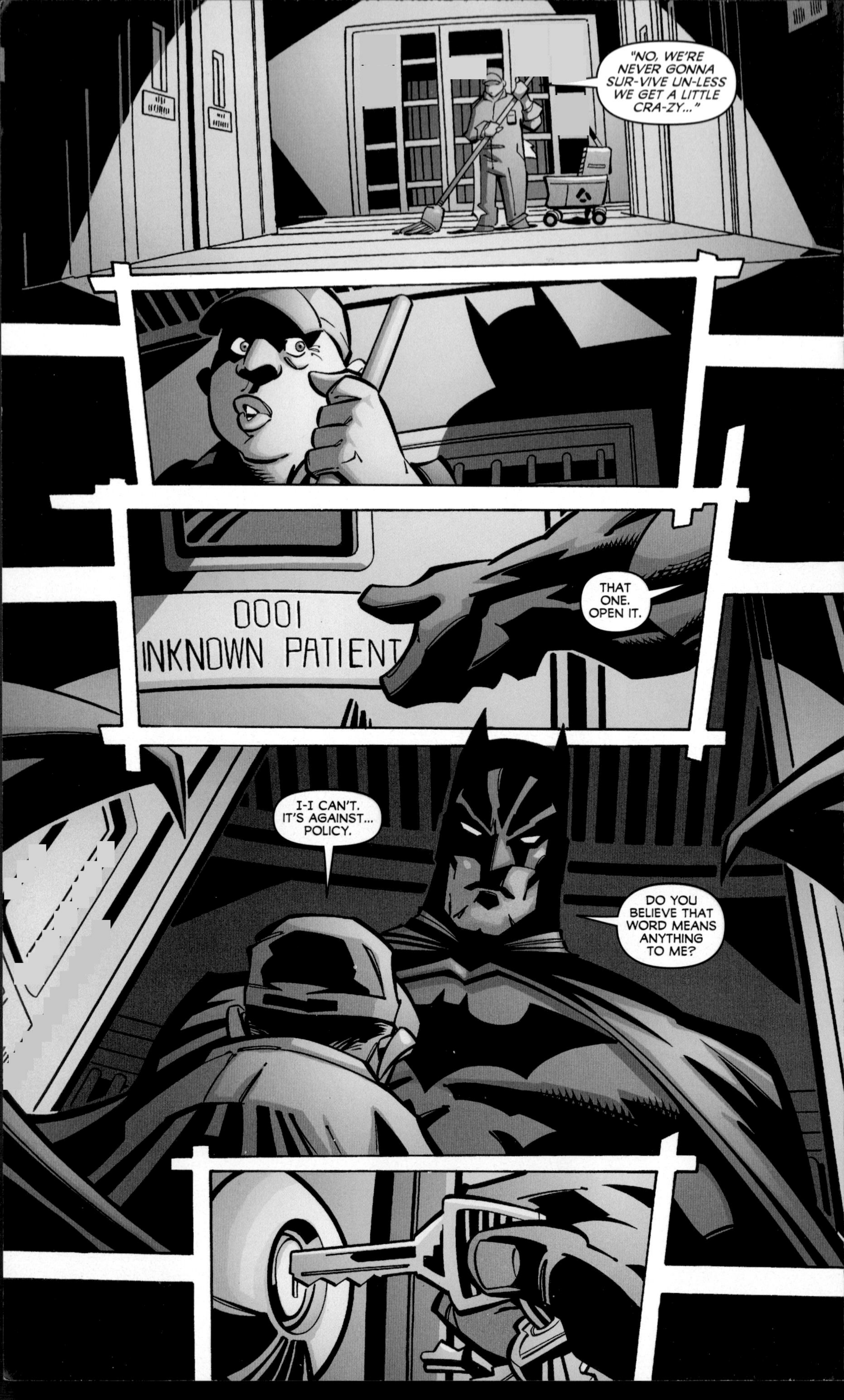
"NO, WE'RE NEVER GONNA SUR-VIVE UN-LESS WE GET A LITTLE CRA-ZY..."
0001
INKNOWN PATIENT
THAT ONE. OPEN IT.
I-I CAN'T. IT'S AGAINST... POLICY.
DO YOU BELIEVE THAT WORD MEANS ANYTHING TO ME?

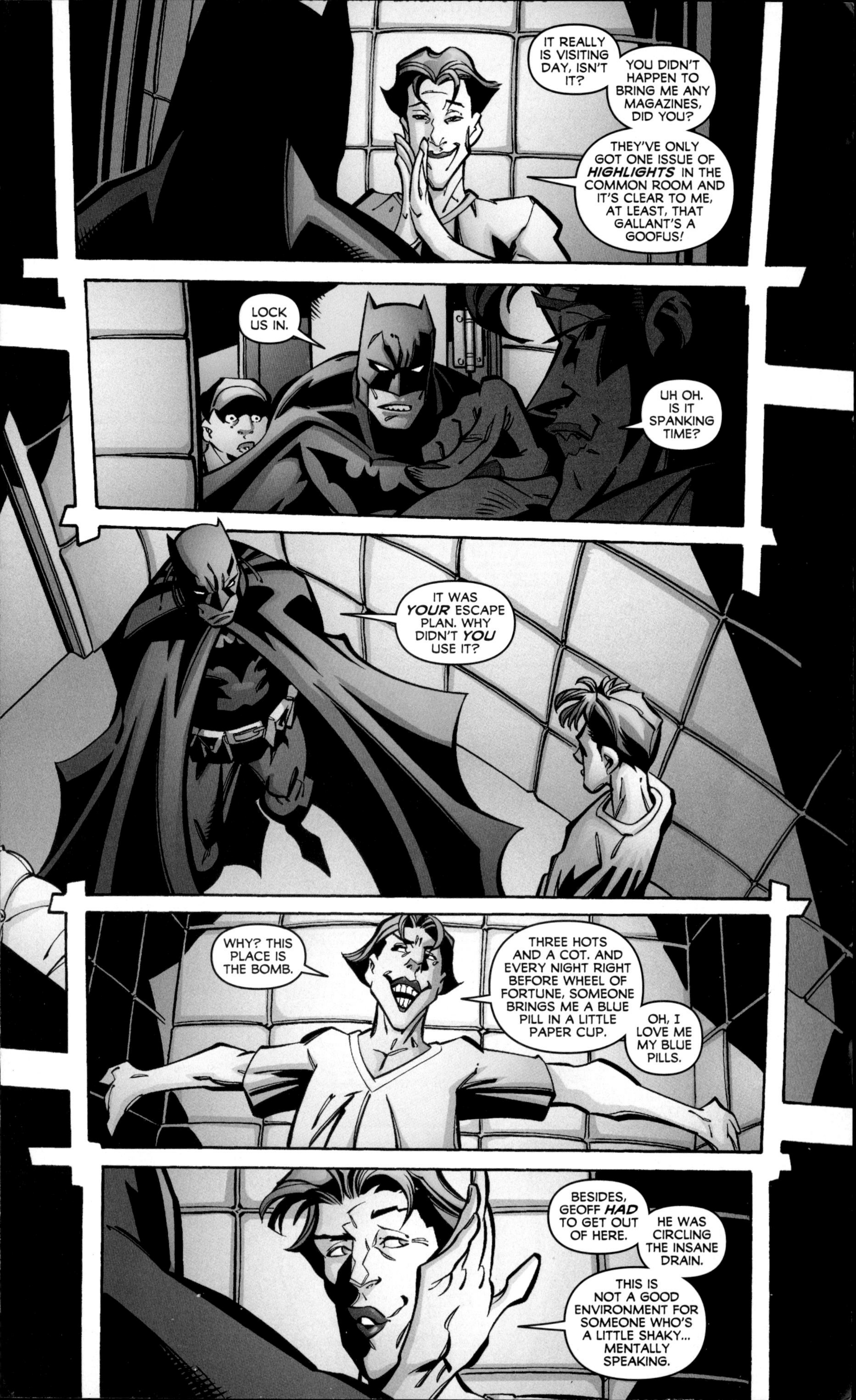
IT REALLY IS VISITING DAY, ISN'T IT?
YOU DIDN'T HAPPEN TO BRING ME ANY MAGAZINES, DID YOU?
THEY'VE ONLY GOT ONE ISSUE OF *HIGHLIGHTS* IN THE COMMON ROOM AND IT'S CLEAR TO ME, AT LEAST, THAT GALLANT'S A GOOFUS!
LOCK US IN.
UH OH. IS IT SPANKING TIME?
IT WAS *YOUR* ESCAPE PLAN. WHY DIDN'T *YOU* USE IT?
WHY? THIS PLACE IS THE BOMB.
THREE HOTS AND A COT. AND EVERY NIGHT RIGHT BEFORE WHEEL OF FORTUNE, SOMEONE BRINGS ME A BLUE PILL IN A LITTLE PAPER CUP.
OH, I LOVE ME MY BLUE PILLS.
BESIDES, GEOFF *HAD* TO GET OUT OF HERE.
HE WAS CIRCLING THE INSANE DRAIN.
THIS IS NOT A GOOD ENVIRONMENT FOR SOMEONE WHO'S A LITTLE SHAKY... MENTALLY SPEAKING.

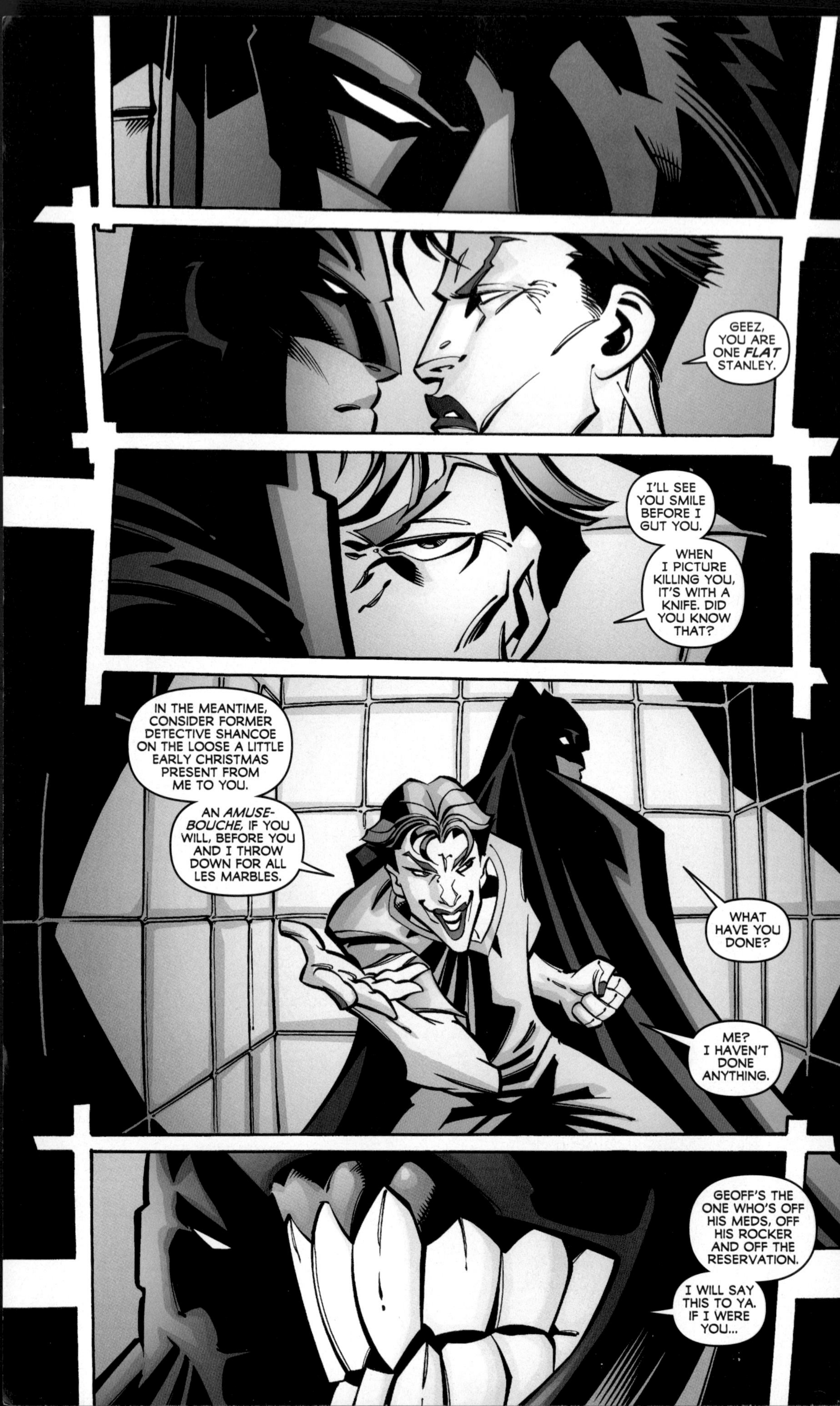
GEEZ, YOU ARE ONE *FLAT* STANLEY.
I'LL SEE YOU SMILE BEFORE I GUT YOU.
WHEN I PICTURE KILLING YOU, IT'S WITH A KNIFE. DID YOU KNOW THAT?
IN THE MEANTIME, CONSIDER FORMER DETECTIVE SHANCOE ON THE LOOSE A LITTLE EARLY CHRISTMAS PRESENT FROM ME TO YOU.
AN *AMUSE-BOUCHE,* IF YOU WILL, BEFORE YOU AND I THROW DOWN FOR ALL LES MARBLES.
WHAT HAVE YOU DONE?
ME? I HAVEN'T DONE ANYTHING.
GEOFF'S THE ONE WHO'S OFF HIS MEDS, OFF HIS ROCKER AND OFF THE RESERVATION.
I WILL SAY THIS TO YA. IF I WERE YOU...

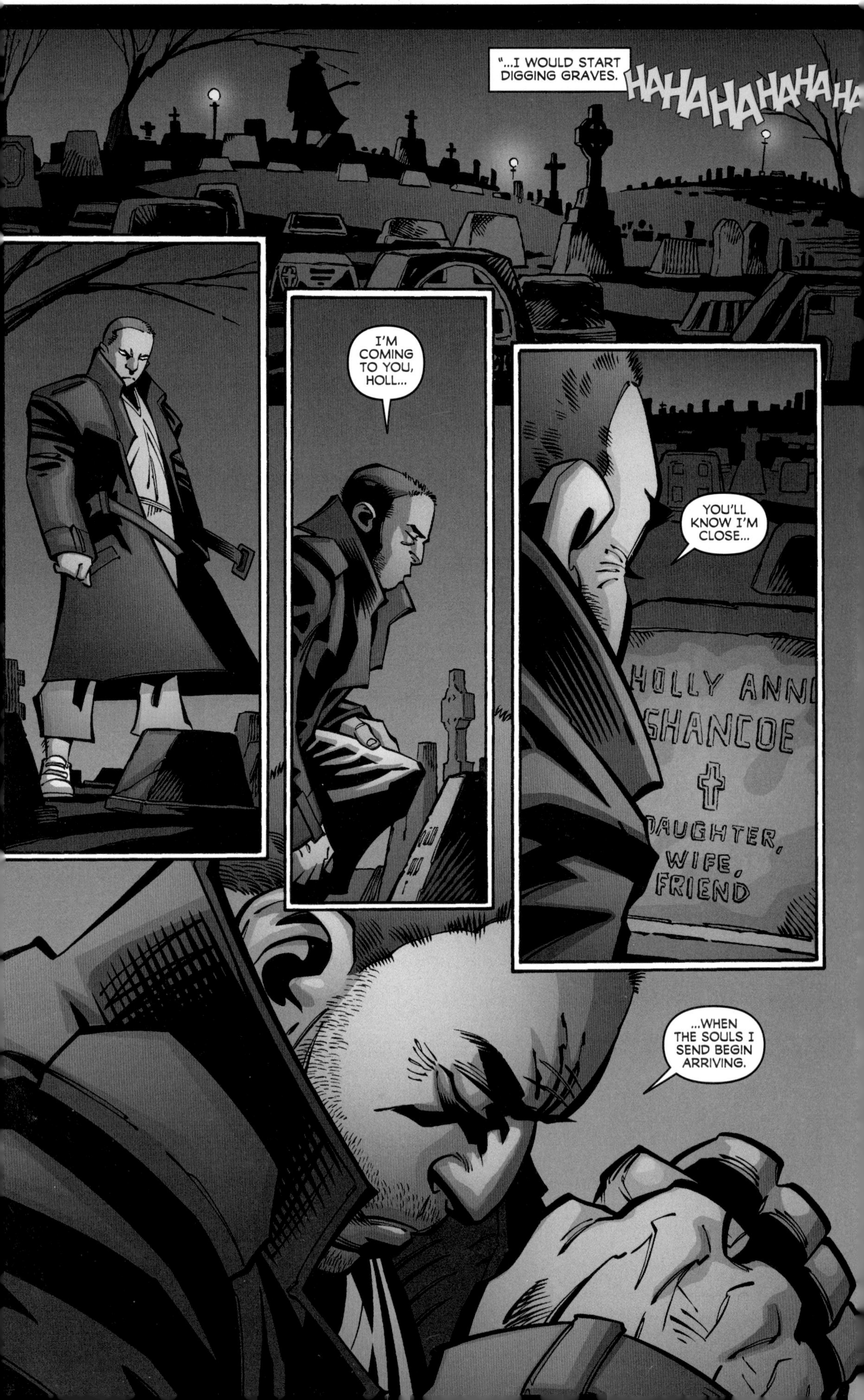
"...I WOULD START DIGGING GRAVES.
HAHAHAHAHAHA
I'M COMING TO YOU, HOLL...
YOU'LL KNOW I'M CLOSE...
HOLLY ANN
SHANCOE
DAUGHTER, WIFE, FRIEND
...WHEN THE SOULS I SEND BEGIN ARRIVING.

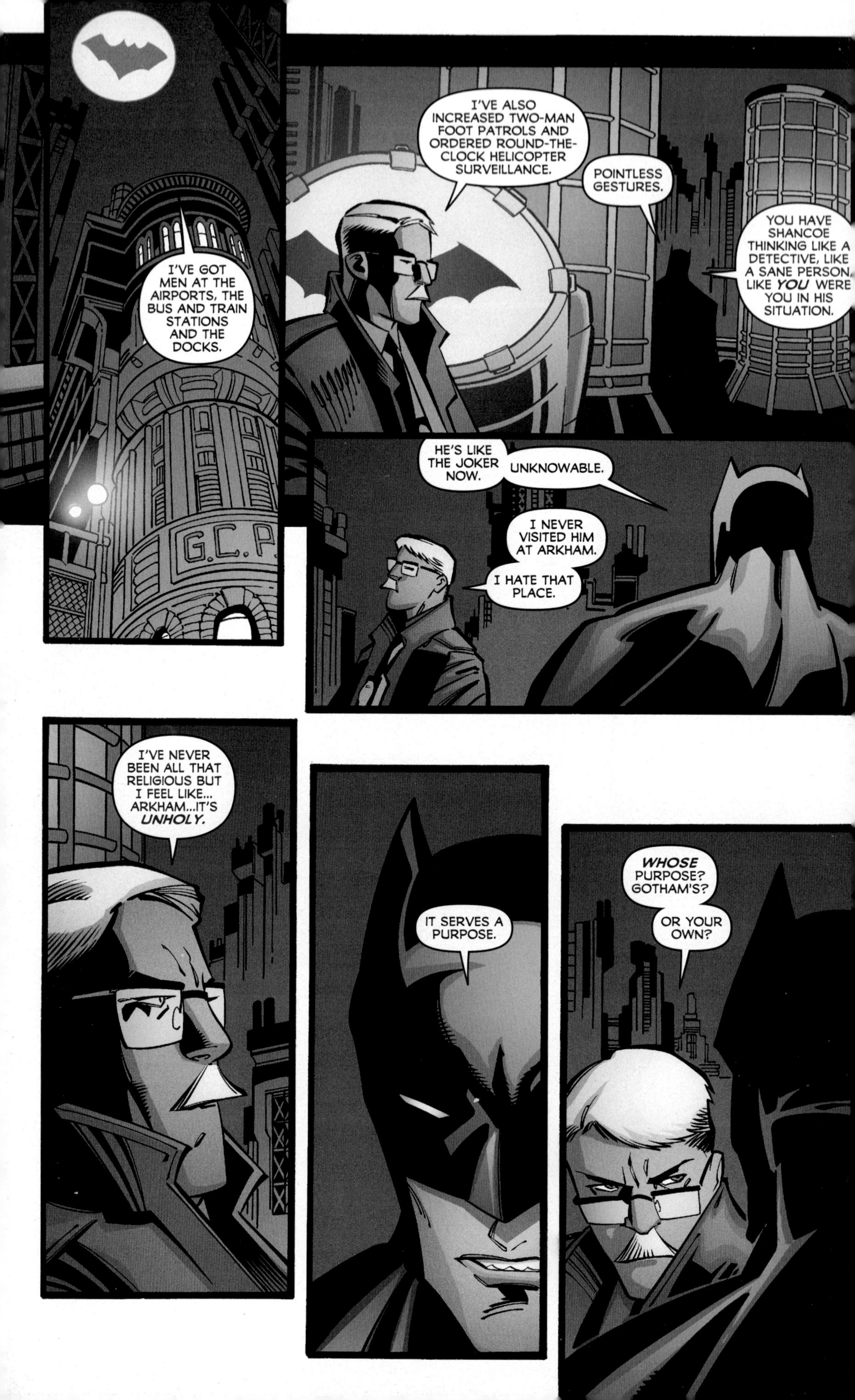
I'VE GOT MEN AT THE AIRPORTS, THE BUS AND TRAIN STATIONS AND THE DOCKS.
G.C.P.
I'VE ALSO INCREASED TWO-MAN FOOT PATROLS AND ORDERED ROUND-THE-CLOCK HELICOPTER SURVEILLANCE.
POINTLESS GESTURES.
YOU HAVE SHANCOE THINKING LIKE A DETECTIVE, LIKE A SANE PERSON, LIKE *YOU* WERE YOU IN HIS SITUATION.
HE'S LIKE THE JOKER NOW.
UNKNOWABLE.
I NEVER VISITED HIM AT ARKHAM.
I HATE THAT PLACE.
I'VE NEVER BEEN ALL THAT RELIGIOUS BUT I FEEL LIKE... ARKHAM...IT'S ***UNHOLY.***
IT SERVES A PURPOSE.
WHOSE PURPOSE? GOTHAM'S?
OR YOUR OWN?

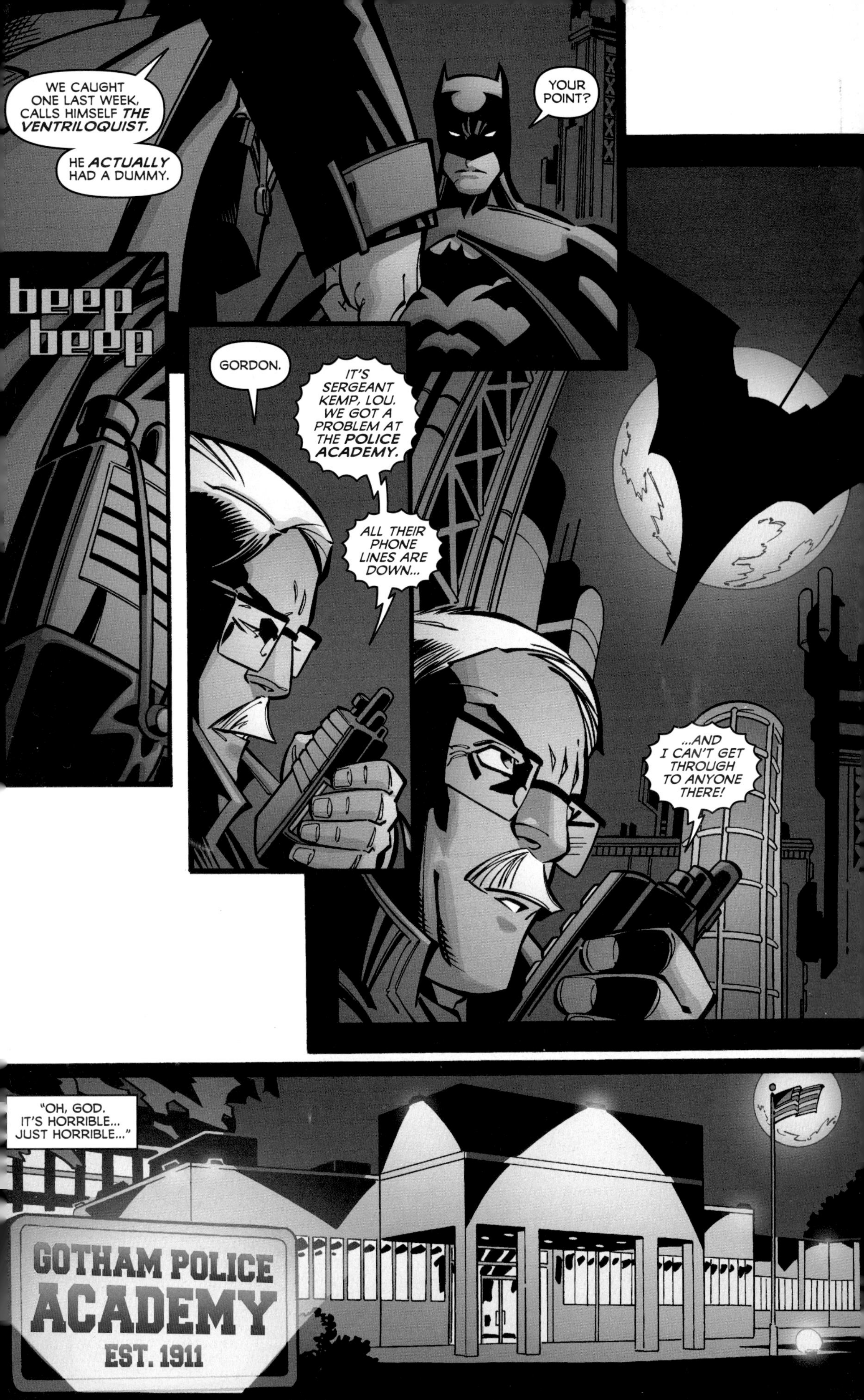
WE CAUGHT ONE LAST WEEK, CALLS HIMSELF *THE VENTRILOQUIST.*
HE *ACTUALLY* HAD A DUMMY.
YOUR POINT?
beep beep
GORDON.
IT'S SERGEANT KEMP, LOU. WE GOT A PROBLEM AT THE *POLICE ACADEMY.*
ALL THEIR PHONE LINES ARE DOWN...
...AND I CAN'T GET THROUGH TO ANYONE THERE!
"OH, GOD. IT'S HORRIBLE... JUST HORRIBLE..."
GOTHAM POLICE ACADEMY
EST. 1911

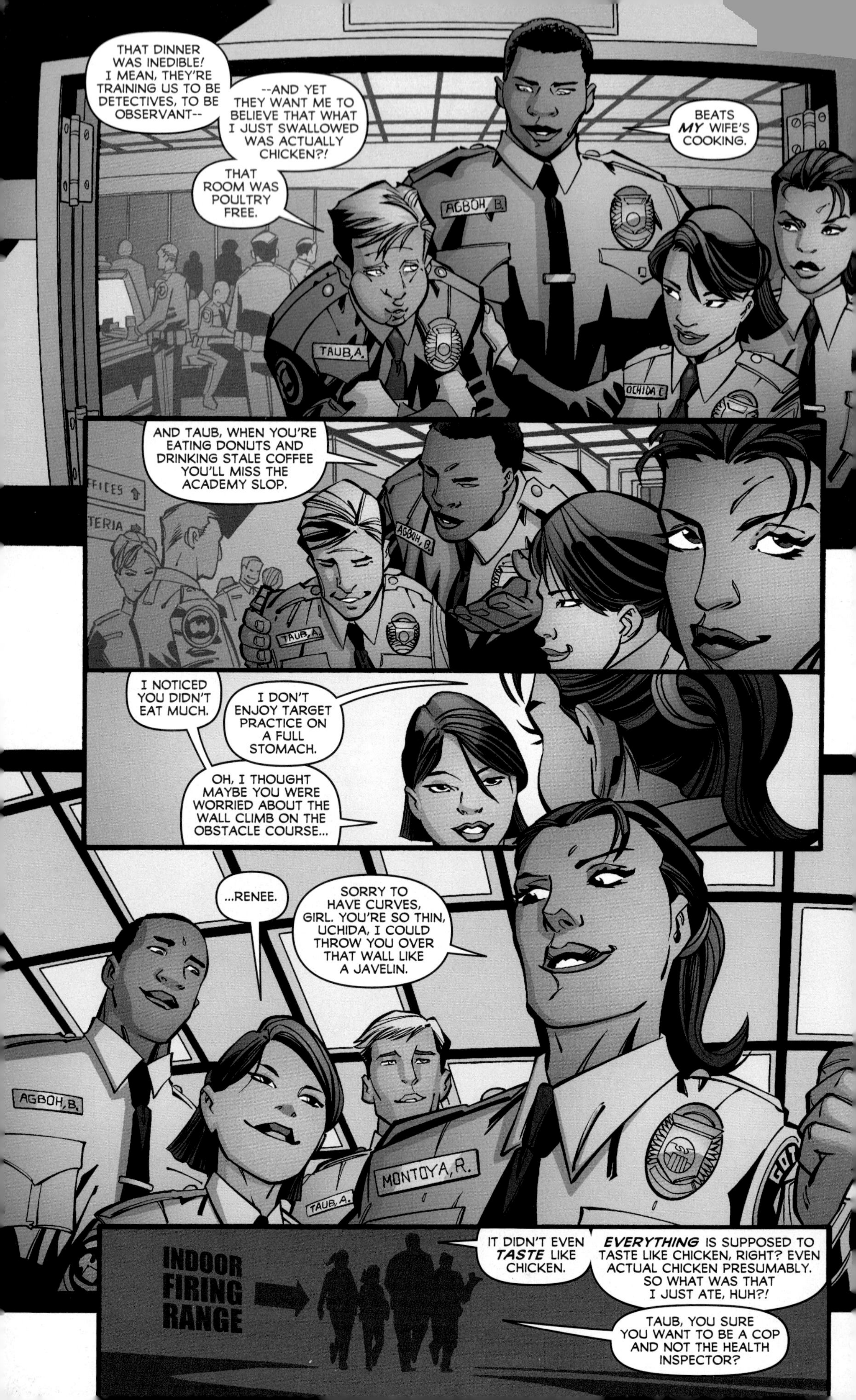
THAT DINNER WAS INEDIBLE! I MEAN, THEY'RE TRAINING US TO BE DETECTIVES, TO BE OBSERVANT--
--AND YET THEY WANT ME TO BELIEVE THAT WHAT I JUST SWALLOWED WAS ACTUALLY CHICKEN?!
THAT ROOM WAS POULTRY FREE.
BEATS MY WIFE'S COOKING.
AGBOH, B.
TAUB, A.
OCHIDA C.
AND TAUB, WHEN YOU'RE EATING DONUTS AND DRINKING STALE COFFEE YOU'LL MISS THE ACADEMY SLOP.
FFICES
TERIA
AGBOH, B.
TAUB, A.
I NOTICED YOU DIDN'T EAT MUCH.
I DON'T ENJOY TARGET PRACTICE ON A FULL STOMACH.
OH, I THOUGHT MAYBE YOU WERE WORRIED ABOUT THE WALL CLIMB ON THE OBSTACLE COURSE...
...RENEE.
SORRY TO HAVE CURVES, GIRL. YOU'RE SO THIN, UCHIDA, I COULD THROW YOU OVER THAT WALL LIKE A JAVELIN.
AGBOH, B.
MONTOYA, R.
TAUB, A.
INDOOR FIRING RANGE
IT DIDN'T EVEN TASTE LIKE CHICKEN.
EVERYTHING IS SUPPOSED TO TASTE LIKE CHICKEN, RIGHT? EVEN ACTUAL CHICKEN PRESUMABLY. SO WHAT WAS THAT I JUST ATE, HUH?!
TAUB, YOU SURE YOU WANT TO BE A COP AND NOT THE HEALTH INSPECTOR?

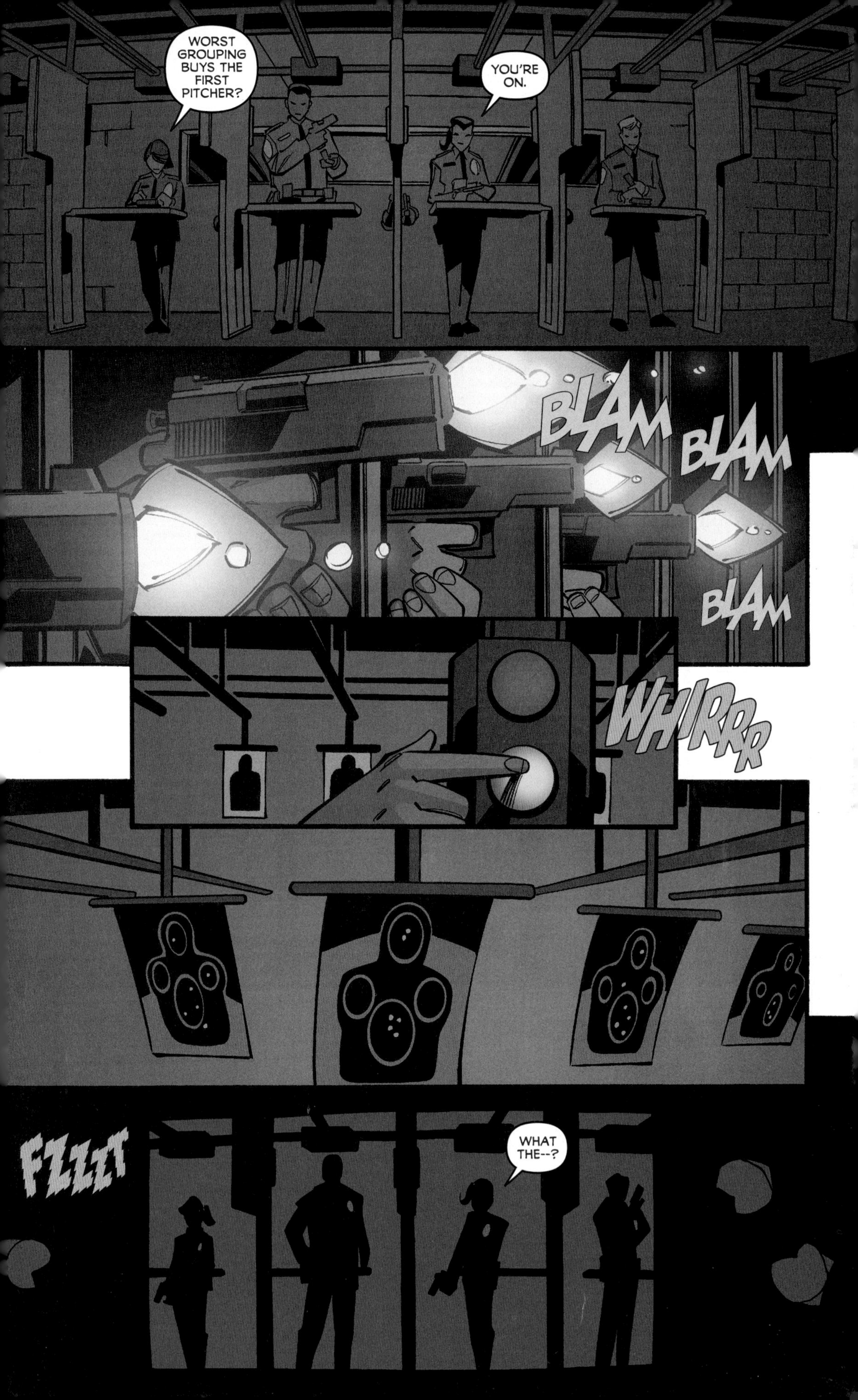
WORST GROUPING BUYS THE FIRST PITCHER?
YOU'RE ON.
BLAM
BLAM
BLAM
WHIRRR
FZZZT
WHAT THE--?

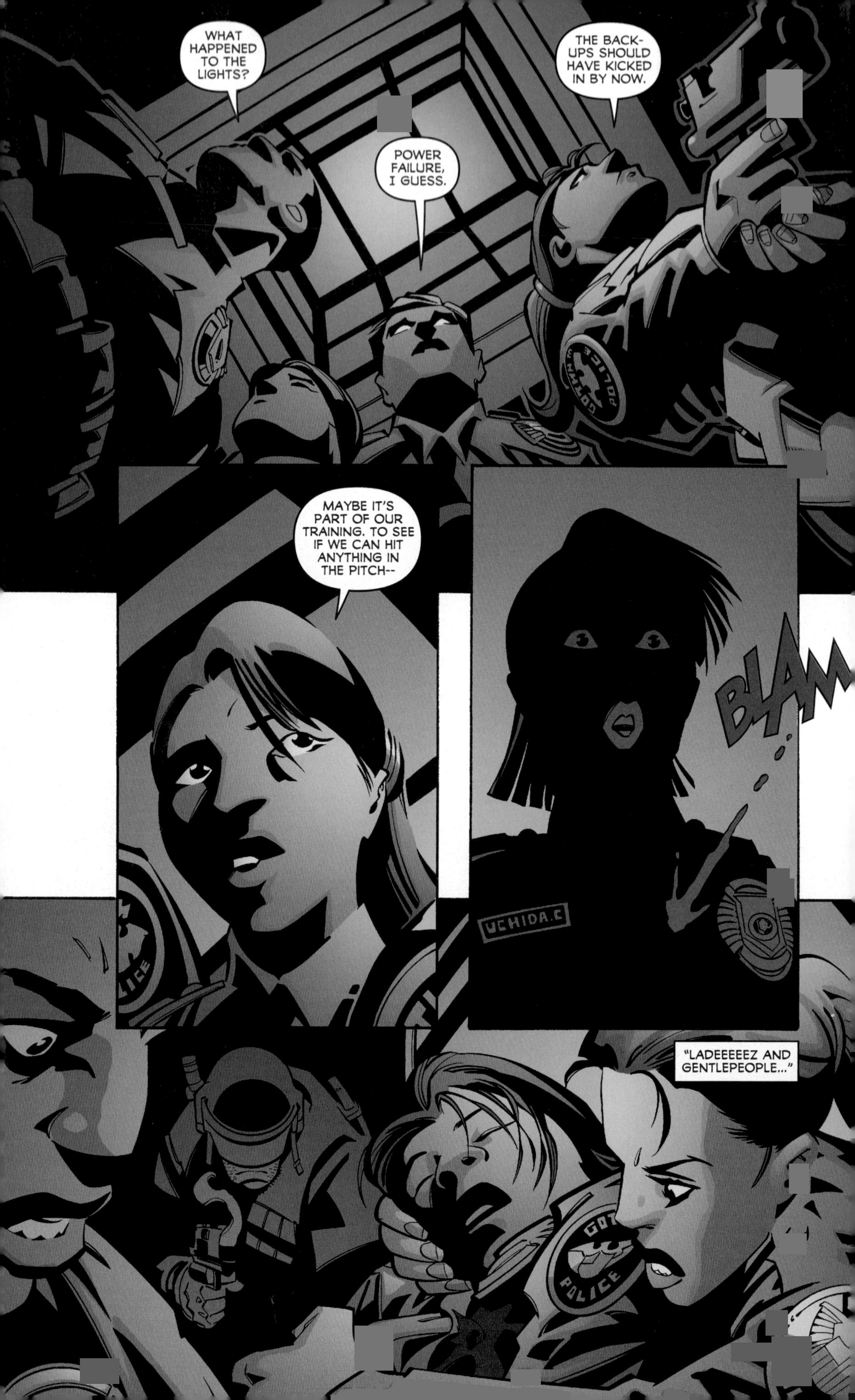
WHAT HAPPENED TO THE LIGHTS?
POWER FAILURE, I GUESS.
THE BACK-UPS SHOULD HAVE KICKED IN BY NOW.
MAYBE IT'S PART OF OUR TRAINING. TO SEE IF WE CAN HIT ANYTHING IN THE PITCH--
UCHIDA.C
BLAM
"LADEEEEEZ AND GENTLEPEOPLE..."
POLICE

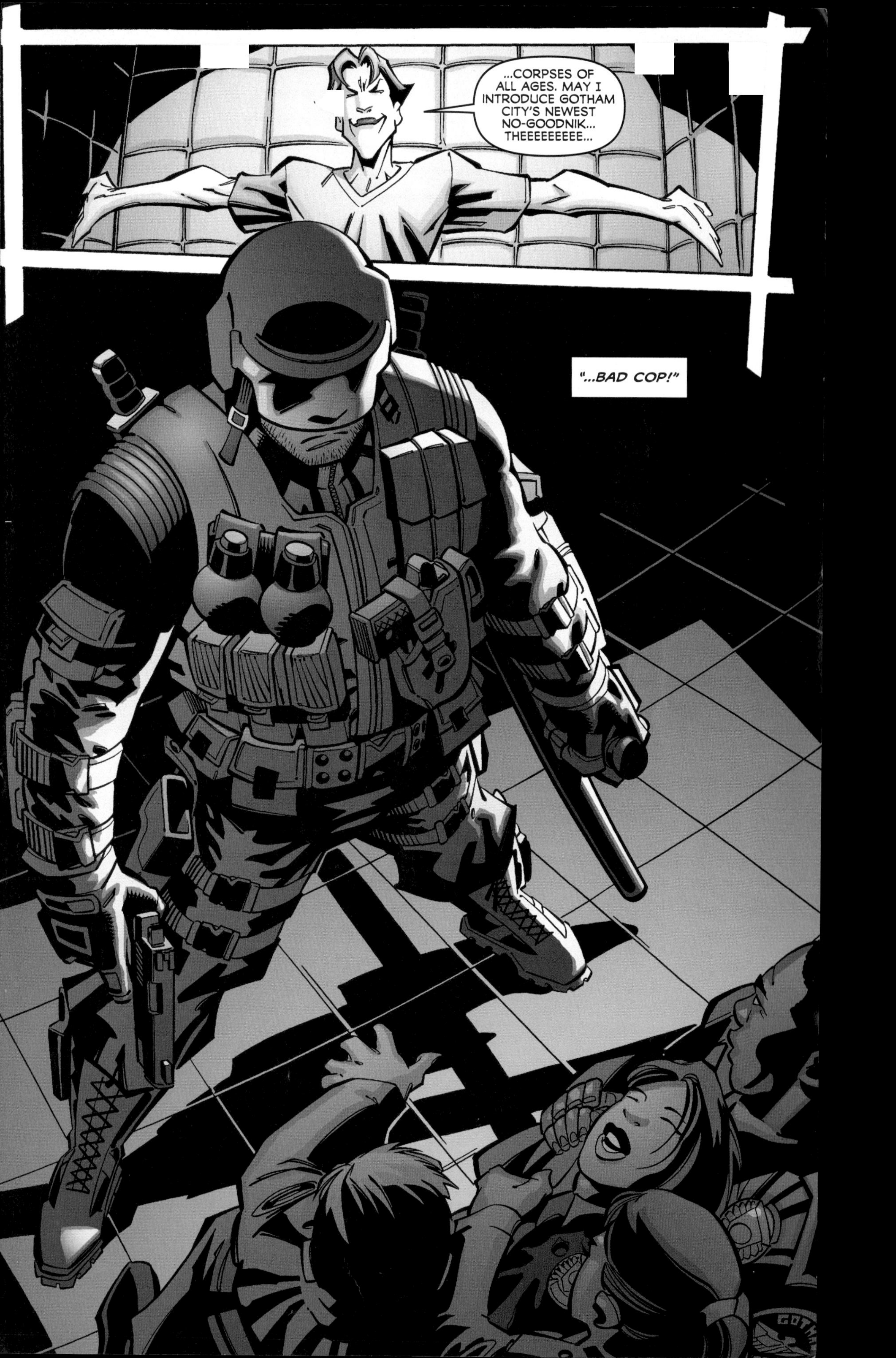
...CORPSES OF ALL AGES. MAY I INTRODUCE GOTHAM CITY'S NEWEST NO-GOODNIK... THEEEEEEEEE...
"...BAD COP!"

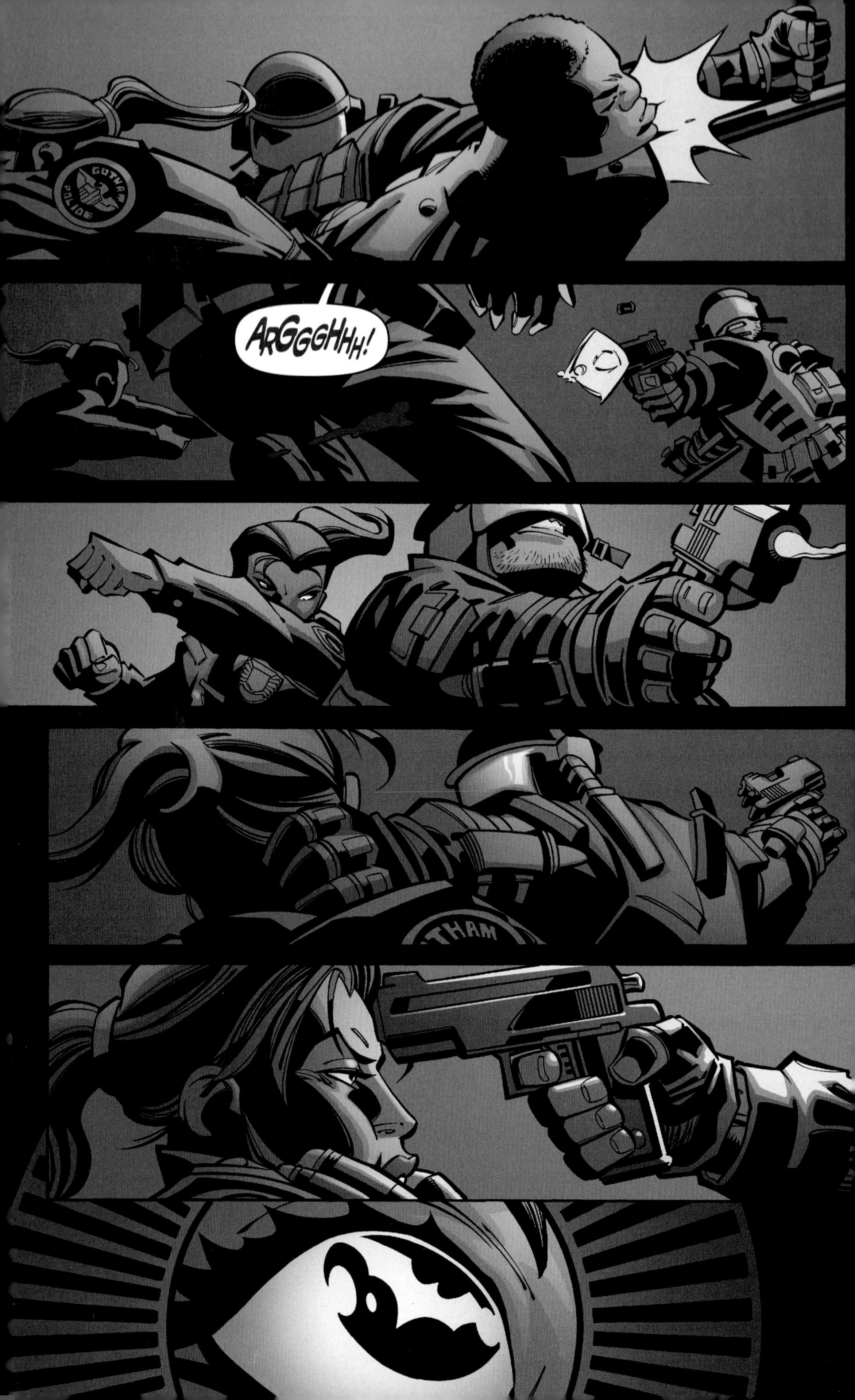
ARGGGHHH!

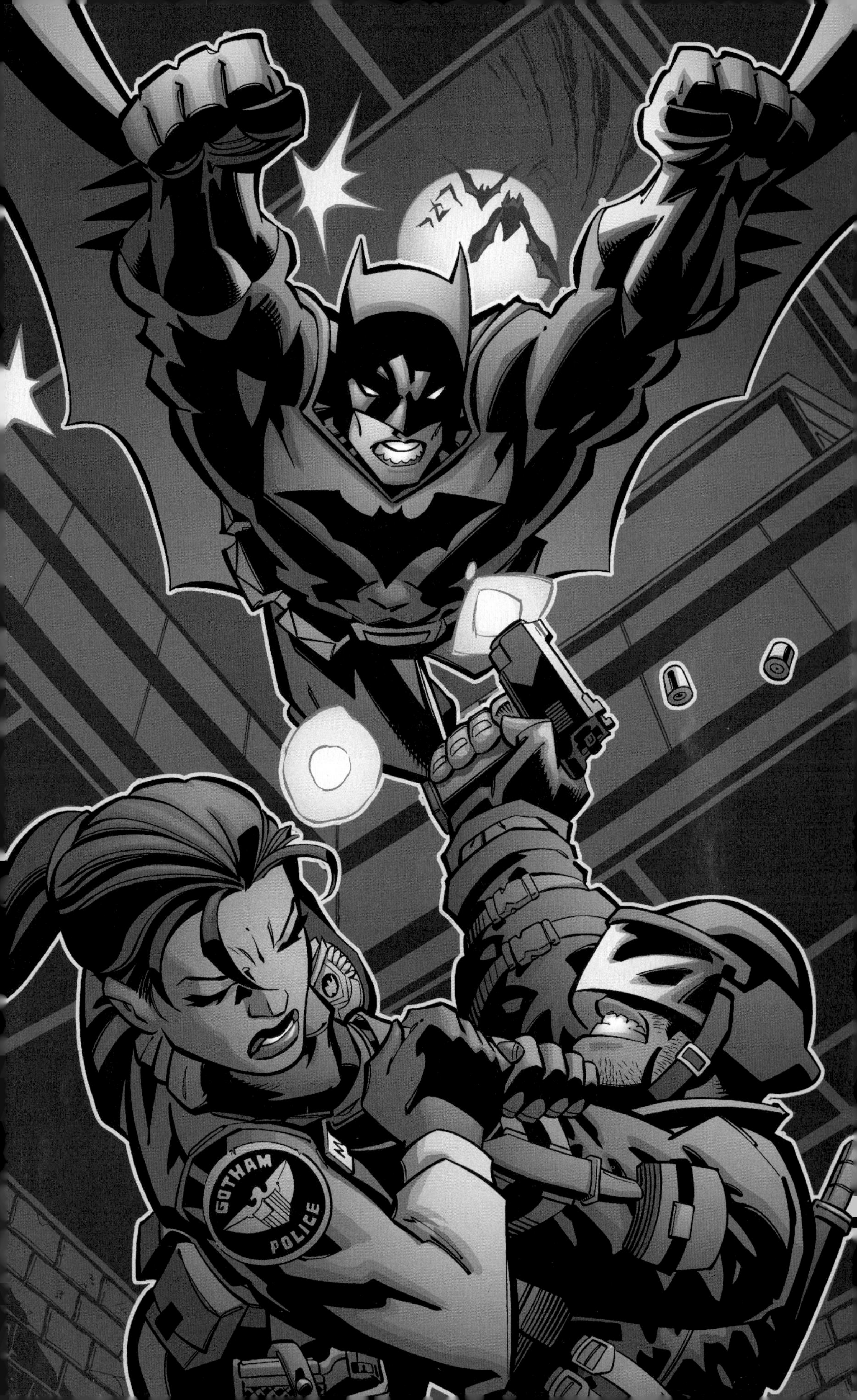
GOTHAM
POLICE

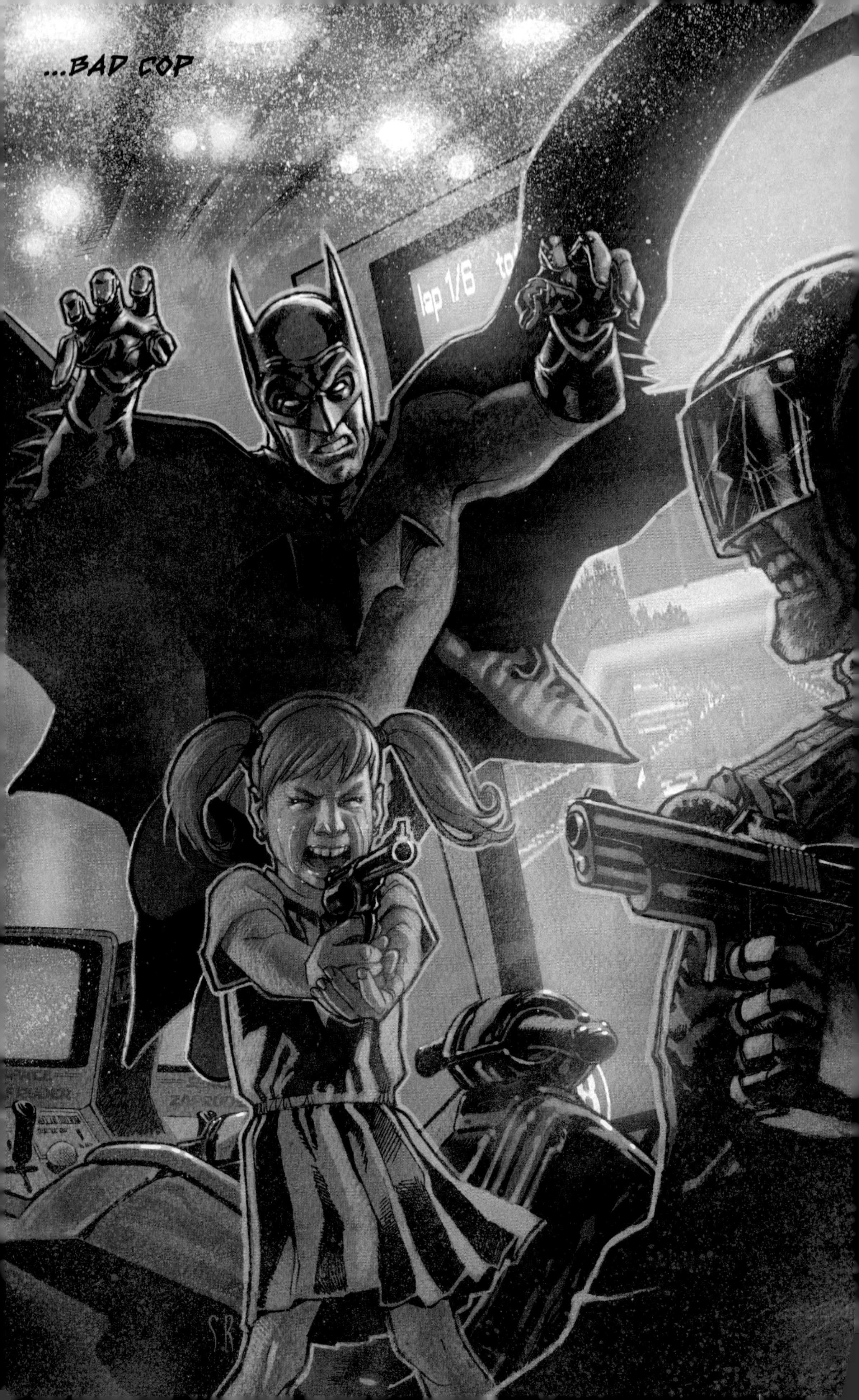
...BAD COP
lap 1/6

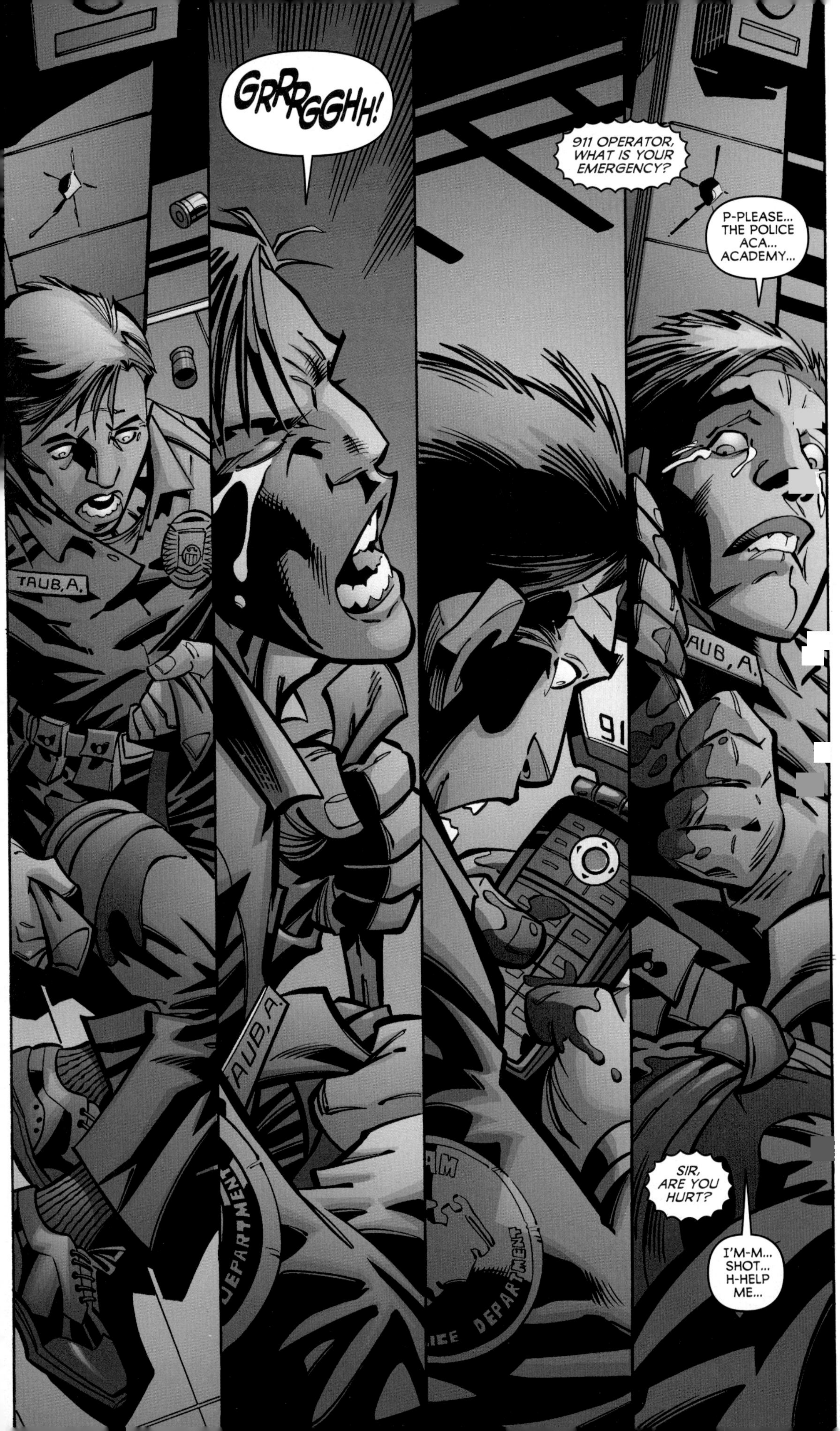
GRRRGGHH!
911 OPERATOR, WHAT IS YOUR EMERGENCY?
P-PLEASE... THE POLICE ACA... ACADEMY...
SIR, ARE YOU HURT?
I'M-M... SHOT... H-HELP ME...

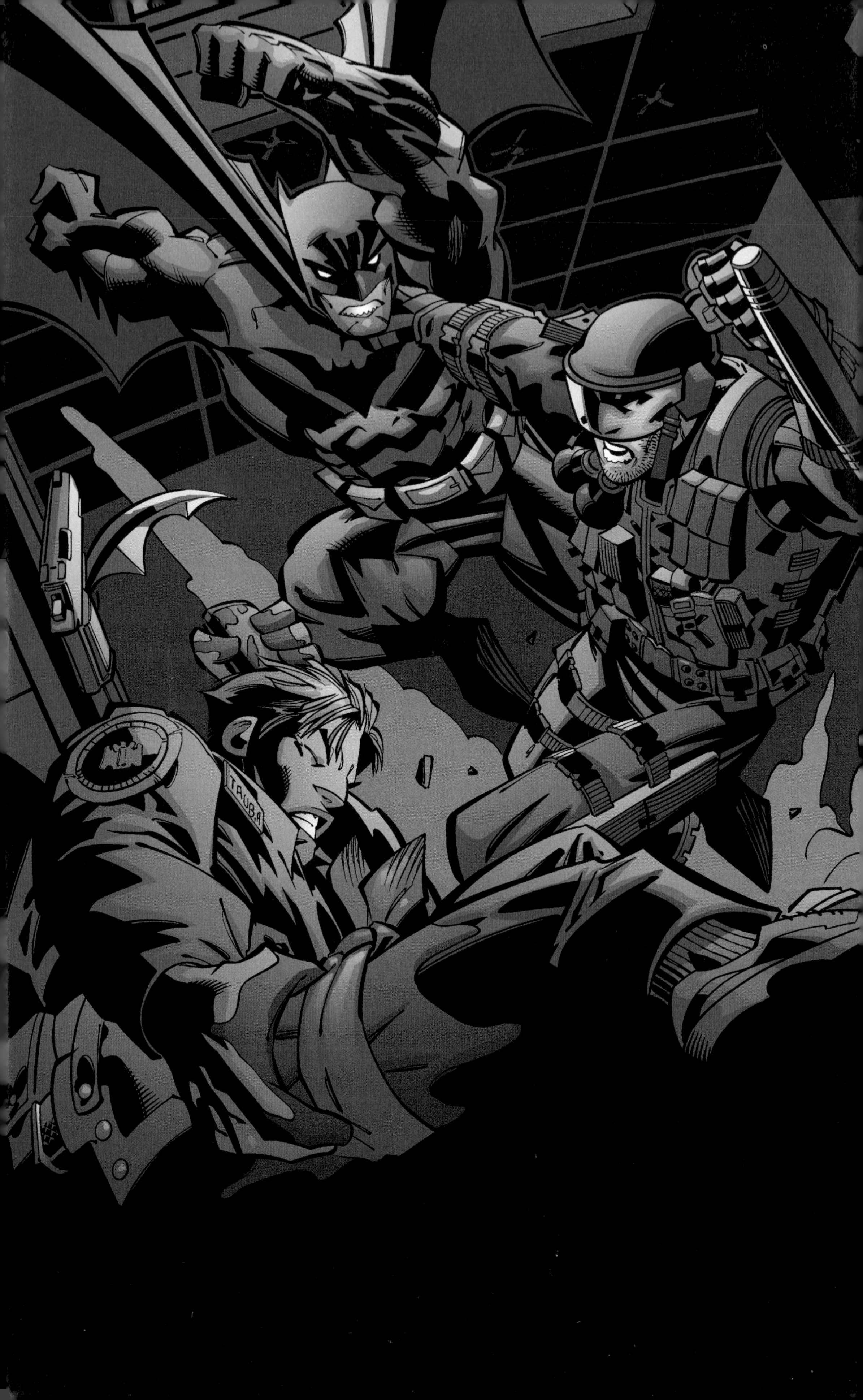
TAUBA

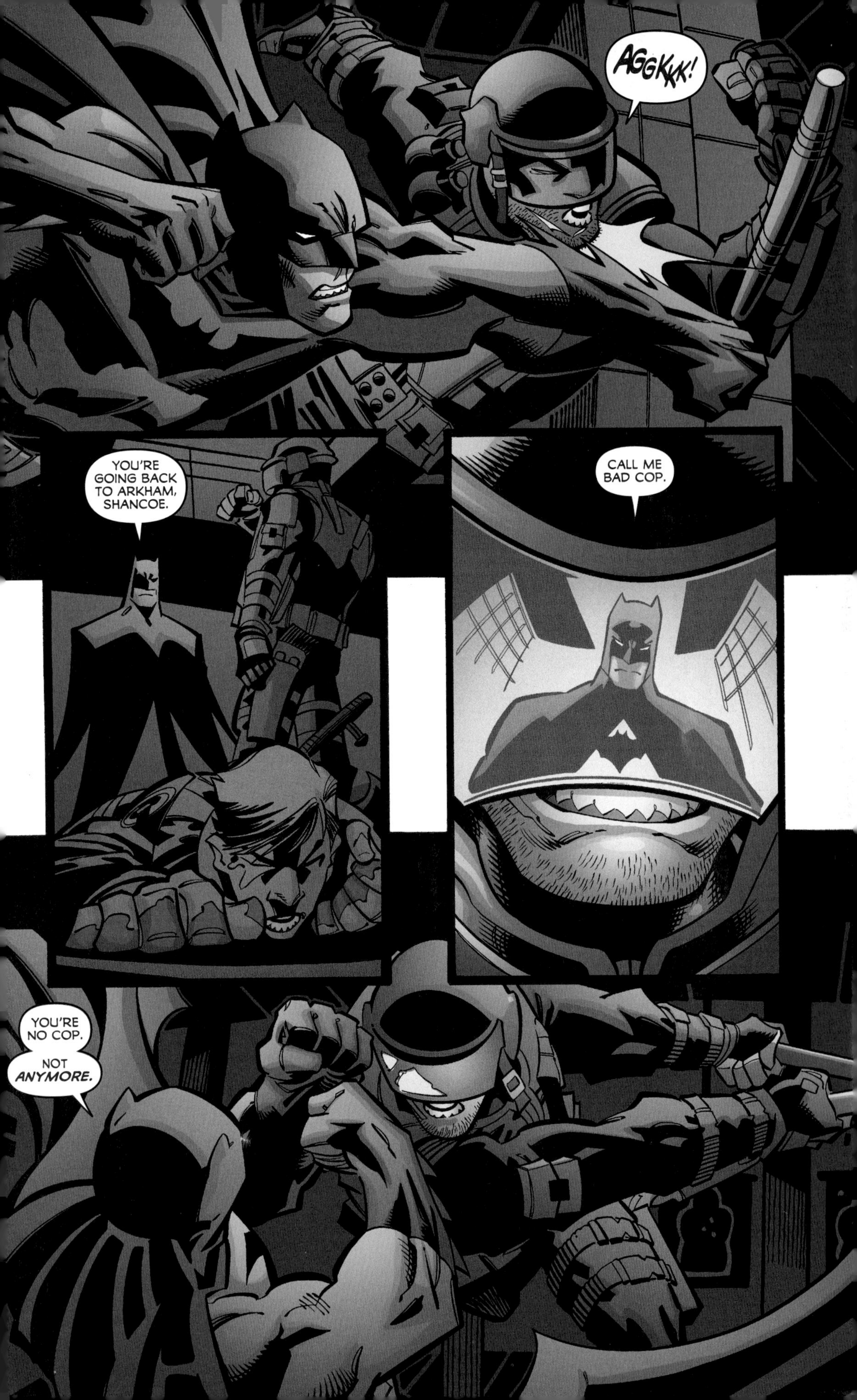
AGGKKK!
YOU'RE GOING BACK TO ARKHAM, SHANCOE.
CALL ME BAD COP.
YOU'RE NO COP.
NOT *ANYMORE.*

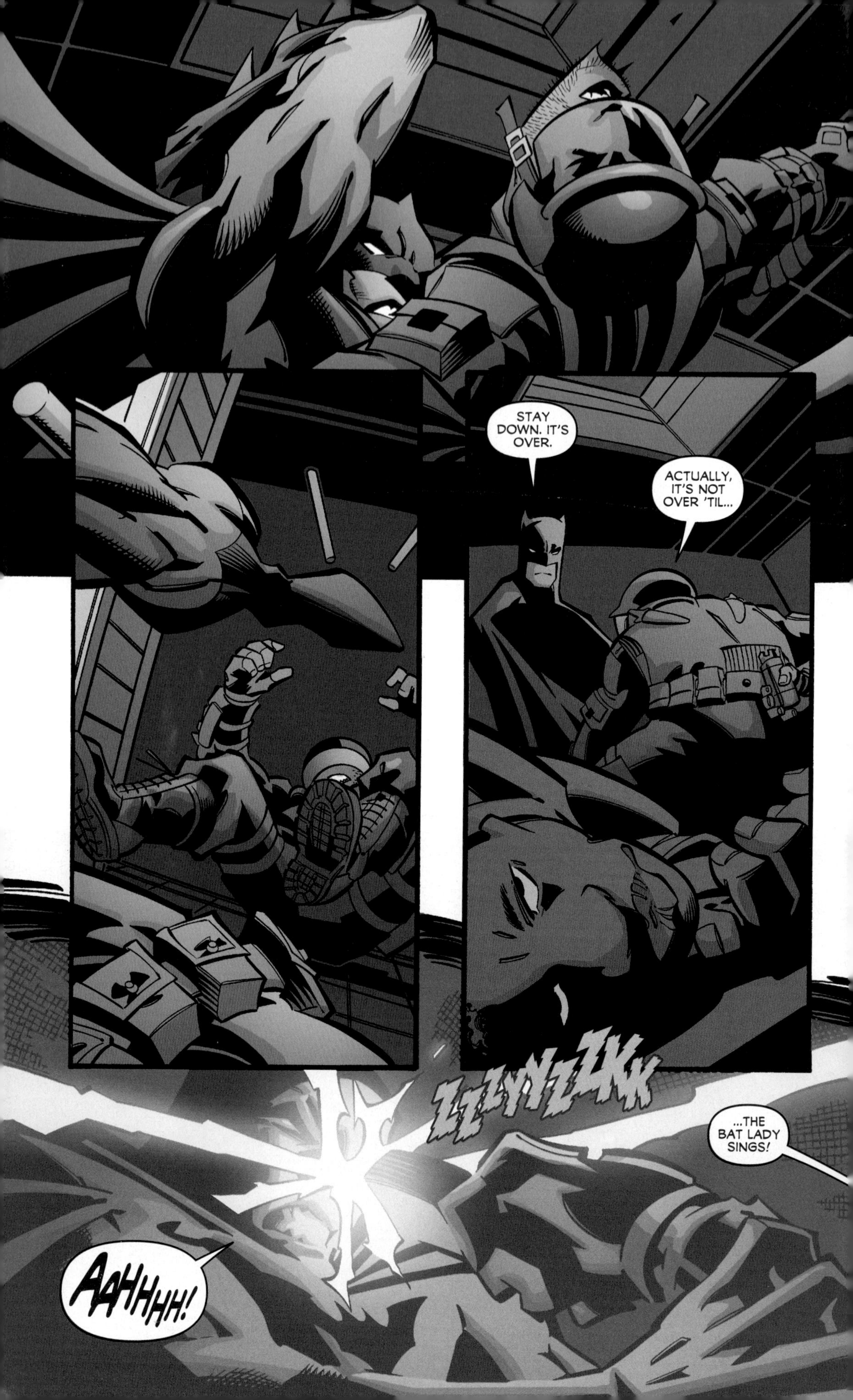
STAY DOWN. IT'S OVER.
ACTUALLY, IT'S NOT OVER 'TIL...
ZZZYYYZZZKK
...THE BAT LADY SINGS!
AAHHHH!

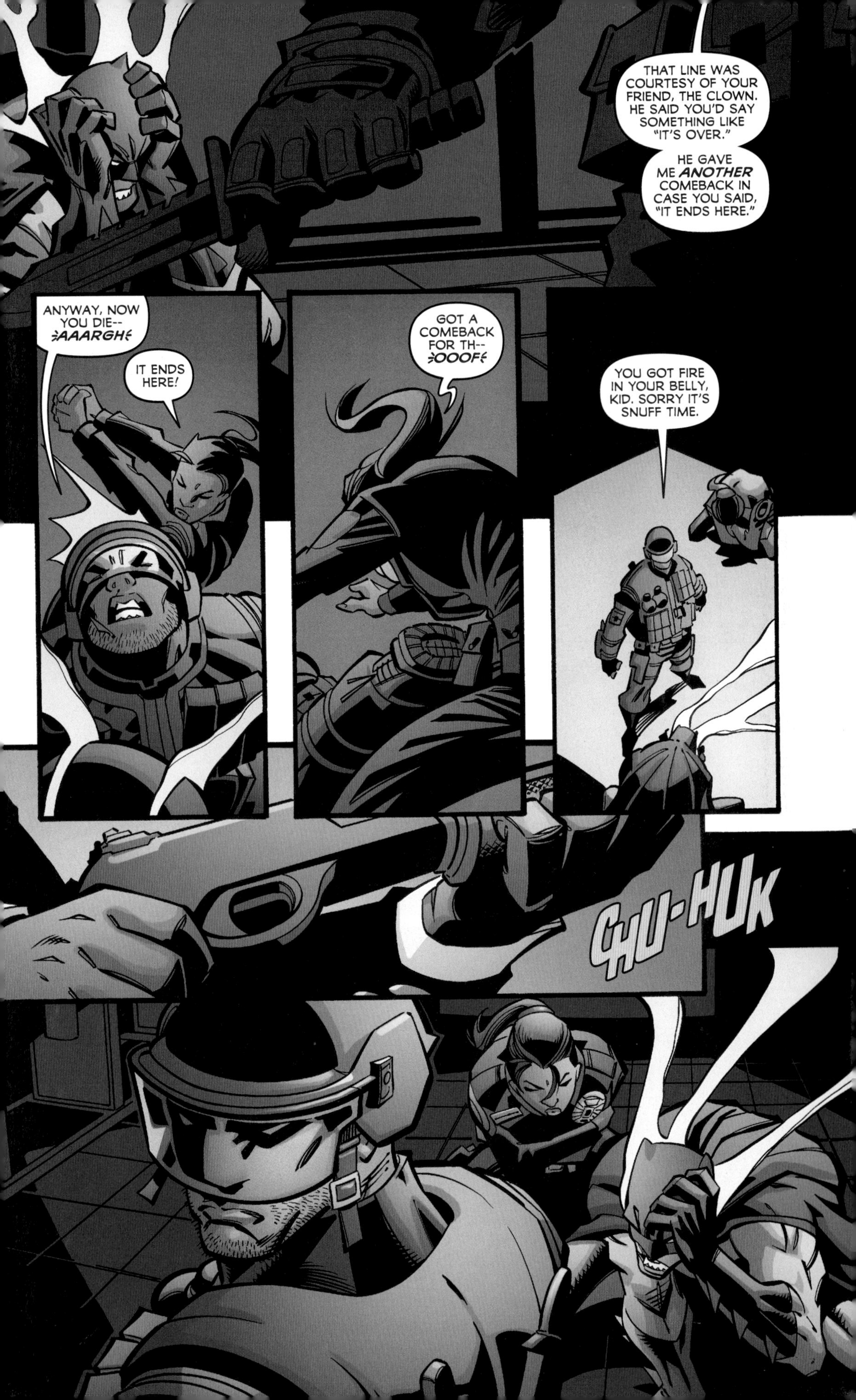
THAT LINE WAS COURTESY OF YOUR FRIEND, THE CLOWN. HE SAID YOU'D SAY SOMETHING LIKE "IT'S OVER."
HE GAVE ME ANOTHER COMEBACK IN CASE YOU SAID, "IT ENDS HERE."
ANYWAY, NOW YOU DIE-- AAARGH
IT ENDS HERE!
GOT A COMEBACK FOR TH-- OOOF
YOU GOT FIRE IN YOUR BELLY, KID. SORRY IT'S SNUFF TIME.
CHU-HUK

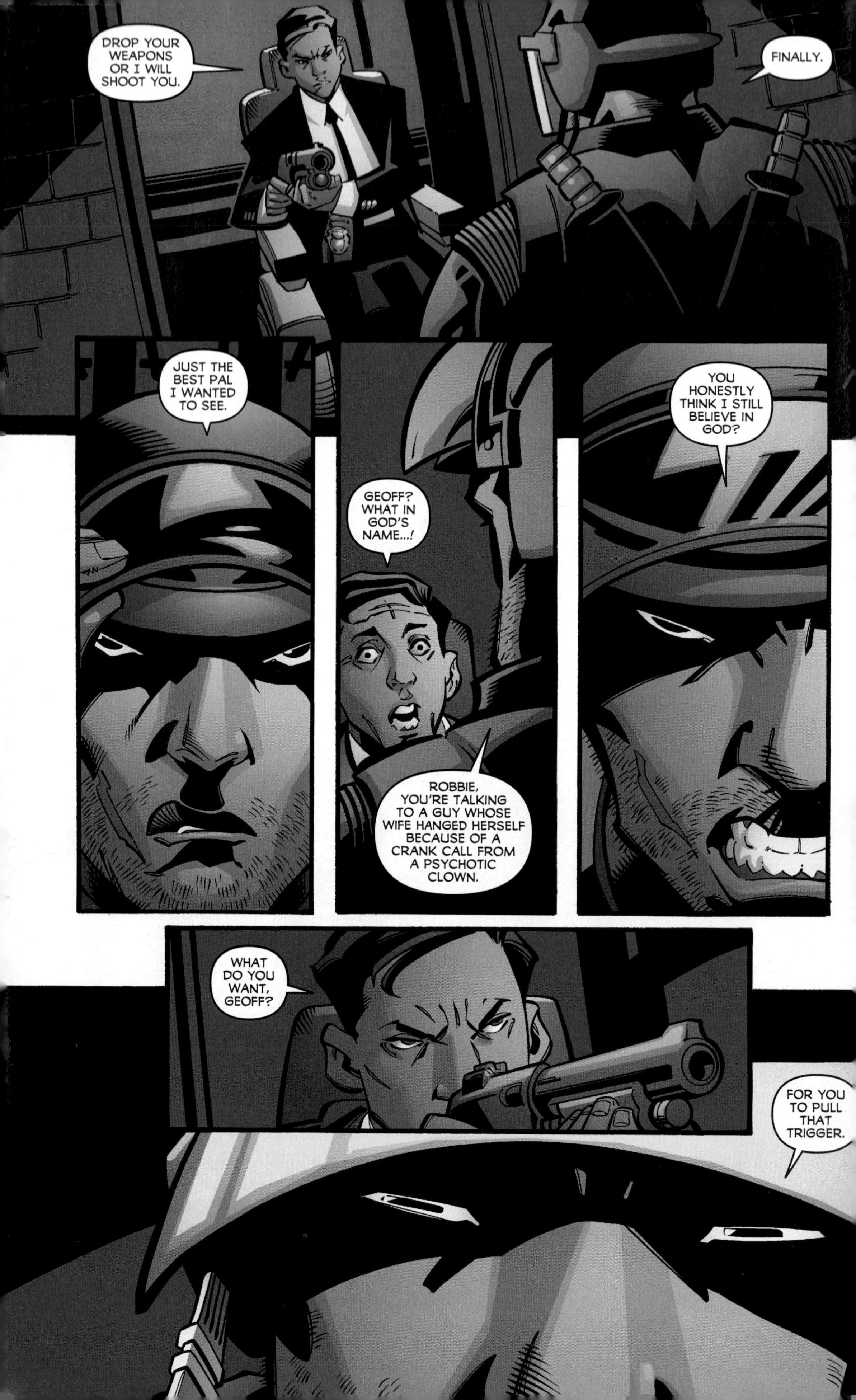
DROP YOUR WEAPONS OR I WILL SHOOT YOU.
FINALLY.
JUST THE BEST PAL I WANTED TO SEE.
GEOFF? WHAT IN GOD'S NAME...!
ROBBIE, YOU'RE TALKING TO A GUY WHOSE WIFE HANGED HERSELF BECAUSE OF A CRANK CALL FROM A PSYCHOTIC CLOWN.
YOU HONESTLY THINK I STILL BELIEVE IN GOD?
WHAT DO YOU WANT, GEOFF?
FOR YOU TO PULL THAT TRIGGER.

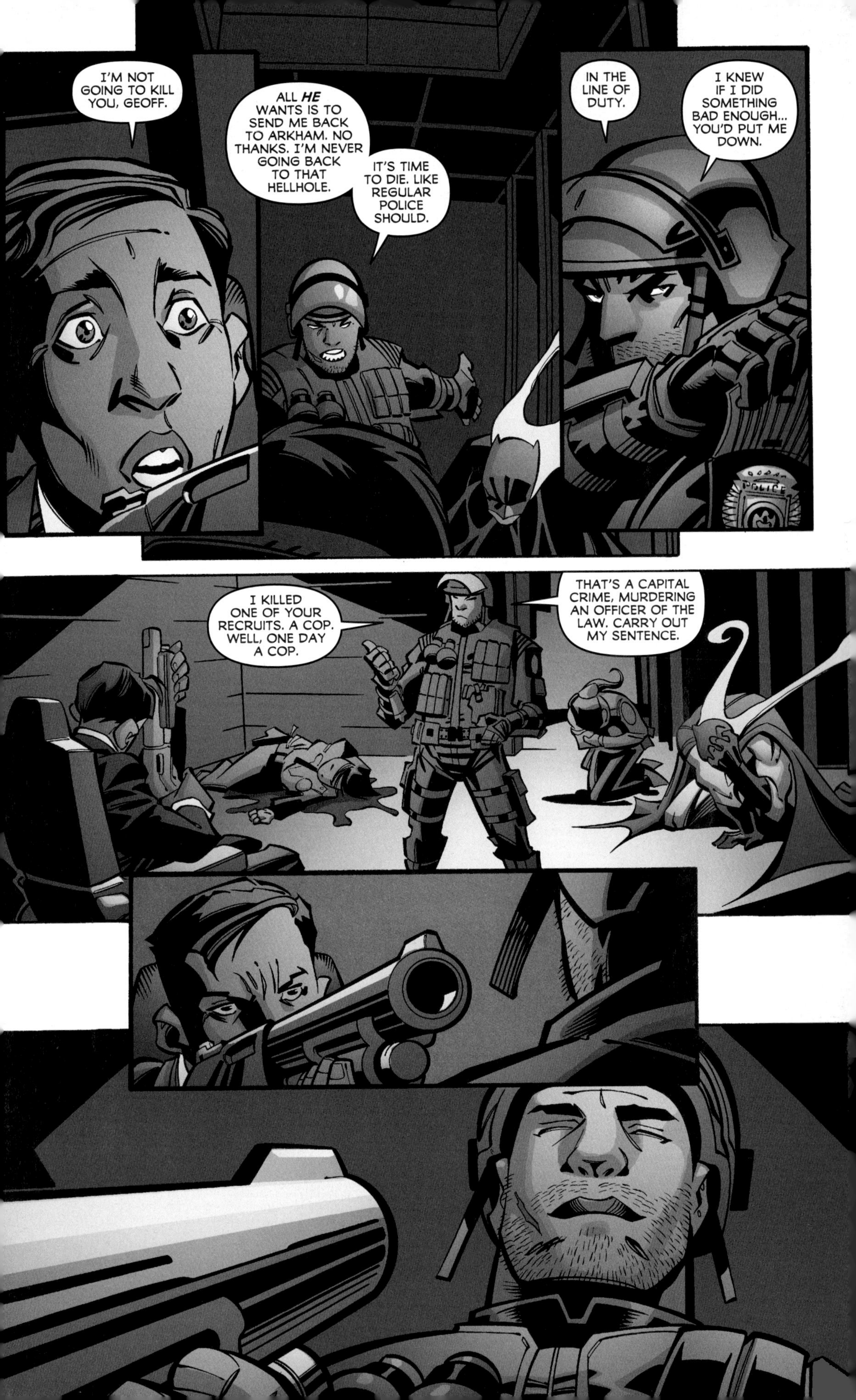
I'M NOT GOING TO KILL YOU, GEOFF.
ALL *HE* WANTS IS TO SEND ME BACK TO ARKHAM. NO THANKS. I'M NEVER GOING BACK TO THAT HELLHOLE.
IT'S TIME TO DIE. LIKE REGULAR POLICE SHOULD.
IN THE LINE OF DUTY.
I KNEW IF I DID SOMETHING BAD ENOUGH... YOU'D PUT ME DOWN.
POLICE
I KILLED ONE OF YOUR RECRUITS. A COP. WELL, ONE DAY A COP.
THAT'S A CAPITAL CRIME, MURDERING AN OFFICER OF THE LAW. CARRY OUT MY SENTENCE.

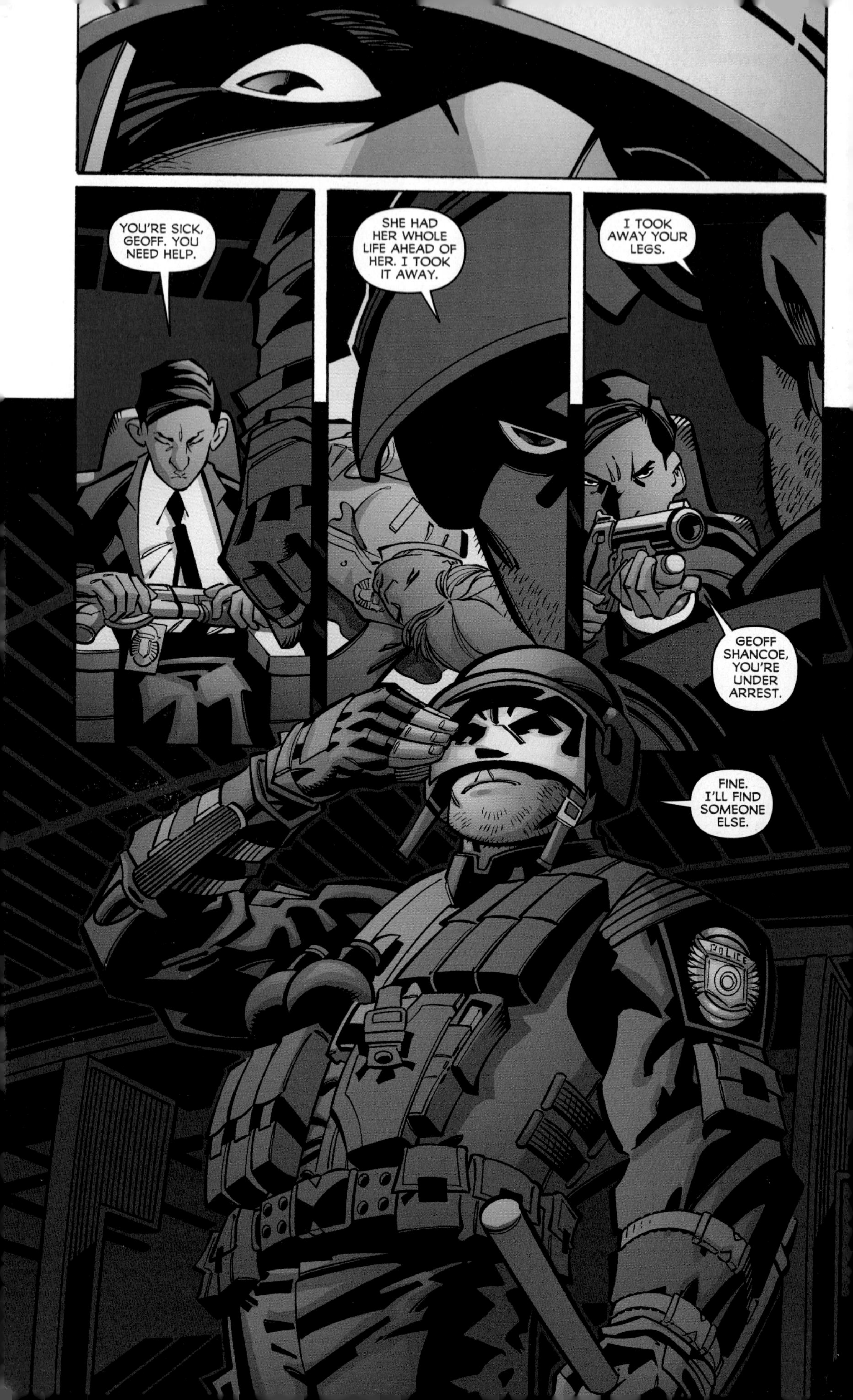
YOU'RE SICK, GEOFF. YOU NEED HELP.
SHE HAD HER WHOLE LIFE AHEAD OF HER. I TOOK IT AWAY.
I TOOK AWAY YOUR LEGS.
GEOFF SHANCOE, YOU'RE UNDER ARREST.
FINE. I'LL FIND SOMEONE ELSE.
POLICE

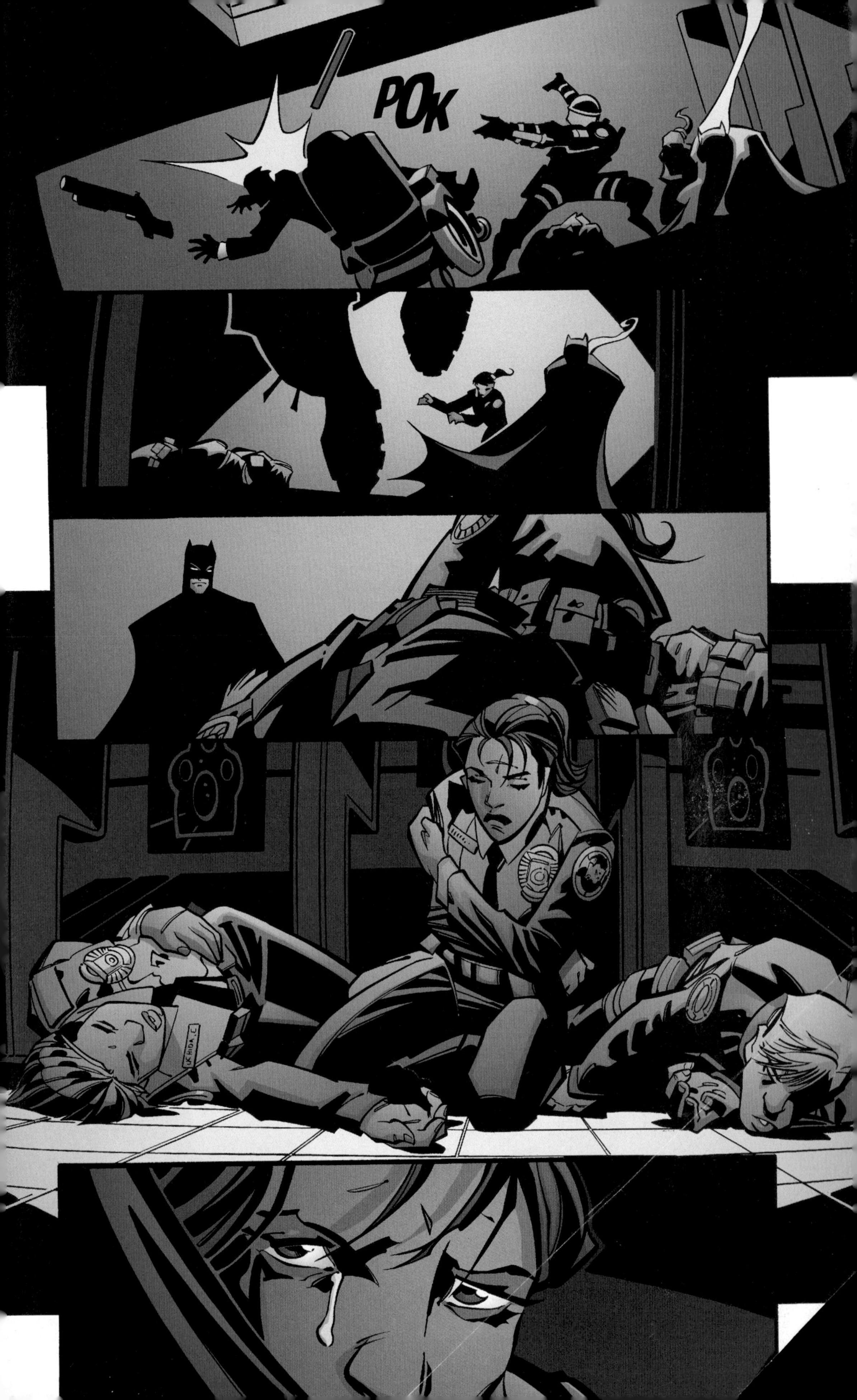
POK
UCHIDA, C

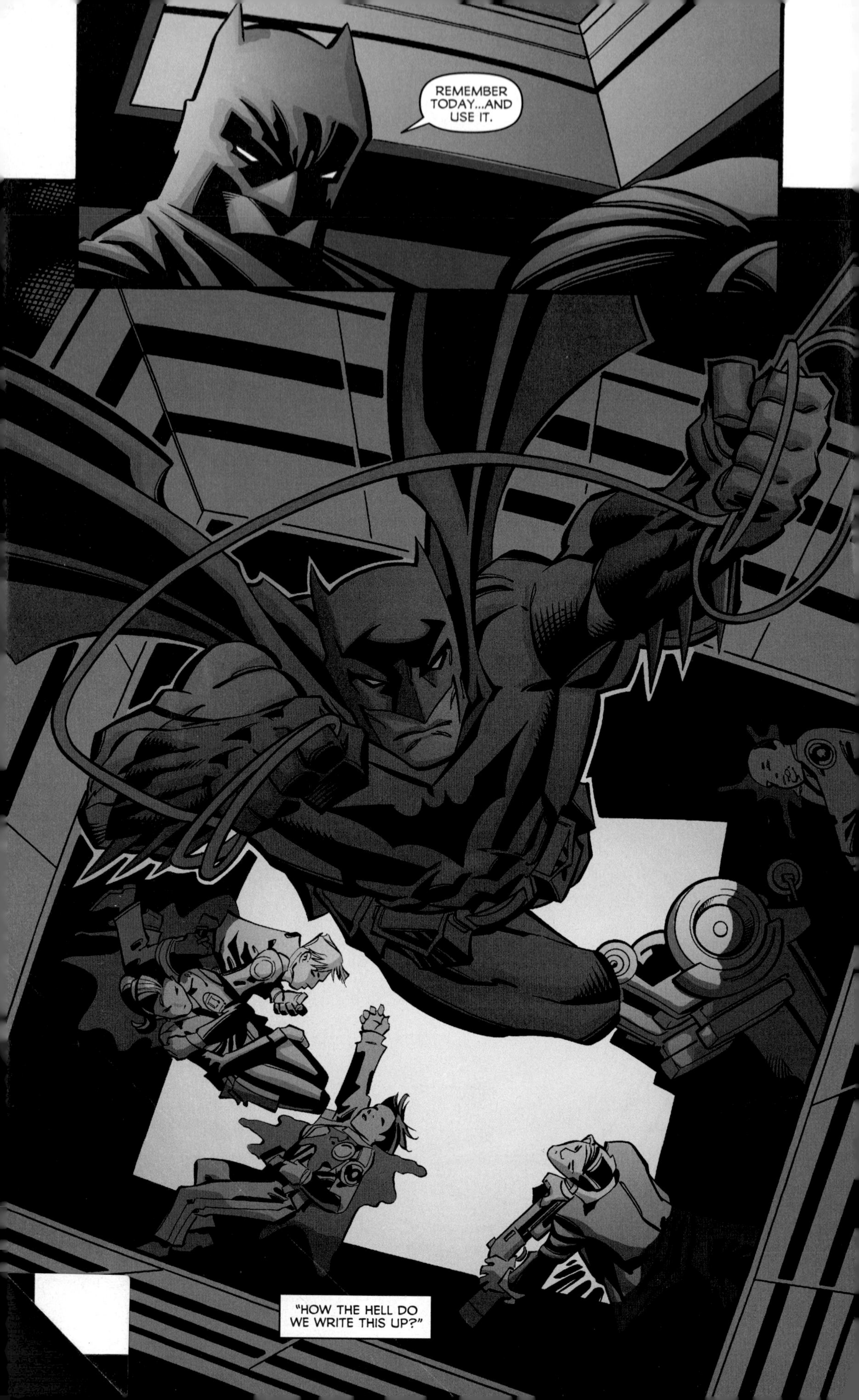
REMEMBER TODAY...AND USE IT.
"HOW THE HELL DO WE WRITE THIS UP?"

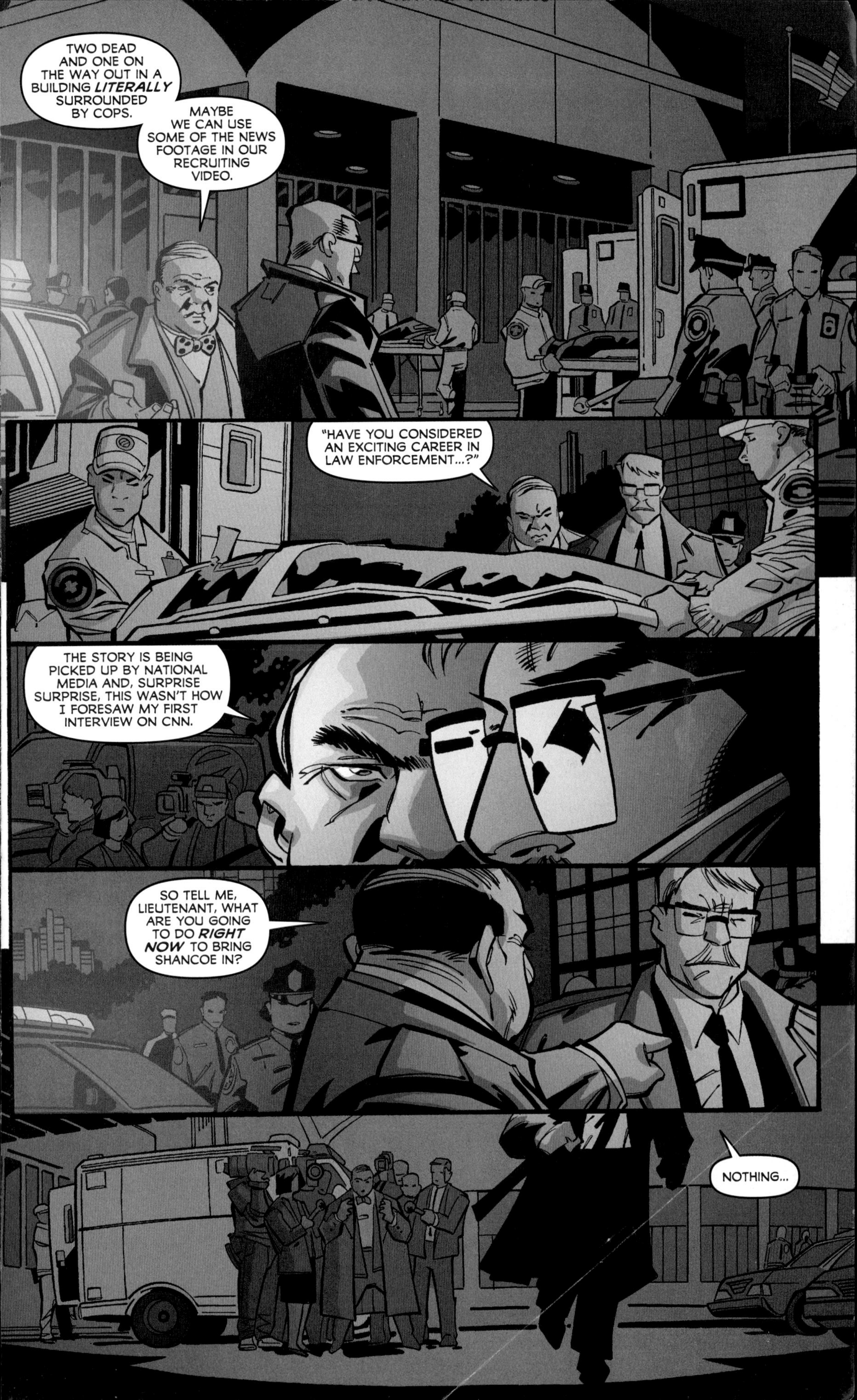
TWO DEAD AND ONE ON THE WAY OUT IN A BUILDING *LITERALLY* SURROUNDED BY COPS.
MAYBE WE CAN USE SOME OF THE NEWS FOOTAGE IN OUR RECRUITING VIDEO.
"HAVE YOU CONSIDERED AN EXCITING CAREER IN LAW ENFORCEMENT...?"
THE STORY IS BEING PICKED UP BY NATIONAL MEDIA AND, SURPRISE SURPRISE, THIS WASN'T HOW I FORESAW MY FIRST INTERVIEW ON CNN.
SO TELL ME, LIEUTENANT, WHAT ARE YOU GOING TO DO *RIGHT NOW* TO BRING SHANCOE IN?
NOTHING...

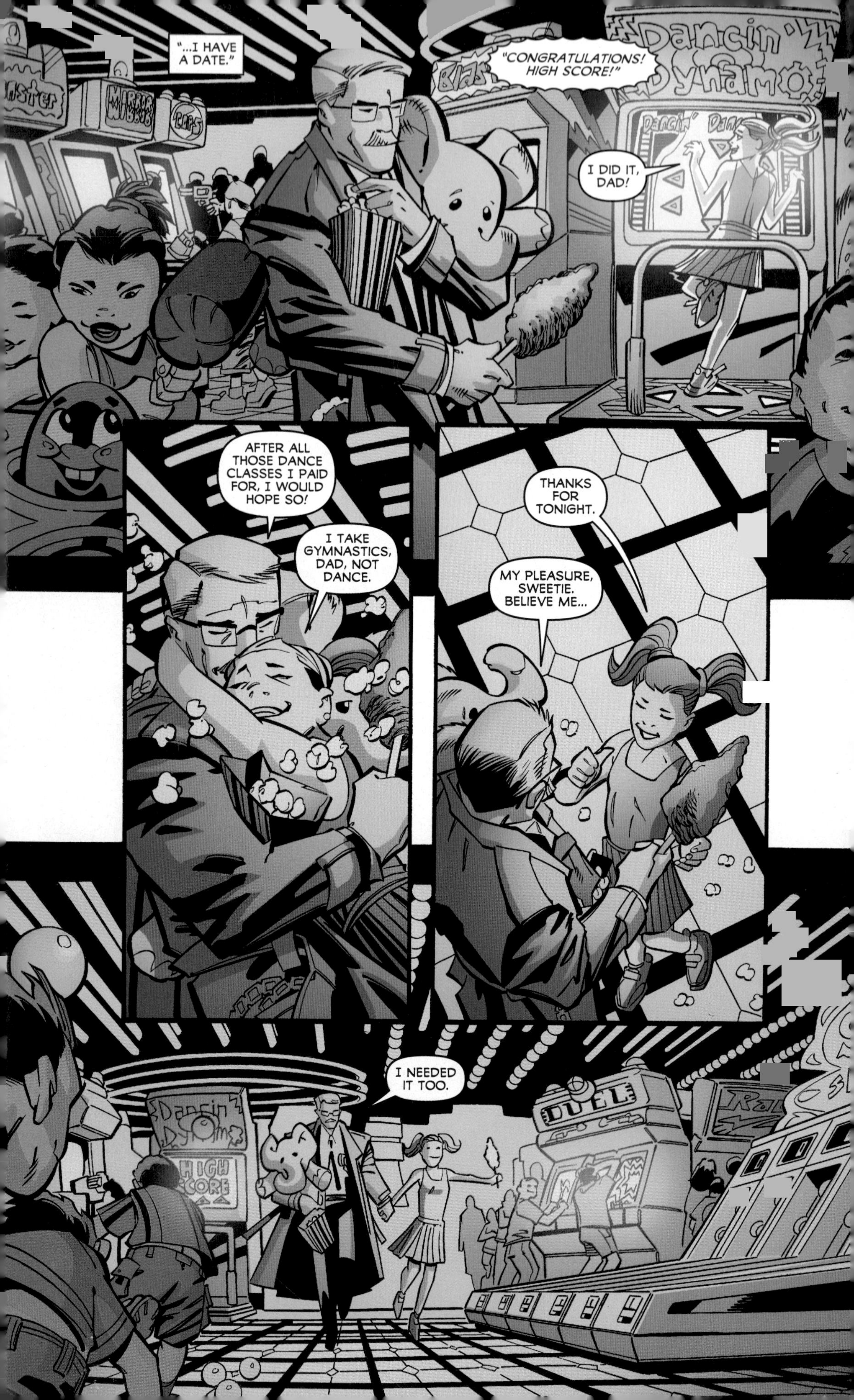
"...I HAVE A DATE."
"CONGRATULATIONS! HIGH SCORE!"
I DID IT, DAD!
AFTER ALL THOSE DANCE CLASSES I PAID FOR, I WOULD HOPE SO!
I TAKE GYMNASTICS, DAD, NOT DANCE.
THANKS FOR TONIGHT.
MY PLEASURE, SWEETIE. BELIEVE ME...
I NEEDED IT TOO.

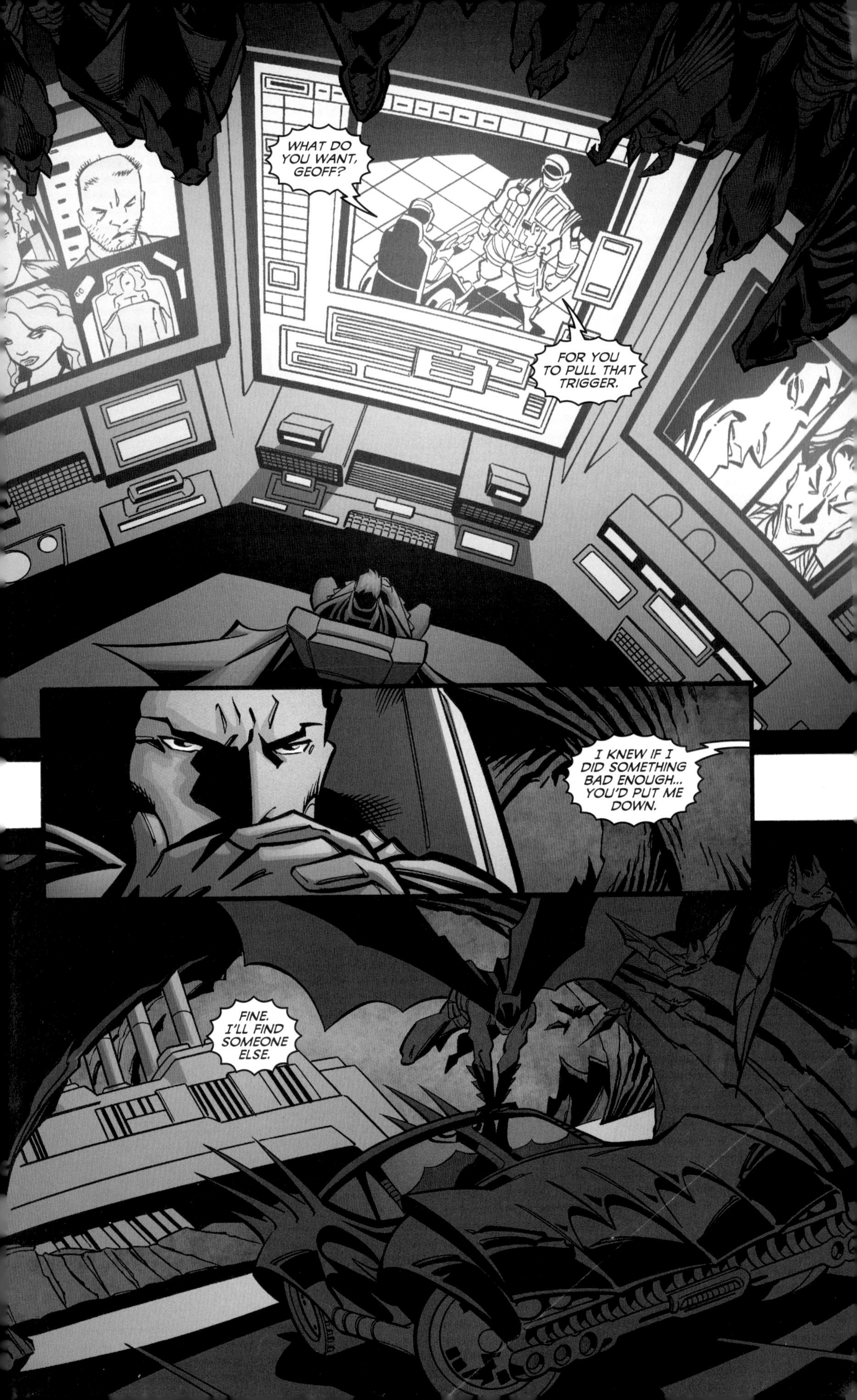
WHAT DO YOU WANT, GEOFF?
FOR YOU TO PULL THAT TRIGGER.
I KNEW IF I DID SOMETHING BAD ENOUGH... YOU'D PUT ME DOWN.
FINE. I'LL FIND SOMEONE ELSE.

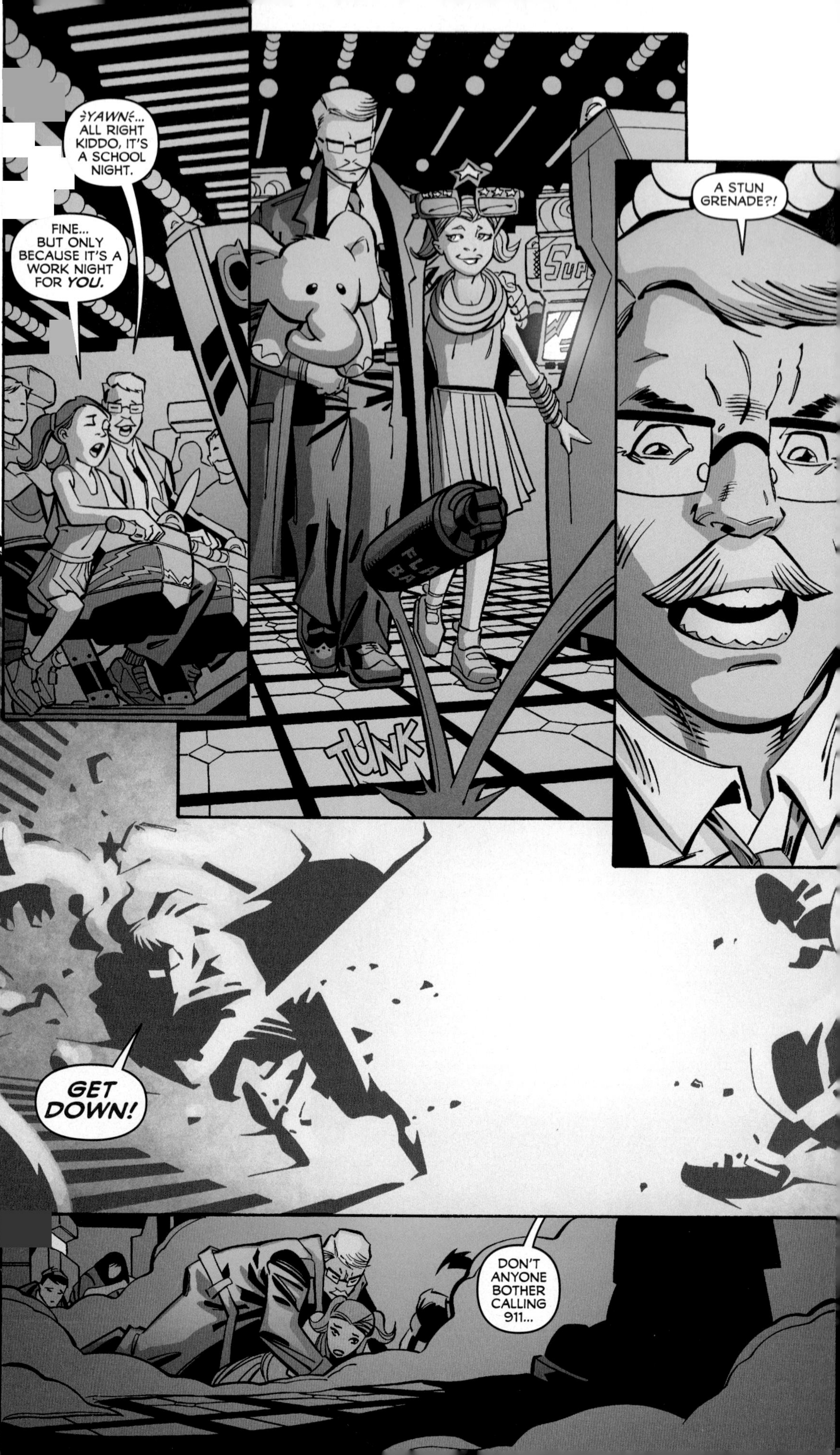

ƎYAWNƐ... ALL RIGHT KIDDO, IT'S A SCHOOL NIGHT.
FINE... BUT ONLY BECAUSE IT'S A WORK NIGHT FOR *YOU.*
TUNK
A STUN GRENADE?!
GET DOWN!
DON'T ANYONE BOTHER CALLING 911...

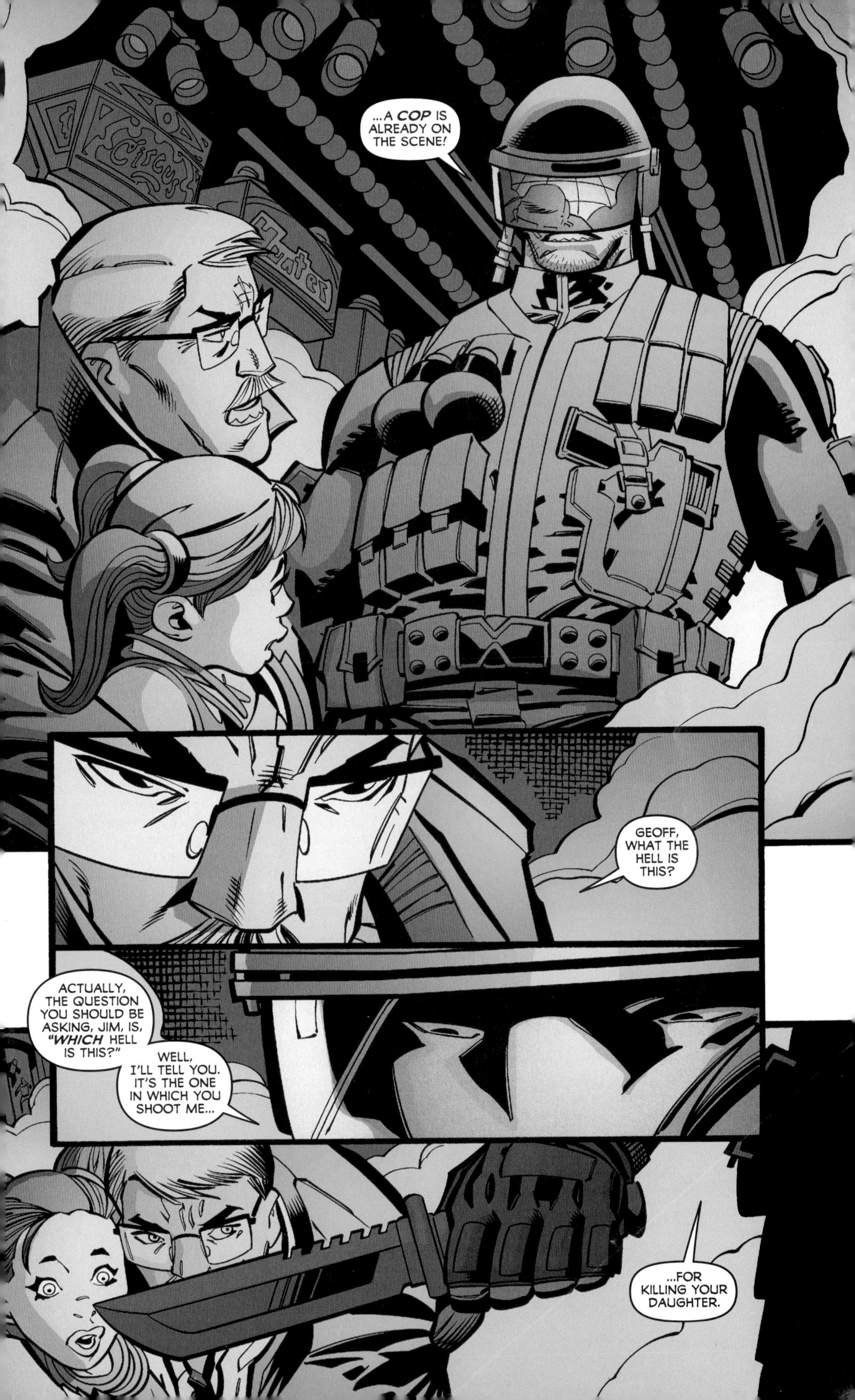
...A COP IS ALREADY ON THE SCENE!
GEOFF, WHAT THE HELL IS THIS?
ACTUALLY, THE QUESTION YOU SHOULD BE ASKING, JIM, IS, "WHICH HELL IS THIS?"
WELL, I'LL TELL YOU. IT'S THE ONE IN WHICH YOU SHOOT ME...
...FOR KILLING YOUR DAUGHTER.

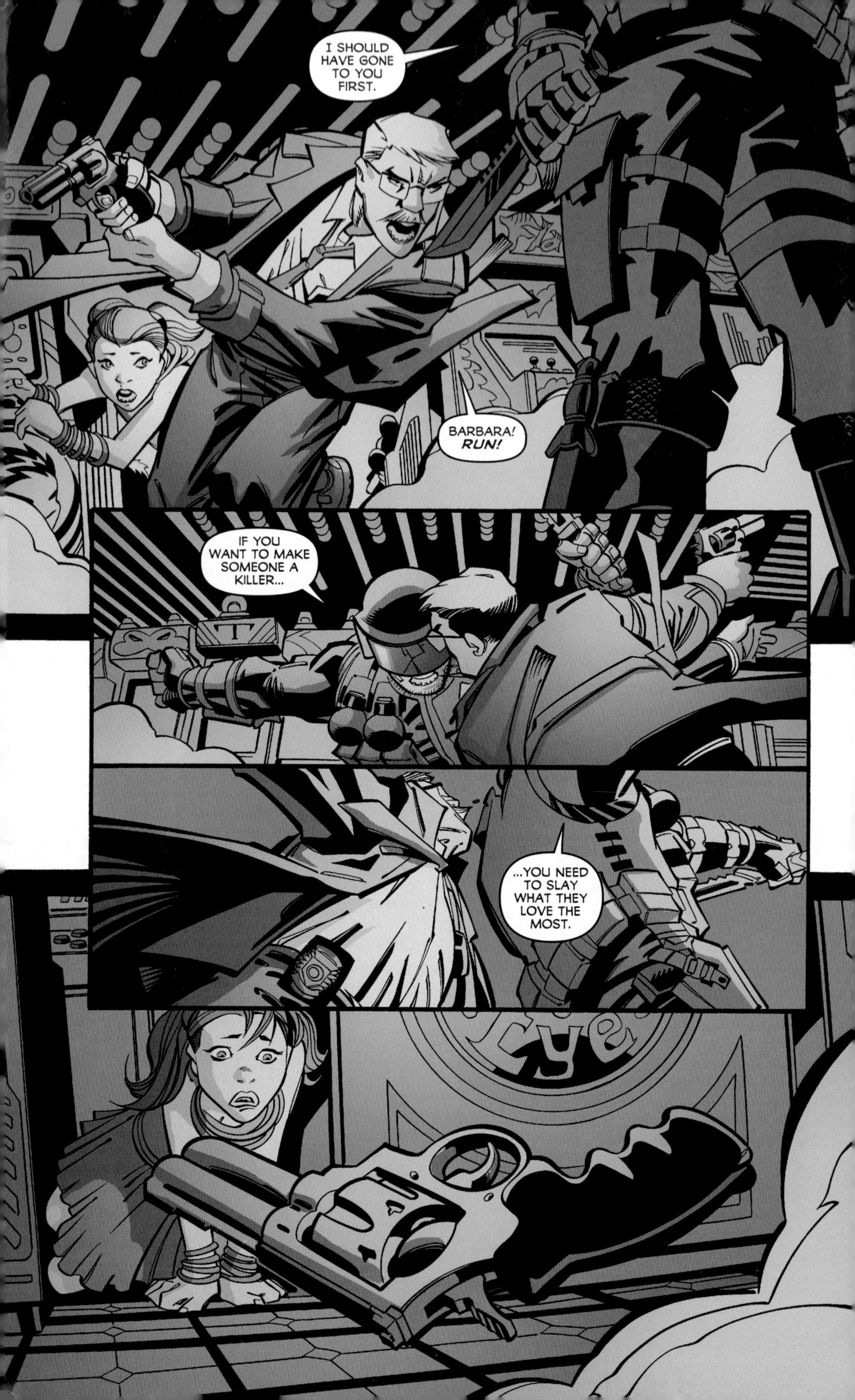
I SHOULD HAVE GONE TO YOU FIRST.
BARBARA! *RUN!*
IF YOU WANT TO MAKE SOMEONE A KILLER...
...YOU NEED TO SLAY WHAT THEY LOVE THE MOST.

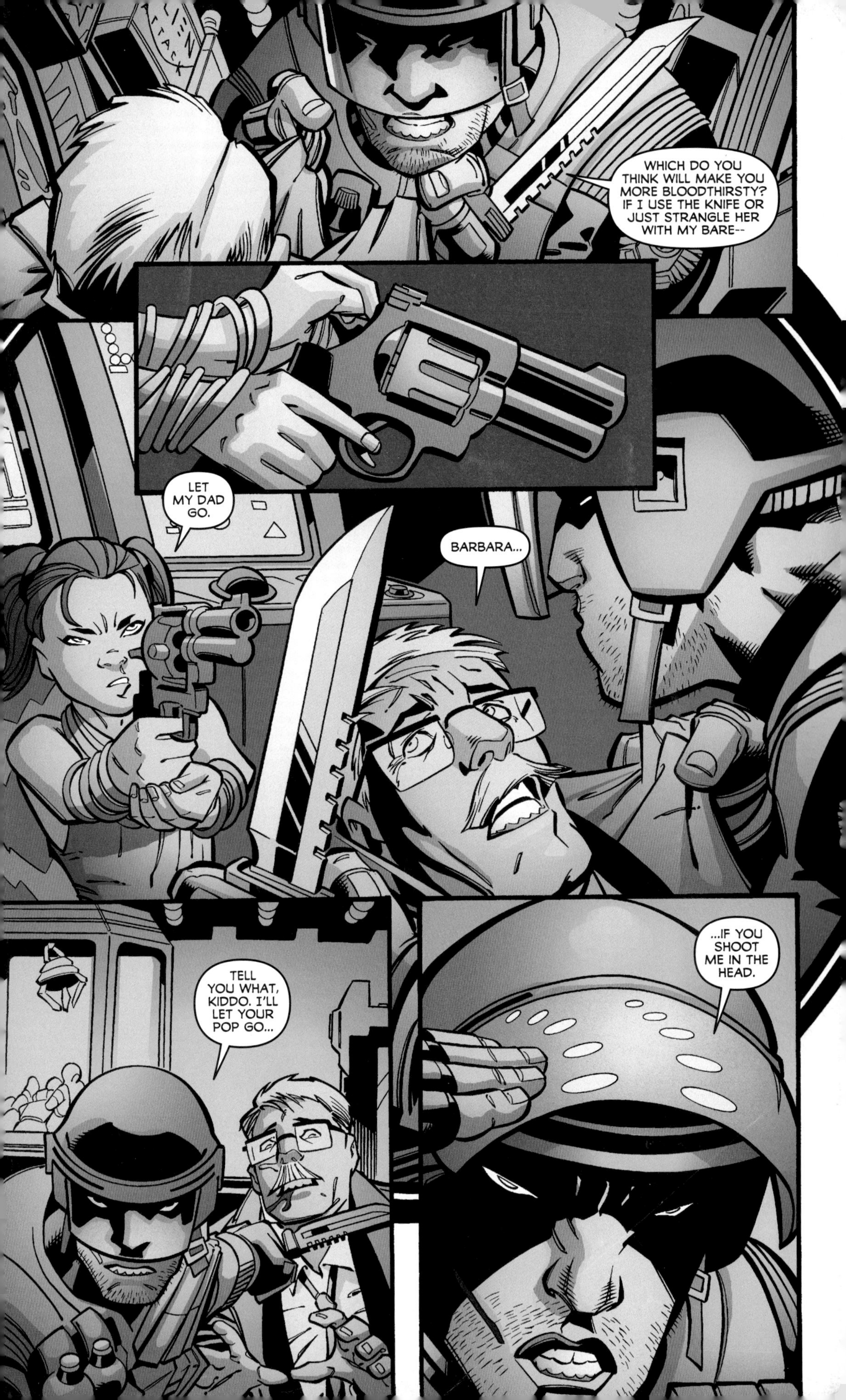
WHICH DO YOU THINK WILL MAKE YOU MORE BLOODTHIRSTY? IF I USE THE KNIFE OR JUST STRANGLE HER WITH MY BARE--
LET MY DAD GO.
BARBARA...
TELL YOU WHAT, KIDDO. I'LL LET YOUR POP GO...
...IF YOU SHOOT ME IN THE HEAD.

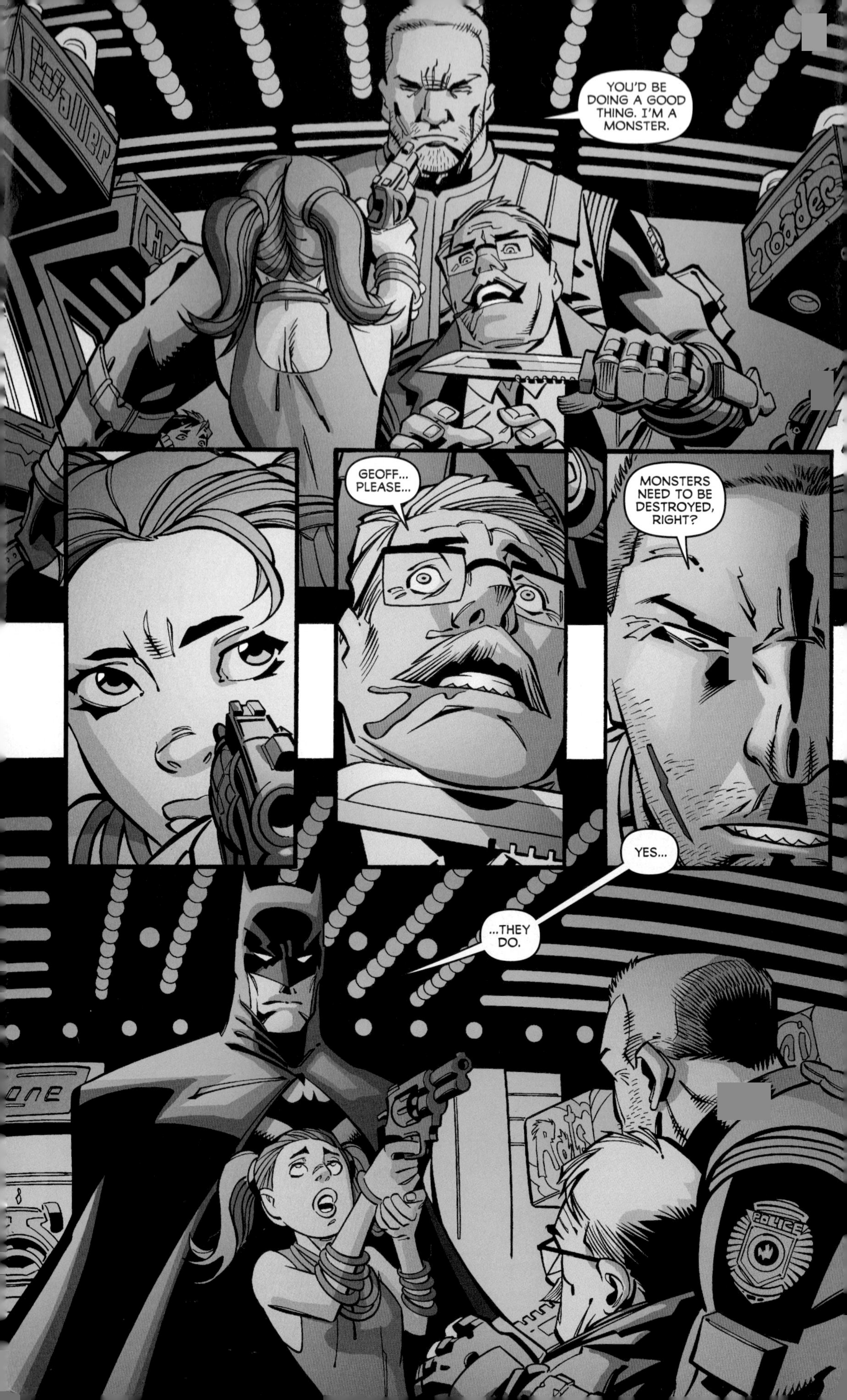
YOU'D BE DOING A GOOD THING. I'M A MONSTER.
GEOFF... PLEASE...
MONSTERS NEED TO BE DESTROYED, RIGHT?
YES...
...THEY DO.

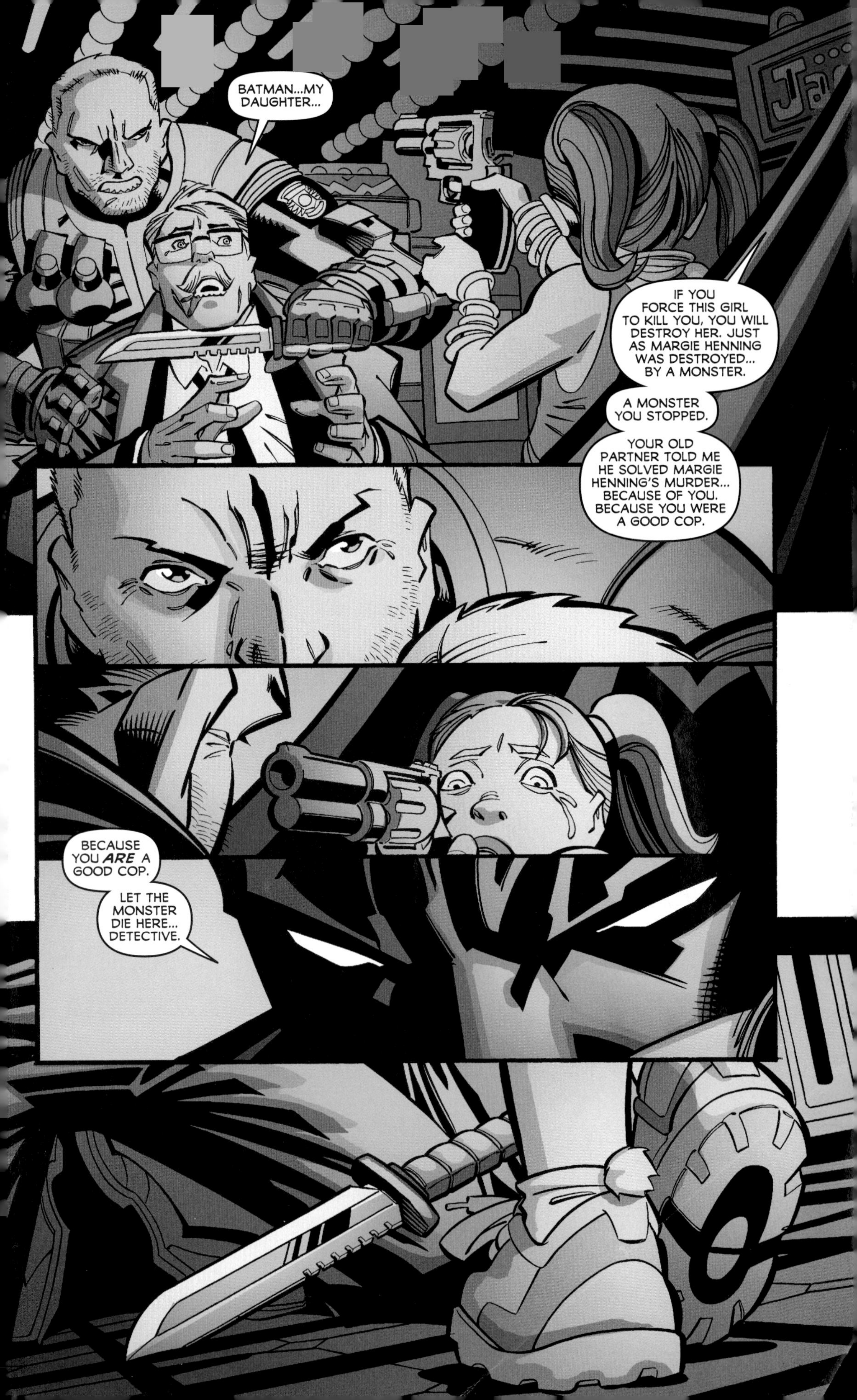
BATMAN...MY DAUGHTER...
IF YOU FORCE THIS GIRL TO KILL YOU, YOU WILL DESTROY HER. JUST AS MARGIE HENNING WAS DESTROYED... BY A MONSTER.
A MONSTER YOU STOPPED.
YOUR OLD PARTNER TOLD ME HE SOLVED MARGIE HENNING'S MURDER... BECAUSE OF YOU. BECAUSE YOU WERE A GOOD COP.
BECAUSE YOU *ARE* A GOOD COP.
LET THE MONSTER DIE HERE... DETECTIVE.

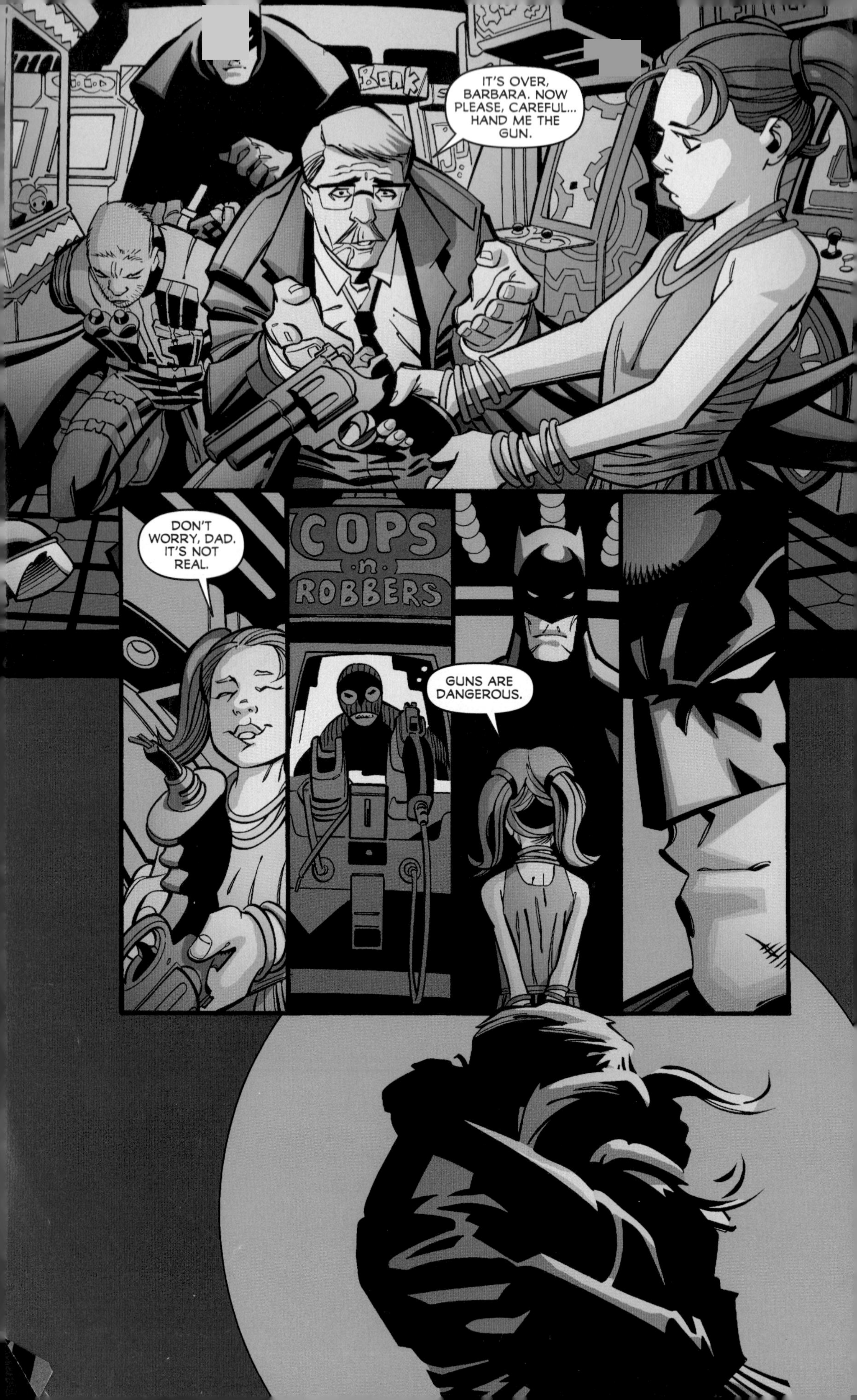
BONK
IT'S OVER, BARBARA. NOW PLEASE, CAREFUL... HAND ME THE GUN.
DON'T WORRY, DAD. IT'S NOT REAL.
COPS -n- ROBBERS
GUNS ARE DANGEROUS.

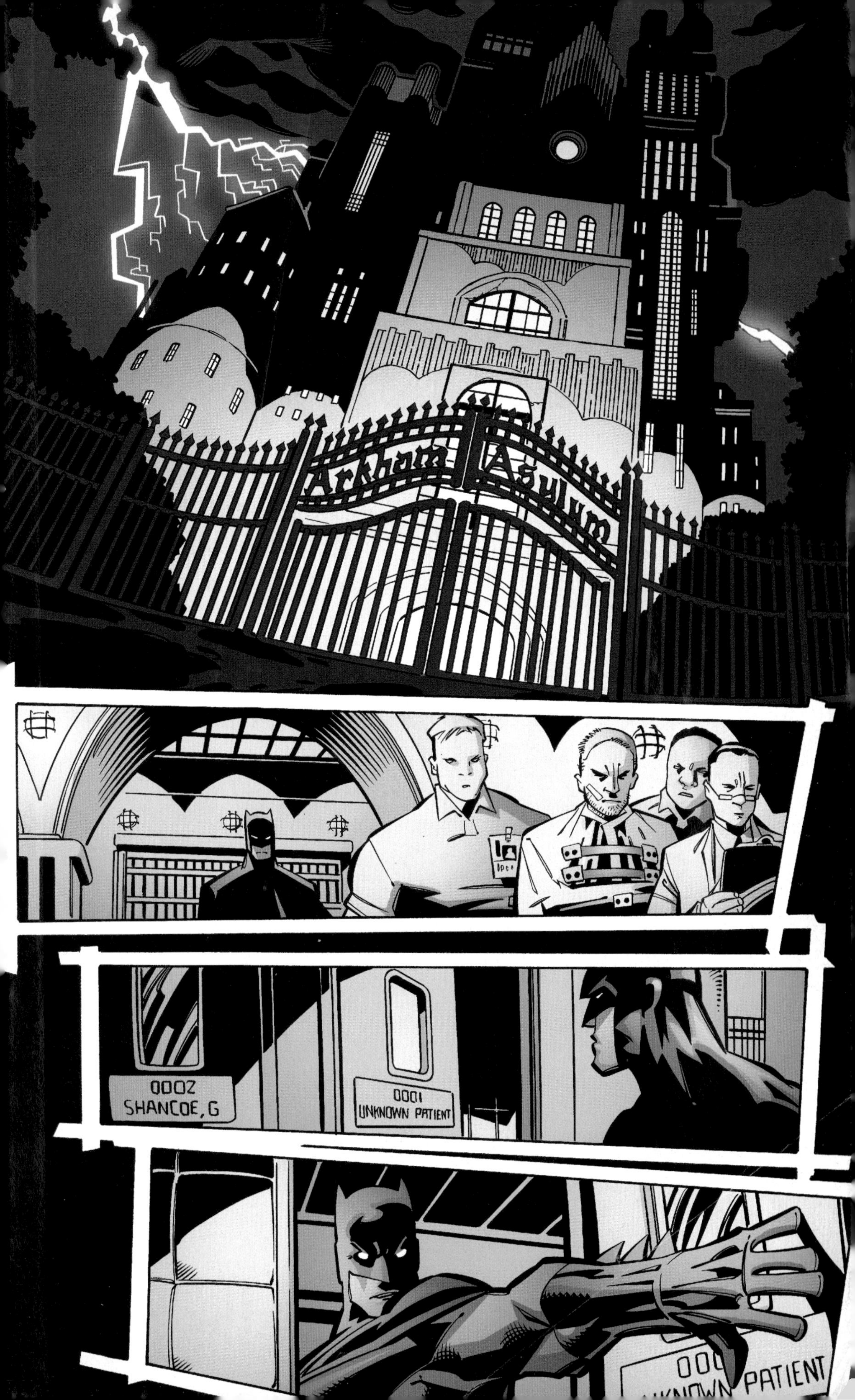
Arkham Asylum
0002
SHANCOE, G
0001
UNKNOWN PATIENT
UNKNOWN PATIENT

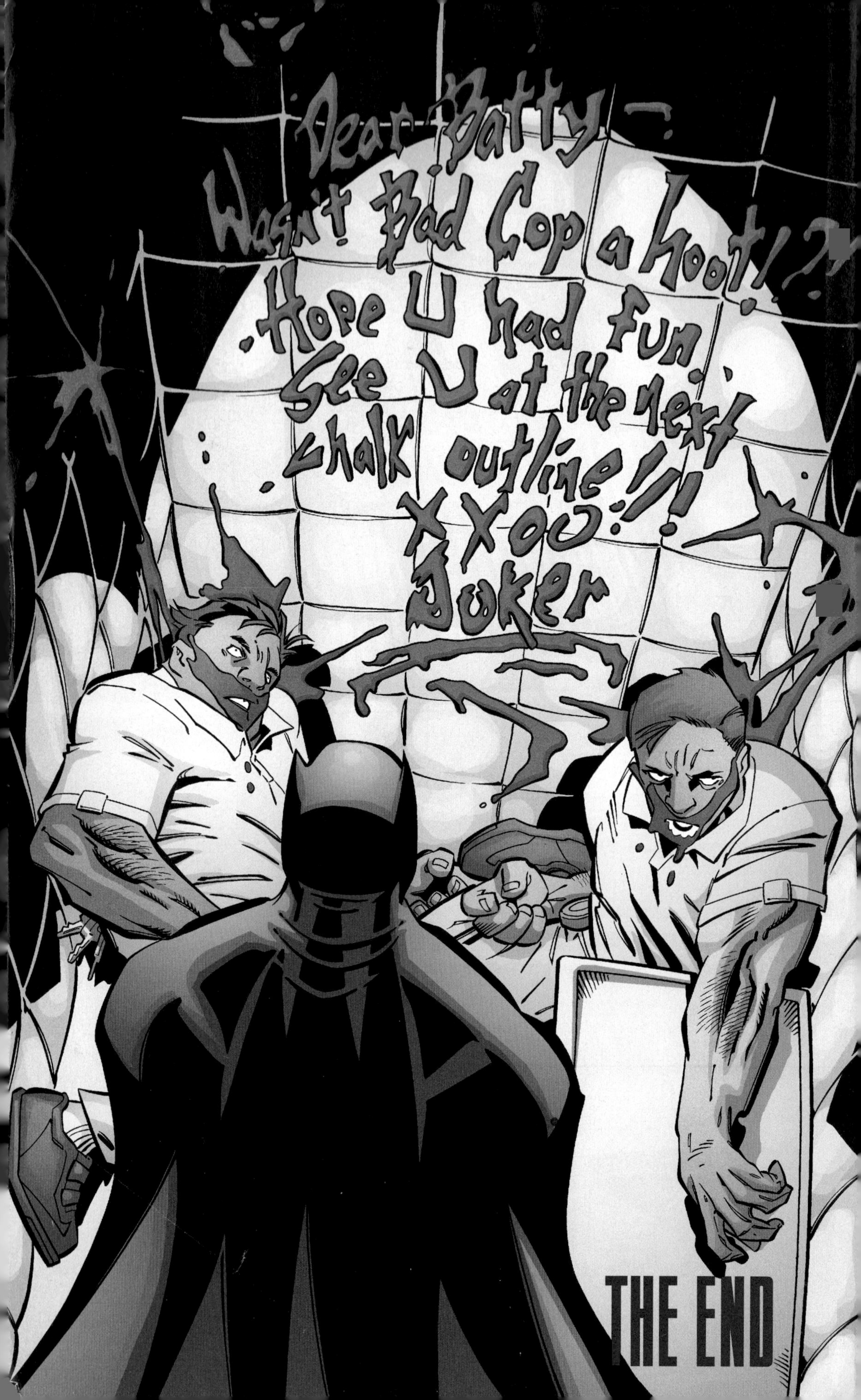
Dear Batty–
Wasn't Bad Cop a hoot!?
Hope U had fun.
See U at the next chalk outline!!
XXOO!!
Joker
THE END

MORE CLASSIC TALES OF THE DARK KNIGHT

BATMAN: HUSH

**JEPH LOEB
JIM LEE**

BATMAN: UNDER THE HOOD
VOLS. 1 & 2

**JUDD WINICK
DOUG MAHNKE**

BATMAN:
THE LONG HALLOWEEN

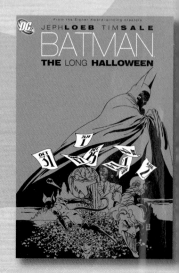

**JEPH LOEB
TIM SALE**

BATMAN:
DARK VICTORY

**JEPH LOEB
TIM SALE**

BATMAN:
HAUNTED KNIGHT

**JEPH LOEB
TIM SALE**

BATMAN:
YEAR 100

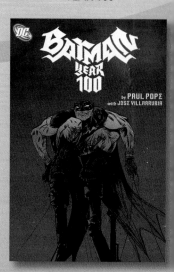

PAUL POPE

SEARCH THE GRAPHIC NOVELS SECTION OF
DCCOMICS.COM
FOR ART AND INFORMATION ON ALL OF OUR BOOKS!